REWARDS

Reading Excellence: Word Attack & Rate Development Strategies

Multisyllabic Word Reading Strategies

Teacher's Guide
Intermediate Level

Anita L. Archer, Ph.D.
Mary M. Gleason, Ph.D.
Vicky Vachon, Ph.D.

Assisted by
Johnathan King
Pat Pielaet

SOPRIS WEST™ EDUCATIONAL SERVICES
A CAMBIUM LEARNING COMPANY

BOSTON, MA • LONGMONT, CO

12 11 10 09   12 13 14

Teacher's Guide ISBN 13 Digit: 978-1-59318-551-0
Teacher's Guide ISBN 10 Digit: 1-59318-551-0
Student Book ISBN 13 Digit: 978-1-59318-552-7
Student Book ISBN 10 Digit: 1-59318-552-9
Packet of Overhead Transparencies ISBN 13 Digit: 978-1-59318-553-4
Packet of Overhead Transparencies ISBN 10 Digit: 1-59318-553-7

Cover images: ©Brand X Pictures, ©Masterfile Royalty Free,
©Inmagine, ©Comstock Royalty Free/Fotosearch
JELL-O is a registered trademark of Kraft Foods Holdings, Inc.

Printed in the United States of America

Published and Distributed by

Sopris West™
EDUCATIONAL SERVICES

A Cambium Learning Company

4093 Specialty Place ■ Longmont, Colorado 80504
(303) 651-2829 ■ www.sopriswest.com

116345/291/5-07

About the Authors

Anita L. Archer, Ph.D.

Dr. Anita Archer serves as an educational consultant to school districts on effective instruction, classroom management, language arts instruction, and study skills instruction. She has taught elementary and middle school students and is the recipient of eight Outstanding Educator awards. She has been a faculty member at San Diego State University, the University of Washington, and the University of Oregon. Dr. Archer is nationally known for her presentations and publications on instructional procedures and design. She has authored many other curriculum and training materials as well as book chapters and books.

Mary M. Gleason, Ph.D.

Dr. Mary Gleason is an educational consultant to school districts on implementation of literacy programs. Previously, Dr. Gleason was director of training for the National Institute for Direct Instruction. She began her career by teaching for eight years in general and special education classrooms. For 20 years as a professor at the University of Oregon, she designed and taught more than 40 college courses, including supervision and coaching, instructional design, methods for special education and general education, and technology in education. She is the author or coauthor of many journal articles, books, and curriculum materials. Her research focuses on academic interventions for students with learning disabilities.

Vicky Vachon, Ph.D.

 Dr. Vicky Vachon is an educational consultant to school districts in the United States and Canada. She began her career as a classroom teacher in 1971. In 1983, she completed a master's degree in education at the University of Oregon. On returning to Canada, she worked as a teacher for the Toronto Board of Education. She was assigned to a multidisciplinary assessment team at the Child Development Clinic, Hospital for Sick Children, for nine years. In 1995, Vicky returned to the University of Oregon to complete a doctoral degree in special education. Her doctoral dissertation was about the effects of mastery of multisyllabic word reading component skills and the effects of context on the word and text reading skills of middle school students with reading deficiencies. She is a project director for the National Institute for Direct Instruction, overseeing the usage of language arts and math curricula in several schools.

Contents

Introduction

Overview

What is *REWARDS Intermediate*?

REWARDS Intermediate is a specialized reading program designed to teach intermediate students (grades 4, 5, and 6) in elementary schools a flexible strategy for decoding long words and to increase their oral and silent reading fluency. The letters in the acronym stand for:

R—Reading

E—Excellence:

W—Word

A—Attack and

R—Rate

D—Development

S—Strategies.

What are the goals of *REWARDS Intermediate*?

As a result of participation in this program, students will:

- Decode previously unknown multisyllabic words containing two to eight word parts.

- Accurately read more multisyllabic words within sentences.

- Accurately read more multisyllabic words found in science, social studies, and health textbooks and in other classroom materials.

- Have expanded vocabulary.

- Read narrative and expository text not only accurately but fluently.

- Experience increased comprehension as their accuracy, fluency, and vocabulary increase.

- Have more confidence in their reading ability.

Which students would benefit from participating in this program?

REWARDS Intermediate is designed for use with students in the intermediate grades (fourth, fifth, and sixth grades) who have mastered the decoding of single-syllable words and are ready for multisyllabic words. Eligible students should have mastered the basic reading skills associated with first and second grade expectations but are unable to accurately and fluently read grade-level passages. Students who read at the 2.5 to 5th grade reading level and who orally read between 60 and 120 words per minute would particularly benefit from *REWARDS Intermediate*.

If students read below the 2.5 reading level or read fewer than 60 words per minute, they should **not** be placed in *REWARDS Intermediate*. Instead, these students would benefit from a program that explicitly and systematically increases their word identification skills for one- and two-syllable words and provides them with fluency practice at their instructional level before moving into *REWARDS Intermediate*.

In what types of settings has *REWARDS Intermediate* been used?

Because *REWARDS Intermediate* is a short-term intervention, it has been taught in several settings including:

1. **General Education Classes**

   REWARDS Intermediate has been used at the beginning of the school year to review and expand the decoding skills of intermediate students (fourth, fifth, and sixth graders) in general education classes. The increased decoding and fluency skills that resulted allowed students more ease in reading anthology selections, chapter books, and content-area textbooks.

2. **Remedial Reading Classes**

   REWARDS Intermediate has also been used with struggling readers in remedial reading classes, special education resource rooms, and specialized tutoring programs. Once *REWARDS Intermediate* has been taught, teachers are encouraged to continue decoding and fluency exercises similar to those found in Lessons 20–25 using selections from their core reading program or content-area materials.

3. **Intensive Remedial Programs** (summer school programs, after-school programs)

REWARDS Intermediate has proven to be a very effective intervention, particularly in summer school programs. The fact that the program consists of only 25 lessons has made it a perfect match to summer school.

Why might you want to teach *REWARDS Intermediate*?

• **Word recognition is a necessary, though not sufficient, skill to allow comprehension.**

Although the ultimate goal of reading instruction is comprehension, not word recognition, all of us recognize the importance of word recognition skills. If I am unable to read the words, I have no pathway to comprehension. In fact, many researchers have concluded that poorly developed word recognition skills are the most pervasive and debilitating source of reading challenges (Adams, 1990; Perfetti, 1985; Share & Stanovich, 1995).

In addition, if students' word recognition skills and fluency are low, making reading laborious, they are unlikely to select reading as a recreational activity or to complete class assignments. Thus, as Stanovich (1986) summarized in *Matthew Effects in Reading*, "The rich get richer. The poor poorer." Students who have difficulty with word recognition and fluency are less likely to get the practice they need to increase these very skills. For these reasons, it is important that we equip students with word recognition strategies as well as comprehension strategies.

• **Intermediate materials include many more multisyllabic words than primary materials.**

Nagy and Anderson (1984) determined that average students, from fifth grade on, encounter approximately 10,000 new words in print each year. Most of these new words are longer words having two or more syllables (Cunningham, 1998). Although multisyllabic words still do not make up all the words that students read, they do carry most of the meaning in a passage.

Assume that you cannot read multisyllabic words. Read the following passage, deleting the underlined multisyllabic words. How much would you gain from reading this science passage?

"At high <u>altitudes</u>, air <u>pressure</u> is much <u>lower</u>, and so the <u>boiling</u> point is <u>reduced</u>. If you could go many <u>kilometers</u> <u>above</u> the Earth's <u>surface</u>, the <u>pressure</u> of the air would be so low that you could boil <u>water</u> at <u>ordinary</u> room <u>temperature</u>! <u>However</u>, this <u>boiling</u> <u>water</u> would be cool. You would not be able to cook <u>anything</u> in this <u>water</u>. For it is the heat in <u>boiling</u> <u>water</u> that cooks food, not <u>simply</u> the <u>boiling</u> <u>process</u>."

—*Matter: Building Block of the Universe* (1994) published by Prentice Hall.

- **For many students, decoding instruction ended with second grade.**

Most systematic word recognition instruction occurs only in the primary grades. In fact, the document "Becoming a Nation of Readers" (Anderson, Hiebert, Scott, & Wilkinson, 1985) actually recommends that phonics instruction be completed by the end of second grade. This is unfortunate, given that the number of multisyllabic words dramatically increases in third grade materials, leaving students with strategies for monosyllabic words but without strategies for longer words.

- **Many students in intermediate grades are hampered by their inability to read multisyllabic words.**

If you picked up this program, you probably have personal experience working with intermediate students who are intimidated by long words and lack systematic strategies for attacking these words. Several researchers have validated your personal observations. Poor decoders, even those who can decode single-syllable words, have a difficult time with multisyllabic words (Just & Carpenter, 1987; Samuels, LaBerge, & Bremer, 1978). Shefelbine and Calhoun (1991) analyzed the decoding errors of low and high-intermediate decoders. They determined that low decoders correctly pronounced fewer affixes and vowel sounds, disregarded large portions of letter information, and were two to four times more likely to omit syllables. Perfetti (1986) concluded that the ability to decode long words increases the qualitative differences between good and poor readers.

- **Students need to be taught flexible strategies for unlocking the pronunciation of long words.**

When you were an elementary student, you were probably taught a set of syllabication rules for segmenting words. After breaking the words into syllables, you were to apply your phonics knowledge to the parts and to say the word. These rules are seldom taught today as a decoding strategy partially because teachers realized that the rules didn't improve decoding. Actually, Canney and Schreiner (1977) found no relationship between knowing syllabication rules and successful reading.

The strategy taught in *REWARDS Intermediate* is based on our current knowledge of word recognition. Words are identified on the basis of the brain's processing letter by letter and then using context to ensure that what has been read makes sense (Cunningham, 1998; Stanovich, 1991). The eye-movement research done with computerized tracking indicates that readers look at every word and almost every letter of each word (Rayner & Pollatsek, 1989). Thus, the *REWARDS* strategy teaches students to examine the letters and patterns in words rather than guess the word's pronunciation from context. Second, we understand that the major word-recognition function of the brain is pattern detection (Cunningham, 1998). The strategy taught in *REWARDS Intermediate* is based on the two most useful patterns found in multisyllabic words: (1) Affixes (prefixes and suffixes) are present in about 80 percent of multisyllabic words; and (2) All parts of multisyllabic words contain a vowel grapheme (a letter or letters that correspond to a vowel sound). In order to decode a word, a student doesn't need to segment the word into perfect dictionary syllables but rather into manageable chunks that can be decoded. The student also doesn't need to emerge with the exact pronunciation of the word on the first attempt. Instead, the student achieves a close approximation of the word's pronunciation and corrects it using his/her knowledge of language and the context in which the word appears. A flexible strategy rather than a rigid, rule-bound strategy is taught in *REWARDS Intermediate*.

- **Teaching strategies for reading longer words is very helpful to students.**

  Several studies have shown that teaching students strategies for decoding longer words improves their decoding ability. Shefelbine (1990) taught fourth and sixth graders having difficulty decoding multisyllabic words to use affixes and vowels to pronounce long words. When compared with a control group, they made significant gains in their ability to pronounce long words.

  Using an earlier version of the *REWARDS* program (now revised based on research and feedback), the authors of *REWARDS Intermediate* conducted two formal studies that verified the power of the *REWARDS* strategy for improving students' word recognition skills.

  In the first study, statistically significant differences in reading skills were observed between reading-deficient fourth and fifth graders receiving the multisyllabic (*REWARDS*) strategy instruction and those receiving monosyllabic word instruction. Similar student gains were observed in the second controlled study, in which reading-deficient sixth, seventh, and eighth graders served as subjects. Significant increases in word reading accuracy and fluency were observed in students using the *REWARDS* program. More complete descriptions of these studies are found in Appendix G at the end of the *Teacher's Guide*.

What is the content of *REWARDS*?

As noted previously, students are taught a flexible strategy for reading longer words rather than a set of rigid syllabication rules. This strategy is based on two realities of the English language: (1) Eighty percent of multisyllabic words contain at least one prefix or suffix; and (2) All decodable parts of a word contain vowels. Thus, the students are taught to identify prefixes, suffixes, and vowel sounds in the rest of the word to assist them in segmenting the word into manageable, decodable "chunks." The students are then taught to say the word parts and to say the whole word. No decoding strategy in English will yield accurate pronunciation of every word. Instead, the goal is to achieve a close approximation to the actual pronunciation and to correct that pronunciation using oral-aural language and context.

- In *REWARDS Intermediate,* students are initially taught a strategy containing *overt* behaviors (circling and underlining). The steps of this strategy include:

Overt Strategy

1. Circle the prefixes.

2. Circle the suffixes.

3. Underline the vowels.

4. Say the parts of the word.

5. Say the whole word.

6. Make it a real word.

EXAMPLE

(re)(con)str<u>u</u>c(tion)

Because students would not be expected to stop reading when encountering a multisyllabic word in order to circle the prefixes and suffixes and underline the vowels, circling and underlining behaviors are gradually faded. In the end, students use the following *covert strategy.* The steps of this strategy include:

Covert Strategy

1. Look for prefixes, suffixes, and vowels.

2. Say the parts of the word.

3. Say the whole word.

4. Make it a real word.

As you would expect, many students would have difficulty learning this strategy, not because of the strategy's complexity, but rather because of unknown preskills. To apply these strategies, the students must be able to:

1. Say the correct vowel sound (phoneme) when shown the corresponding letter or letters (grapheme).

2. Say the sound (short sound) and name (long sound) for single vowel letters.

3. Underline vowel graphemes within words.

4. Sound out parts of words containing various vowel graphemes.

5. Say the correct pronunciation for common prefixes and suffixes.

6. Circle prefixes and suffixes.

7. Blend auditorily presented word parts into a word.

8. Adjust incorrect pronunciations of longer words when the words are presented in context.

Because of the importance of these preskills to student success, Lessons 1–15 of *REWARDS Intermediate* are dedicated to preskill training. In Lessons 16–25, students are introduced to the *REWARDS* flexible decoding strategy. To increase the probability that students will transfer this strategy to their classroom reading assignments, practice activities are provided in which students read longer words within sentences and passages. Because accuracy without automaticity will not serve students, rate development exercises are also provided. In addition, students are taught that many of the prefixes and suffixes carry specific meanings and that those meanings can assist in deciphering the meaning of an unknown word.

How to Use This Program

What are the components of *REWARDS Intermediate*?

1. *Teacher's Guide*

   The *Teacher's Guide* consists of the following three sections:

   a. **Introduction**

      This section provides information about the program and how the program is implemented. The introduction should be carefully read before implementation.

   b. **Lessons**

      Twenty-five comprehensive teacher-directed lessons provide information for the teacher to ensure successful implementation of the program. Each lesson contains instructional activities, activity procedures, and lesson blueprints (scripts) that outline suggested teacher wording and student responses.

      The activities for the preskill lessons (Lessons 1–15) are similar each day, as are activities for the strategy lessons (Lessons 16–25). For each activity, two "lesson plans" are given. First, there is a general description of the activity. Next, there is a teacher script that includes wording a teacher could use when teaching the lesson. The scripts were developed for the formal research projects and field-testing of the *REWARDS* program to ensure fidelity of treatment across teachers.

      Please read the lessons prior to instruction, including the activity procedures and the scripts. You may then choose to follow the general procedure or the script, maintaining the essence of the activity in either case.

   c. **Additional Materials**—In the back of the *Teacher's Guide*, you will find:

      - Blackline Masters for Overhead Transparencies*

      - Strategies for Reading Long Words (Appendix A)*

      - Student Reference Chart: Prefixes, Suffixes, and Vowel Combinations (Appendix B)*

      - Pretest/Posttest and Generalization Test (Appendix C)

      - Pretest/Posttest Reading Fluency (Appendix D)

      - Fluency Graph: Correct Words Per Minute (Appendix E)*

* A complete set of transparencies may be purchased separately.

- Incentive Program (Appendix F)
- Research on *REWARDS* (Appendix G)
- Word List for *REWARDS Intermediate* (Appendix H)

2. **Student Book**

The *Student Book* contains the student material used in the lessons for the various teacher-directed and practice activities. All student materials needed for the program are found in the *Student Book*.

What activities are included in the *REWARDS Intermediate* program?

1. **Preskill Lesson Activities (Lessons 1–15)**

The first 15 lessons present the preskills necessary for applying the flexible decoding strategy taught in *REWARDS Intermediate*. Please read the description of each preskill activity so that you will understand the rationale for the activity.

a. **Oral Activity—Blending Word Parts Into Words**

When a student sounds out a long word, he/she must blend the parts into a recognizable whole. This blending skill can be practiced auditorily even before the decoding strategy is introduced. In this activity, the teacher says a word, separating its parts (e.g., for the word *intermission*, say *in ter mis sion*), and the students say the whole word quickly. The words used in this activity appear later in decoding exercises in order to expand students' familiarity with the pronunciation of the words. When pronouncing the words by parts, pause for a second between parts. This will not only make the task more challenging but also will parallel what students experience when sounding out words.

b. **Vowel Combinations**

Most students know consonant sounds, but many struggling readers have not yet mastered the sounds of vowel combinations (digraphs and diphthongs). In this book, students are introduced to the common sounds (major sounds) for high-frequency vowel combinations (**ay, ai, au, er, ir, ur, ar, or, a-e, o-e, i-e, e-e, u-e, oi, oy, ee, oa, ou**) and the major and minor sounds for **ow** (*low, down*), **oo** (*moon, book*), and **ea** (*meat, thread*). After each vowel combination is presented, it is reviewed in subsequent lessons to ensure accurate and quick recognition.

Before you introduce a phoneme-grapheme association, check the pronunciation using the following table. Accurate pronunciation is essential in all lessons.

Vowel Combinations Shown in the Order of Introduction (See Appendix B for a vowel combination reference chart grouped by type.)			
Vowel Combination	Key Word	Vowel Combination	Key Word
ay	say	**i - e**	side
ai	rain	**e - e**	Pete
au	sauce	**u - e**	use
er	her	**oi**	boil
ir	bird	**oy**	boy
ur	turn	**ee**	deep
ar	farm	**oa**	boat
or	torn	**ou**	loud
a - e	make	**ow**	low, down
o - e	hope	**oo**	moon, book
		ea	meat, thread

c. **Vowel Conversions**

When a student encounters a single vowel letter in a word, the student should first try the short sound (referred to as "the sound" in *REWARDS Intermediate*). If the student does not emerge with a recognizable word, he/she should then say the long sound (referred to as "the name"). In this activity, the students practice saying the sound and then the name for the letters **a**, **i**, **o**, **u**, and **e**. (This order of introduction was used to separate the easily confused sounds of **i** and **e**.)

d. **Reading Parts of Real Words**

In this activity, students practice reading parts of words (e.g., *pede, murd, mi*). Although these appear to be nonsense words, they are actually parts of multisyllabic words that students will encounter later in the program. The purposes of this activity are to: (1) Provide students with decoding practice using recently introduced vowel graphemes in short word parts initially rather than in multisyllabic words; (2) Increase the speed at which students decode; and (3) Make reading longer words easier.

e. **Underlining Vowels in Words**

Each part of a long word contains a vowel grapheme. Thus, locating the vowel graphemes is very helpful in segmenting a word into decodable chunks. In this activity, students locate and underline vowel graphemes within words (e.g., sp_o_rtsm_a_n, destr_oy_). Next, the teacher segments the word into parts. Students say the parts and then the whole word. Thus, practice reading long words begins in the preskill lessons with the teacher segmenting the words for the students by looping under the word parts.

f. **Oral Activity—Correcting Close Approximations Using Context**

No matter what strategy is used to determine the pronunciation of an unknown word, perfection cannot be guaranteed given the nature of English. Therefore, use of a decoding strategy often yields a pronunciation that is a close approximation to the word, but not the exact pronunciation. These close approximations must be turned into real words using oral/aural language in conjunction with the context. In this oral activity, the teacher intentionally mispronounces a word in a manner similar to common decoding errors (e.g., *hot el*, stressing the *hot* in *hotel*), repeats the mispronunciation within a sentence (We stayed in a *hot el.*), and asks the students to produce the accurate pronunciation of the word. While enjoying this "detective" game activity, students are learning a critical decoding skill—the words we read must be real words that other English speakers have said or heard.

g. **Prefixes and Suffixes**

About 80 percent of multisyllabic words have one or more affix. Thus, the ability to quickly identify and pronounce prefixes (e.g., *re, un, dis*) and suffixes (e.g., *tion, al, able*) facilitates the accurate, fluent decoding of longer words. Prefixes and suffixes have four characteristics: a specific pronunciation, a specific spelling, a specific meaning, and an attachment to a root word. Thus, affixes assist us in decoding and spelling the word and, if the root word is known, assist us with word meaning.

However, in many cases the root word is not familiar to us. For example, the root may be an archaic form or may have meaning in another language, such as Greek or Latin. In other situations, peeling off the affixes leaves a part that is an unfamiliar root word. In these instances, affixes may be helpful only with decoding and spelling because the affix does not carry a familiar meaning that is easily identifiable. Though these elements may not technically be acting as prefixes and suffixes within a specific word, they are still tremendously useful decoding elements.

In this activity, students listen to the pronunciation of prefixes and suffixes, practice saying these affixes, and review previously introduced affixes, the goal being accurate and quick pronunciation.

The following high-frequency prefixes and suffixes are introduced in this program. On the day a new affix is introduced, we suggest that you write the affix on an index card and place it on a chart labeled "Prefixes and Suffixes." This will assist students in many of the activities until mastery has been achieved. After completion of the program, you may wish to add less frequent affixes that you and your students encounter. An alphabetized reference chart is found at the back of this *Teacher's Guide* (Appendix B) and at the back of the *Student Book* as well as being available as a classroom wall poster. Refer students to this chart for use during Lessons 16–25.

Before you introduce a prefix or suffix, check the pronunciation. Accurate pronunciation is essential in all lessons. Because many of these affixes are not pronounced as you would expect, they are introduced with a key word.

Prefixes Shown in the Order of Introduction		
(See Appendix B for an alphabetized reference chart.)		
Prefix	Key Word	Meaning
dis	disagree	away, apart; negative
mis	mistake	wrong; not
ab	absent	from; away; off; not
ad	addition	to, toward; against
in	incomplete	in, into; not; really
im	immature	in, into; not
com	compare	with; together; really
con	continue	with; together; really
be	belong	really; by; to make
pre	prevent	before
de	depart	away from; down; negative
re	return	again, back, really
pro	protect	in favor of; before; forward
per	permit	through; really
un	unfair	not; reversal of; remove

a	above	in, on, at; not, without
ex	export	out, away
en	enlist	in; within; on

Suffixes Shown in the Order of Introduction (See Appendix B for an alphabetized reference chart.)		
Suffix	Key Word	Meaning
s	birds	more than one, verb marker
ing	running	when you do something; quality, state
ed	landed	in the past; quality
ness	kindness	that which is; state, quality
less	useless	without; not
ic	athletic	like; related to
ate	regulate	to make, act; having the quality of
ish	selfish	like, related to; to make
ist	artist	one who
ism	realism	state, quality; act
est	biggest	the most
ful	careful	full of
or	tailor	one who; that which
er	farmer	more; one who, that which
al	final	related to, like
age	courage	that which; state
le	cradle	—
tion	action	state, quality; act
sion	discussion	state, quality; act
tive	attentive	one who; quality of
sive	expensive	one who; quality of
y	thirsty	having the quality of; in the manner of; small
ly	safely	how something is
ary	missionary	related to
ity	oddity	quality; state

ant	dormant	one that performs; thing that promotes; being
ent	persistent	one that performs; thing that promotes; being
ment	argument	that which; quality, act
ance	disturbance	action, process; quality or state
ence	influence	action, process; quality or state
ous	famous	having the quality of
ture	picture	state; quality; that which
able	comfortable	able to be
ible	reversible	able to be
ize	memorize	to become

h. **Circling Prefixes and Suffixes**

"Peeling off" the prefixes and suffixes is a critical part of the strategy taught in this program that makes the task of reading long words significantly easier. In this exercise, the students identify, circle, and pronounce and then—with teacher assistance in segmenting—read words with prefixes and suffixes. The goal is to quickly recognize very common affixes embedded within words and to see their usefulness as a decoding tool.

i. **Vocabulary**

While *REWARDS Intermediate* is primarily a decoding and fluency program, expansion of student vocabulary is also a focus. In each of the preskill lessons, word meanings for select words are introduced using two procedures. First, to show the students how the addition of a prefix or suffix can systematically alter the meaning of a word, students are given a definition that stresses the meaning of the affix (e.g., *not loyal*) and asked to locate the corresponding word (e.g., *disloyal*). Second, students are provided explicit vocabulary instruction on two "special vocabulary" terms. In this instruction, students are given a "student-friendly explanation" for the word, and their understanding is checked using examples and non-examples or questions that require deep processing of the word's meaning.

j. **Spelling Dictation**

Many students who have poor decoding skills also have low spelling knowledge and are intimidated by longer words. In this activity, the teacher dictates a lesson word; the students say the parts in the word as they put up one finger for each part, and then they write the word. Next, the students compare their spellings to the correct spelling of the word. Finally, they cross out any misspellings and rewrite those words.

2. **Strategy Lesson Activities (Lessons 16–25)**

In Lessons 16–25, all of the preskills are incorporated into the flexible decoding strategy that is the heart of this program. Students practice the strategy using word lists, complex sentences, and expository passages. The following activities are found in each of these lessons.

a. **Vowel Combinations Review**

Students quickly review all of the vowel combinations taught in the initial 15 lessons. The goals of this practice are automaticity, instant recognition, and pronunciation of the vowels.

b. **Vowel Conversions Review**

Students practice saying the sound and then the name of each letter.

c. **Prefixes and Suffixes Review**

To sharpen their ability to recognize and correctly pronounce affixes, students review them each day. Again, as with the vowel review, developing automaticity is another goal.

d. **Strategy Instruction**

In this activity, the teacher demonstrates each step in the overt strategy and guides students in applying the strategy steps. This, of course, is the most important activity in the program. You will need to carefully read the instructional procedures to ensure clarity.

e. **Strategy Practice**

To take any skill to the point of automaticity, extensive practice is needed. In this activity, students circle prefixes and suffixes, underline the vowels in the rest of the word, and read the words by parts, thus applying the strategy with less teacher assistance.

f. **Independent Strategy Practice**

The final goal of the program is to decode long words without the use of the overt steps of circling and underlining. Therefore, in this activity, which begins in Lesson 22, students visually examine long words looking for prefixes, suffixes, and vowels, and determine the pronunciation of the word. If students have difficulty, they are encouraged to pick up their pencils and circle the prefixes and suffixes and underline the vowels so that they can segment the word into decodable chunks.

g. **Word Families**

To visually reinforce the morphographic nature of English, in Lessons 16–25, students read "word families," which are groups of words having the same base. For example, students read the family "*manage, manager, management, manageable, mismanage, mismanaged, and unmanageable.*" After reading the first word in the family, students figure out the remaining words in the list on their own, then read the list with the teacher twice, and finally read the list to a partner.

h. **Spelling**

The spelling activity introduced in the preskill lessons continues throughout the program, using four words from the decoding instruction of each lesson.

i. **Vocabulary**

As in the preskill lessons, vocabulary instruction is provided on selected words in each lesson.

j. **Sentence and Passage Reading**

As you have probably already experienced when teaching various strategies to your students, the challenge is not always teaching the strategy but getting students to use the strategy. For this reason, specific generalization activities are included to promote generalization of the strategy to daily reading. In Lessons 16–20, students practice reading sentences laden with multisyllabic words. In the final lessons, students will practice their multisyllabic word reading strategies while reading interesting expository passages.

Sentences. Initially, the generalization practice involves reading sentences containing many multisyllabic words that were introduced in the same and previous lessons. First, the students read the sentence silently, allowing them time to apply the *REWARDS* strategy to any particularly difficult words. Next, the students read the sentence orally so the teacher and students can monitor their reading accuracy. Three oral reading options are suggested: choral reading with the teacher, partner reading, and calling on an individual to read if the group size is small.

Passages. To further promote generalization of the strategy to daily reading, students practice the strategy as they read expository passages. Prior to passage reading, the teacher tells students the pronunciation of some difficult words and leads them in applying the *REWARDS* strategy to other difficult-to-pronounce words. In addition, definitions of all of the words are presented, with more extensive instruction given on four critical passage-word meanings.

After the passage preparation, students are guided in reading the passage. They read the passage segment by segment, first reading each segment silently and then orally, answering questions about the content.

k. **Passage Reading—Fluency**

Several studies have determined that students' oral reading fluency is correlated with reading comprehension. As students read words more fluently, they can turn their attention from decoding to comprehension.

The following oral reading rate goals represent the number of words read correctly in one minute at different reading levels (not grade levels).

Reading Level	Words Read Correctly in a Minute (CWPM)*
Grades 4 and 5	120–150 CWPM
Grade 6	150–180 CWPM

* CWPM = correct words per minute

Oral reading fluency can be increased through multiple rereadings of passages for which the reader already has a high level of accuracy. After practicing the passage for the purpose of accuracy, the students whisper-read the passage for a minute, noting their ending points. This is then repeated, with students trying to read beyond their initial ending points. Next, the students exchange books, listen to their partners read for a minute, and record their partners' errors. At the close of this activity, students determine and graph (using the Fluency Graph at the back of the *Student Book*) the number of correctly read words on the last timing. Teachers have consistently reported that this activity was a student favorite.

Student Motivation

How can I motivate my students?

As in all academic and nonacademic areas, students are significantly more motivated if they experience success. Thus, we must teach in such a way that students can obtain as much success as possible. Careful lesson preparation, intentional modeling of skills and strategies, and effective correction of errors are three teacher behaviors that increase students' success. In addition, the lesson delivery must be lively, with lots of responses garnered from the students.

Student motivation is also influenced by your personal enthusiasm. If you reflect a belief that this program is important and will make a difference in students' reading ability, that enthusiasm will affect your students' view of the program. Your enthusiasm can be conveyed both through your positive comments and body language (smiles, nods).

Motivation can also be increased by sharing with students the relevance of the program content: why reading long words accurately and fluently is important, when they can use the strategies, and where they can use the strategies. In the first lesson, the purpose of the program is introduced to the students. However, you can continue to reiterate the importance of the program throughout the 25 lessons.

Students who are involved in this program have often previously experienced reading failure. For this reason, they may be reluctant learners. To establish a positive climate that makes each student comfortable, you should praise students for their academic efforts, accurate reading, and appropriate behavior. In addition to verbal praise, some classes will benefit from a formal incentive program. An example can be found in Appendix F of the *Teacher's Guide*.

What can I do if students' attention begins to wane during the practice activities?

To maintain students' attention without sacrificing the necessary practice that leads to automaticity, the following practice procedures can be used.

1. **Partner Reading**

   After the students read any of the lists with the teacher, have them reread a portion of the list to their partners. One student becomes the reader, the other the coach. If the reader makes an error, the coach tells the reader to use what he/she has learned to figure out the word. If the reader cannot correct the error within three seconds, the coach says the word. Have students switch roles.

2. **Timed Word List Reading**

After a list of words has been read under teacher guidance, engage the students in mini-timings. Have one student whisper-read words for 10 seconds to his/her partner. As the student reads, the partner counts the number of words read. Have the partners switch roles.

3. **Team Practice**

After an initial reading of a list, two partnerships form a team. The four students read the list "round-robin," each student saying a word.

4. **Cross-Out**

After initial reading of the list, students can play cross-out. One student says a word, and everyone crosses out the word on his/her word list. The next student says a word, and students cross out that word. This continues until all words are crossed out.

5. **Cross-Out Variation (Game Format)**

Have each student circle three words on his/her word list. Be sure that the students do not show classmates their circled words. Read any word from the list. Have students locate and cross out the word. Continue reading words from the list in random order. The winner of the game is the person whose circled words are crossed out first.

6. **I'm Thinking of a Word**

After an initial reading of a list, tell the students a statement that relates to the meaning of a word on the list (e.g., "I am thinking of a word that means 'to tell someone the wrong information.'"). Have each student locate the word, compare his/her choice with the partner's, and say the word.

Frequently Asked Questions

How can I actively involve my students in the instruction?

Student achievement is highly related to opportunities to respond. When students constantly say, write, or do things in a lesson, they are much more likely to be attentive and to learn from the resulting practice. The following chart outlines some of the procedures you may wish to use to involve all students in the lessons.

Best Practices for Eliciting Responses	
Type of Response	Best Practice
Group Says Answer (A group response can be used when the wording is short and the same for all students.)	**If students are looking at the teacher.** • The teacher asks a question. • The teacher raises his/her hands to signal when students should start thinking about the question. • The students think of the answer. • The teacher says, "Everyone," and lowers his/her hands. • The students say the answer. **If students are looking at their work.** • The teacher asks a question or gives a directive. • The teacher gives the students thinking time. The students think of the answer. • The teacher signals audibly (e.g., voice signal, such as "Everyone"). • The students respond.
Partners Say Answer	• The teacher assigns a response partner to each student and the numbers 1 and 2. • The teacher asks a question or gives a directive. • The teacher asks Partner 1 to respond. ("Ones, tell your partner …"). • The student tells the answer to his/her partner. • The teacher monitors the class and gives feedback to each group.
Individual Says Answer	• The teacher asks a question. • The teacher raises his/her hands to signal when students should start thinking about the question and gives eye contact to all students to encourage formulation of an answer. • The students think of an answer. • The teacher calls on one student. • The student gives an answer.
Students Write Answer	• The teacher gives a directive or asks a question and tells students to put their pencils down and to look up when they are done. • The students write a response. • The teacher monitors the students. • The teacher gives feedback to students.

How much time do the lessons take?

The amount of time needed to complete each lesson varies greatly depending on the size of the group, the competency of the students, and the pace of the teacher. Generally, though, the teacher should allocate 50 to 60 minutes for each lesson. If teachers do not complete a lesson, they can review the lesson's content and complete it the following day.

How should errors be corrected?

The type of correction is dependent on the type of error. The following chart lists common errors and the recommended correction procedures.

Type of Error	Recommended Correction
The student mispronounces a vowel combination (e.g., *ai*).	• The teacher says the sound. "The sound is /ā/." • Then, the teacher has the group repeat the sound. "Everyone, what sound?"
The student mispronounces a prefix or suffix (e.g., *dis*).	• The teacher says the affix. "The prefix is *dis*." • Then, the teacher has the group repeat the affix. "Everyone, what prefix?"
When reading a long word, the student says a close approximation of the word but not the accurate pronunciation (e.g., the student says *redooction* for *reduction*).	• First, the teacher directs the student to correct the word. "Can you make it a real word?" • If the student cannot correct the pronunciation of the word, the teacher tells the student the word and has the group repeat the word. "The word is *reduction*. Everyone, what word?"
In Lessons 16–25, a student can't pronounce a long word (e.g., the student says, "I don't know the word" or mispronounces the word).	• The teacher directs the student to use the *REWARDS* strategy for figuring out the word. "Use what you have learned to figure out this word." • If the student cannot figure out the word in four seconds, the teacher tells the student the word and has the student or group repeat the word. "The word is *reduction*. Everyone, what word?" • If the word is in a sentence, the teacher may wish to have the student reread the sentence. "Go back to the beginning of the sentence."

What kind of assessment can be used to determine which students would be candidates for the *REWARDS* program?

If students can successfully read second grade material (one- and two-syllable words) but struggle with reading third through fifth grade material, they are candidates for this program. To determine an approximate grade level for word identification for your students, any form of assessment that allows you to designate a grade level for their current skills (e.g., the San Diego Quick Assessment, Woodcock Reading Mastery Tests, Gates-McGinitie Reading Test) can be used. Students who score below the third grade reading level should not be placed in *REWARDS Intermediate.*

How can I measure the progress my students make in this program?

Use the Pretest/Posttests in Appendix C before the program is taught in order to establish the appropriateness of the program for a student and a baseline concerning his/her multisyllabic word reading. This same test can be administered when students complete the program. At the end of the program, you may also wish to administer the Generalization Test, which contains words that were not taught in the program.

In addition, we would recommend that you give a one-minute fluency test to each student before teaching the program and again afterward. You can find the necessary materials and directions in Appendix D.

How does *REWARDS Intermediate* differ from the original *REWARDS* program?

The original *REWARDS* program was designed for use with students who struggle with reading in fourth through twelfth grades. Although the program has been very successful, intermediate teachers provided the authors with a great deal of feedback that led to the redesign of *REWARDS*, specifically for intermediate students. These are the changes requested by teachers and reflected in *REWARDS Intermediate:*

1. The number of lessons was expanded from 20 to 25 to provide more practice for younger students.

2. With an expanded number of lessons, the vowels and affixes were introduced at a slower pace.

3. Words were selected that better matched the vocabulary of younger students.

4. Explicit vocabulary instruction was added to all lessons.

5. Practice reading word families was emphasized.

6. Sentence practice was introduced before passage reading to ensure higher success.

7. Age-appropriate passages were especially written for intermediate students to increase their interest.

Materials Needed	Preparation
• Lesson 1 from the *Student Book* • Overhead Transparency 1 • Washable overhead transparency pen • Paper or cardboard to use when covering the overhead transparency • Paper or cardboard for each student to use during spelling dictation	Write the following words on the board or overhead transparency: • incredible • descriptive • unconventionality

INTRODUCTION

1. In the next few weeks, we are going to learn a strategy for reading longer words. You will learn to figure out words such as (point to each word on the chalkboard or overhead) **incredible**, **descriptive**, and **unconventionality**.

2. In which of your subjects do you have to read longer words? (Call on several students.)

3. Please turn to page 1 in your *Student Book*.

4. Listen as I read the letter from the authors. (Read the letter from the *Student Book*.)

5. Now, we are going to learn the skills that you will need to read longer words. Then we will practice reading longer words.

ACTIVITY A: Oral Activity—Blending Word Parts Into Words

> **Activity Procedure:** In this activity, students learn to hear words pronounced part by part by part, before they blend the word parts together to make a real word. Say each word, pausing between the word parts, then have students blend the parts together and say the whole word.

1.   Open your *Student Book* to Lesson 1.

2.   Listen. I am going to say the parts of a word. You are going to say the whole word. Listen. (Say the word, pausing completely between the word parts.)
     tea spoon ful. What word? __

3.   (Repeat with the following examples.)

     as tro naut

     mis in form

     re con sid er

     pro fes sion al

     per son al i ty

ACTIVITY B: Vowel Combinations (See the *Student Book*, page 3.)

ay	ai
(say)	(rain)

> **Activity Procedure:** In this activity, students learn the sound to say when they see a combination of letters. Have students point to the letters in their *Student Books.* Tell students the sound as it is pronounced in the key word. Have students practice saying the sounds.

1.   Find Activity B. We are going to learn some sounds. You may know some of them already.

2.   Look at the box. Point to the letters **a - y**. The sound of these letters is usually /ā/. What sound? __

3.   Point to the letters **a - i**. The sound of these letters is usually /ā/. What sound? __

4.   Go back to the beginning of the line. Say the sounds again. What sound? __
     Next sound? __

ACTIVITY C: **Vowel Conversions** (See the *Student Book,* page 3.)

a	i

> **Activity Procedure:** In this activity, students learn to switch between saying the sound and saying the name for a particular vowel letter. They learn that when they see a vowel letter in a long word, they should first say the sound. If it doesn't make a real word, they will say the name. Have students point to the letter while you tell them the sound, and have them repeat the sound. Then, have students point to the same letter while you tell them the name, and have students repeat the name. Have students practice saying the sound, then the name for each letter.

1. Find Activity C. When you are reading words and see these letters, first try the sound. If it doesn't make a real word, then try the name.

2. Point to the first letter. The sound is /ă/. What sound? __ The name is **a**. What name? __

3. Point to the next letter. The sound is /ĭ/. What sound? __ The name is **i**. What name? __

4. First letter again. What sound? __ What name? __

5. Next letter. What sound? __ What name? __

ACTIVITY D: **Reading Parts of Real Words** (See the *Student Book*, page 3.)

1.	tain	mit	stract	mid
2.	ta *	id	vict	la *
3.	cay	dain	tri *	tract
4.	hap	trast	mand	trict

Activity Procedure: In this activity, students learn to read parts of words that come from real words. When separated from the whole word, many of these word parts look like nonsense words. When a vowel in a word part could be pronounced with either the sound or name, an asterisk under the vowel indicates that students should say the name. Ask students to say each word part to themselves, then aloud. Remind them what to do when they see the asterisk.

Note:
- On word parts with an asterisk under the vowel, tell students to say the name. Ask: "What name?"

1. Find Activity D. We are going to read parts of real words. Most of these word parts are not real words by themselves, but practicing them will help you read longer words later.

2. Line 1. Read the first word part to yourself. Put your thumb up when you can say the part. __ What part? __

3. Next word part. Thumbs-up when you are ready. __ What part?__

4. Next word part. (Pause.) What part? __

5. Next word part. (Pause.) What part? __

6. Line 2. Look at the vowel with the asterisk. What name? __ What part? __

7. Next word part. (Pause.) What part? __

8. Next word part. (Pause.) What part? __

9. Next word part. Look at the vowel with the asterisk. What name? __ What part? __

10. Line 3. First word part. What part? __

11. (Repeat "What part?" or "What name? What part?" with all remaining word parts.)

Note:
- You may wish to provide additional practice by having students read a line to the group or to a partner.

ACTIVITY E: **Underlining Vowels in Words** (See the *Student Book*, page 4.)

1.	pathway	waist	pigtail
2.	maintain	midday	rapid
3.	backspin	haystack	milkman
4.	railway	panic	strain
5.	midway	mailman	mainsail

Activity Procedure: In this activity, students learn that each part of a word has a vowel sound. They learn to use the vowel sounds to read the word parts, then blend the word parts together to say the whole word. Show students how to find the vowels and say the sounds. Next, ask them to say the word parts. Then, ask them to say the whole word.

Use Overhead 1: Activity E

1. Find Activity E. Listen. Each part of a word has one vowel sound. What does each word part have? __ Finding the vowels in a word helps us read the word.

2. Watch me find the vowels in these words. (Cover all lines on the overhead transparency except Line 1. On the transparency, underline the letters representing vowel sounds in **pathway**. Point to the vowels.) What sound? __ What sound? __ How many vowel sounds? __ So, how many word parts? __

3. Watch again. (Underline the letters representing a vowel sound in **waist**. Point to the vowel.) What sound? __ How many vowel sounds? __ So, how many word parts? __

4. Watch one more. (Underline the vowels in **pigtail**. Point to the vowels.) What sound? __ What sound? __ How many vowel sounds? __ So, how many word parts? __

5. Now, you underline the vowels in the words in Line 1. (Pause.) Now underline the vowels in the rest of the words. Look up when you are done. __

6. (Show the rest of the overhead transparency.) Now check to see if you underlined all the vowels. Fix any mistakes. __

7. (When students are done checking, assist them in reading each word, beginning with the first word in Line 1. Touch the vowels in **pathway**.) What sound? __ What sound? __

   (Then loop under each word part in **path way**.) What part? __ What part? __

   (Run your finger under the whole word.) What word? __

8. (Repeat Step 7 with all words in Activity E.)

Note:
   • You may wish to provide additional practice by having students read a line to the group or to a partner.

ACTIVITY F: **Oral Activity—Correcting Close Approximations Using Context**

> **Activity Procedure:** In this activity, students listen to mispronunciations similar to those that might be made while they decode words. Then they use the context of the sentence and their own language to make the word into a real word. Pronounce the word incorrectly as shown (stressing the word part in bold). When saying the sentence, continue to mispronounce the word. Then, ask students to make the word into a real word.

1. Listen. Sometimes when we read a longer word, the word doesn't sound right. We have to change the pronunciation of the word so it makes sense in the sentence. Let's see if you can change these words to make sense in the sentences.

2. Listen. I read the word "hus **bănd**." Change the word to make sense in this sentence. "Have you met Mrs. Smith's hus **bănd**?" What should the word be? __

3. (Repeat Step 2 with the following examples, stressing the bold word part.)

hŏt el	When we were on vacation, we stayed in a **hŏt** el.
tī mid	The quiet boy was very **tī** mid.
cap **tāīn**	The cap **tāīn** steered the boat to the dock.
ā **strō** naut	The ā **strō** naut went into outer space.

ACTIVITY G: **Prefixes and Suffixes** (See the *Student Book*, page 4.)

(dis)agree	dis
(mis)take	mis
(ab)sent	ab
(ad)dition	ad

Activity Procedure: In this activity, students learn to identify and pronounce prefixes and suffixes. In this lesson, have students first point to the words, then the circled prefixes, while you pronounce them. Ask students to repeat the words and prefixes after you.

1.   Find Activity G. Now, we are going to learn about word parts we call prefixes. Prefixes always come at the beginning of words. Do prefixes come at the beginning or at the end of words? __

2.   Point to the first column in the box. The first word is **disagree**. What word? __ Point to the circled prefix. The prefix is /dis/. Say it. __

3.   Point to the next word. The word is **mistake**. What word? __ Point to the circled prefix. The prefix is /mis/. Say it. __

4.   (Repeat with **absent** and /ab/, and **addition** and /ad/.)

5.   Find the second column. Read the prefixes. What prefix? __ Next? __ Next? __ Next? __

6.   The parts of words you just learned come at the beginning of words. What are they called? __ In the next activity, you are going to circle these prefixes.

ACTIVITY H: **Circling Prefixes and Suffixes** (See the *Student Book*, page 5.)

1.	misfit	dismiss	abstract
2.	dash	misplay	addict
3.	disband	misprint	disclaim
4.	dismay	mint	distract
5.	display	admit	mislaid
6.	aim	district	disdain
7.	abstain	mishap	miscast

Activity Procedure: In this activity, students practice identifying the prefixes and suffixes learned in the previous activity. In this lesson, tell students to find the prefixes they have learned and circle them. Then, assist students in checking their worksheets and reading the words, first part by part, then the whole word. For additional fluency building, time students for 10 seconds to see how many words they can read.

 Use Overhead 1: Activity H

1.   Find Activity H. Circle the prefixes you learned in Activity G. Do prefixes come at the beginning or at the end of words? __ Be careful. Some words have no prefixes, and some words have one of the prefixes you just learned. Look up when you are done. __

2.   (Show the overhead transparency.) Now check to see if you circled all the prefixes. Fix any mistakes. __

3.   (When students are done checking, assist them in reading each word on the overhead transparency, beginning with the first word of Line 1.) Look up here. __

      (Loop under each word part in **mis fit**.) What part? __ What part? __

      (Run your finger under the whole word.) What word? __

4.   (Repeat Step 3 with all words in Activity H.)

5.   Get ready for a 10-second rapid read. Partner 1, you will be the first reader. Read as many words as you can until I say "Stop." Partner 2, count the words as your partner reads. Begin. (Time students for 10 seconds, and then say "Stop.")

6.   Partner 2, hold up your fingers and show me how many words your partner read. (Look around the group.) Partner 2, your turn to read. Partner 1, count the words as your partner reads. Begin. (Time students for 10 seconds, and then say "Stop.")

7.   Partner 1, hold up your fingers and show me how many words your partner read. (Look around the group.)

ACTIVITY I: **Vocabulary** (See the *Student Book,* page 5.)

a.	a person who is a wrong fit for a group of people
	e 1, Activity H) __misfit__
b.	.ot claim (Line 3, Activity H) __disclaim__
c.	laid down in the wrong place (Line 5, Activity H) __mislaid__

Special Vocabulary

1.   distract—If someone takes your attention away from what you are doing, they <u>distract</u> you.

2.   dismay—When you feel discouraged about a problem, you feel <u>dismay</u>.

> **Activity Procedure:** In this activity, students focus on the meaning of words when an affix is added. In the first part, they read a definition that includes the root word, and they locate a related word with an affix in Activity H. Read each definition and ask students to find the word that matches the meaning and write it in the space provided. In the second part, students read a word and an explanation of its meaning. Ask students to read each word silently and then read the word and the explanation aloud with you. Give several more examples of how the word might be used. Finally, have students tell their assigned partners a particular application of the word.

Note:
 • Read this activity *carefully* before you teach because the wording changes in each lesson.

1.   Find Activity I. Listen. You are going to learn the meanings of words that have prefixes.

2.   Listen to the first definition, "a person who is a wrong fit for a group of people." Find the word that means "a person who is a wrong fit for a group of people" in Line 1 of Activity H, and write it on the line after **a.** (Pause and monitor.) What word means "a person who is a wrong fit for a group of people"? (*misfit*)

3.   Listen to the next definition, "to not claim." Find the word in Line 3 and write it. (Pause and monitor.) What word means "to not claim"? (*disclaim*)

4.   Next. "Laid down in the wrong place." Find the word in Line 5 and write it. (Pause and monitor.) What word means "laid down in the wrong place"? (*mislaid*)

5.   Find *Special Vocabulary.* Let's learn two vocabulary words. Find Line 1. (Pause.) Read the word to yourself. (Pause.) What word? (*distract*)

6.   Read the explanation with me. "If someone takes your attention away from what you are doing, they <u>distract</u> you."

7.   If you are reading a book and loud music is playing, the music might _____. (*distract you*)

8.   If you are taking a math test and a friend starts talking to you, the friend might _____. (*distract you*)

9. Partner 1, tell your partner some things that might distract you if you were working on a project at home. __

10. Find Line 2. (Pause.) Read the word to yourself. (Pause) What word? (*dismay*)

11. Read the explanation with me. "When you feel discouraged about a problem, you feel <u>dismay</u>."

12. If you couldn't figure out why your friend wasn't talking to you, you would feel _____. (*dismay*)

13. Partner 2, tell your partner about a situation that would cause you dismay. __

ACTIVITY J: **Spelling Dictation** (See the *Student Book,* page 5.)

1. admit	2. display
3. mislaid	4. abstain

> **Activity Procedure:** In this activity, students practice spelling some of the words they've learned to read. For each word, tell students the word, then have students say the parts of the word with you. Have them say the parts to themselves as they write the word. Then, have students compare their words with your word written on an overhead transparency or the board. Finally, have students cross out and rewrite any misspelled words.

Note:
- Distribute a piece of light cardboard to each of the students so they can cover their page during spelling dictation. The cardboard can also be used as a bookmark so students can quickly locate pages at the beginning of the lesson.

1. Find Activity J. At the end of each lesson you will be spelling four of the lesson words. Please cover up the rest of the page with your cardboard.

2. The first word is **admit**. What word? __ Put your fist in the air. Put up one finger for each part and say the parts in **admit** with me. First part? (*ad*) Next part? (*mit*) Say the parts slowly to yourself as you write the word. (Pause and monitor.)

3. (Write **admit** on the board or overhead transparency.) Check **admit**. If you misspelled it, cross it out and write it correctly.

4. The second word is **display**. What word? __ Put your fist in the air. Put up one finger for each part and say the parts of **display** with me. First part? (*dis*) Next part? (*play*) Say the parts slowly to yourself as you write the word. (Pause and monitor.)

5. (Write **display** on the board or overhead transparency.) Check **display**. If you misspelled it, cross it out and write it correctly.

6. (Repeat the procedures for the words **mislaid** and **abstain**.)

Materials Needed

- Lesson 2 from the *Student Book*
- Overhead Transparency 2
- Washable overhead transparency pen
- Paper or cardboard to use when covering the overhead transparency
- Paper or cardboard for each student to use during spelling dictation

ACTIVITY A: **Oral Activity—Blending Word Parts Into Words**

> **Activity Procedure:** Say each word, pausing between the word parts, then have students blend the parts together and say the whole word.

1. Open your *Student Book* to Lesson 2.

2. Listen. I am going to say the parts of a word. You are going to say the whole word. (Say the word, pausing completely between the word parts.)
   re con struct. What word? ___

3. (Repeat with the following examples.)

   max i mum

   op ti mism

   dis a gree ment

   en ter tain ment

   con tam i nate

ACTIVITY B: **Vowel Combinations** (See the *Student Book*, page 6.)

au			
(sauce)			

1.	au	ai	ay	au
2.	ay	au	ai	au

Activity Procedure: Have students point to the combination of letters and tell students the sound as it is pronounced in the key word. Have students practice the new sound and the sounds from the previous lesson.

1. Find Activity B. We are going to learn a new sound. You may know it already.

2. Look at the box. Point to the letters **a - u**. The sound of these letters is usually /aw/. What sound? __

3. Say the sound again. What sound? __

4. Point to the first letters in Line 1. What sound? __ Next sound? __ Next sound? __ Next sound? __

5. Point to the first letters in Line 2. What sound? __ Next sound? __ Next sound? __ Next sound? __

ACTIVITY C: **Vowel Conversions** (See the *Student Book*, page 6.)

a	i

Activity Procedure: Have students point to the letter while you tell them the sound, and have them repeat the sound. Then, have students point to the same letter while you tell them the name, and have students repeat the name. Have students practice saying the sound, then the name for each letter.

1. Find Activity C. When you are reading words and see these letters, first try the sound. If it doesn't make a real word, then try the name.

2. Point to the first letter. The sound is /ă/. What sound? __ The name is **a**. What name? __

3. Point to the next letter. The sound is /ĭ/. What sound? __ The name is **i**. What name? __

4. First letter again. What sound? __ What name? __

5. Next letter. What sound? __ What name? __

ACTIVITY D: **Reading Parts of Real Words** (See the *Student Book,* page 6.)

1.	dit	rai	fant	bla *
2.	hib	tinct	ti *	hab
3.	pact	sist	naut	bi *
4.	flict	val	vic	jaun

Activity Procedure: Have students say each word part to themselves, then aloud. Remind them to say the name when they see the asterisk.

Note:
- On word parts with an asterisk under the vowel, tell students to say the name. Ask: "What name?"

1. Find Activity D. We are going to read parts of real words. Most of these word parts are not real words by themselves.

2. Line 1. Read the first word part to yourself. Put your thumb up when you can say the part. ___ What part? ___

3. Next word part. Thumbs-up when you are ready. ___ What part? ___

4. Next word part. (Pause.) What part? ___

5. Next word part. Look at the vowel with the asterisk. What name? ___ What part? ___

6. Line 2. First word part. What part? ___

7. Next word part. (Pause.) What part? ___

8. Next word part. Look at the vowel with the asterisk. What name? ___ What part? ___

9. Next word part. (Pause.) What part? ___

10. Line 3. First word part. What part? ___

11. (Repeat "What part?" or "What name? What part?" with all remaining word parts.)

Note:
- You may wish to provide additional practice by having students read a line to the group or to a partner.

ACTIVITY E: **Underlining Vowels in Words** (See the *Student Book*, page 7.)

1.	ransack	vault	raisin
2.	victim	waistband	fraud
3.	timid	fault	valid
4.	jaunt	claim	cause
5.	captain	audit	candid

Activity Procedure: Have students underline the vowels and say the sounds. Next, have them say the word parts and the whole word.

 Use Overhead 2: Activity E

1. Find Activity E. Listen. Each word part has one vowel sound. What does each word part have? __ Finding the vowels in a word helps us read the word.

2. Watch me find the vowels in these words. (Cover all lines on the overhead transparency except Line 1. On the transparency, underline the vowels in **ransack**. Point to the vowels.) What sound? __ What sound? __ How many vowel sounds? __ So, how many word parts? __

3. Watch again. (Underline the vowel in **vault**. Point to the vowel.) What sound? __ How many vowel sounds? __ So, how many word parts? __

4. Watch one more. (Underline the vowels in **raisin**. Point to the vowels.) What sound? __ What sound? __ How many vowel sounds? __ So, how many word parts? __

5. Now, you underline the vowels in the words in Line 1. (Pause.) Now underline the vowels in the rest of the words. Look up when you are done. __

6. (Show the rest of the overhead transparency.) Now check to see if you underlined all the vowels. Fix any mistakes. __

7. (When students are done checking, assist them in reading each word, beginning with the first word in Line 1. Touch the vowels in **ransack**.) What sound? __ What sound? __

    (Then loop under each word part in **ran sack**.) What part? __ What part? __

    (Run your finger under the whole word.) What word? __

8. (Repeat Step 7 with all words in Activity E.)

Note:
*   You may wish to provide additional practice by having students read a line to the group or to a partner.

ACTIVITY F: **Oral Activity—Correcting Close Approximations Using Context**

> **Activity Procedure:** Pronounce the word incorrectly as shown. When saying the sentence, continue to mispronounce the word. Then, ask students to make the word into a real word.

1. Listen. Sometimes when we read a longer word, the word doesn't sound right. We have to change the pronunciation of the word so that it makes sense in the sentence. Let's see if you can change these words to make sense in the sentences.

2. Listen. I read the word "vĭt **ā** mins." Change the word to make sense in this sentence. "Many people take vĭt **ā** mins to improve their health." What should the word be? __

3. (Repeat Step 2 with the following examples, stressing the bold word part.)

    hol ī day   In some countries, Thanksgiving Day is a special hol ī day.

    cur tāīn   To keep the sun out of your eyes, close the **cur** tāīn.

    a **bōve**   When something is over a table, it is a **bōve** the table.

    tor năd ō   The **tor** năd ō destroyed more than 100 houses.

ACTIVITY G: **Prefixes and Suffixes** (See the *Student Book,* page 7.)

(in)complete		in
(im)mature		im
(com)pare		com
(con)tinue		con

Prefixes						
1.	in	com	dis	mis	im	con
2.	im	ad	con	in	ab	com

> **Activity Procedure:** Have students first point to the words, then the circled prefixes, while you pronounce them. Ask students to repeat the words and prefixes after you. Then, have students practice saying the new prefixes and the ones from the previous lesson.

1. Find Activity G. We are going to learn more prefixes. Remember, prefixes always come at the beginning of words. Do prefixes come at the beginning or at the end of words? __

2. Point to the first column in the box. The first word is **incomplete**. What word? __ Point to the circled prefix. The prefix is /in/. Say it. __

3. Point to the next word. The word is **immature**. What word? __ Point to the circled prefix. The prefix is /im/. Say it. __

4. (Repeat with **compare** and /com/, and **continue** and /con/.)

5. Find the second column. Read the prefixes. What prefix? __ Next? __ Next? __ Next? __

6. Go to Line 1 in the next box. Point to the first prefix. What prefix? __ Next? __ Next? __ Next? __ Next? __ Next? __

7. Line 2. Point to the first prefix. What prefix? __ Next? __ Next? __ Next? __ Next? __ Next? __

8. The parts of words you just learned come at the beginning of words. What are they called? __ In the next activity, you are going to circle all the prefixes you have learned.

ACTIVITY H: **Circling Prefixes and Suffixes** (See the *Student Book*, page 8.)

1.	insist	commit	imprint
2.	camp	inlaid	consist
3.	distinct	inhabit	dim
4.	convict	ingrain	implant
5.	complain	impact	cash
6.	inflict	command	mislay
7.	impair	contrast	infant

Activity Procedure: Tell students to find the prefixes they have learned and circle them. Then, assist students in checking their worksheets and reading the words, first part by part, then the whole word. Finally, time students for 10 seconds to see how many words they can read.

 Use Overhead 2: Activity H

1. Find Activity H. Circle all the prefixes you have learned in Activity G. Do prefixes come at the beginning or at the end of words? __ Remember, some words have no prefixes, and some words have one of the prefixes you have learned. Look up when you are done. __

2. (Show the overhead transparency.) Now check to see if you circled all the prefixes. Fix any mistakes. __

3. (When students are done checking, assist them in reading each word on the overhead transparency, beginning with the first word of Line 1.) Look up here. __

    (Loop under each word part in **in sist**.) What part? __ What part? __

    (Run your finger under the whole word.) What word? __

4. (Repeat Step 3 with all words in Activity H.)

5. Get ready for a 10-second rapid read. Partner 2, you will be the first reader. Read as many words as you can until I say "Stop." Partner 1, count the words as your partner reads. Begin. (Time students for 10 seconds, and then say "Stop.")

6. Partner 1, hold up your fingers and show me how many words your partner read. (Look around the group.) Partner 1, your turn to read. Partner 2, count the words as your partner reads. Begin. (Time students for 10 seconds, and then say "Stop.")

7. Partner 2, hold up your fingers and show me how many words your partner read. (Look around the group.)

ACTIVITY I: **Vocabulary** (See the *Student Book*, page 8.)

a.	laid into a surface, such as a table (Line 2, Activity H)	**inlaid**
b.	something planted in the body during surgery (Line 4, Activity H)	**implant**
c.	to lay down in the wrong place (Line 6, Activity H)	**mislay**

Special Vocabulary

1.   contrast—When you show or tell the differences between two things, you <u>contrast</u> those things.

2.   insist—If you speak very strongly about something, you <u>insist</u>.

Activity Procedure: In the first part, read each definition and ask students to find the word that matches the meaning and write it in the space provided. In the second part, ask students to read each word silently and then read the word and explanation aloud with you. Give several more examples of how the word might be used. Finally, have students tell their assigned partners a particular application of the word.

Note:
• Read this activity *carefully* before you teach because the wording changes in each lesson.

1. Find Activity I. You are going to learn the meanings of words that have prefixes.

2. Listen to the first definition, "laid into a surface, such as a table." Find the word that means "laid into a surface, such as a table" in Line 2 of Activity H and write it on the line after **a**. (Pause and monitor.) What word means "laid into a surface, such as a table"? (*inlaid*)

3. Listen to the next definition, "something planted in the body during surgery." Find the word in Line 4 and write it. (Pause and monitor.) What word means "something planted in the body during surgery"? (*implant*)

4. Next definition. "To lay down in the wrong place." Find the word in Line 6 and write it. (Pause and monitor.) What word means "To lay down in the wrong place"? (*mislay*)

5. Find *Special Vocabulary*. Let's learn two vocabulary words. Find Line 1. (Pause.) Read the word to yourself. (Pause.) What word? (*contrast*)

6. Read the explanation with me. "When you show or tell the differences between two things, you <u>contrast</u> those things."

7. If you tell the differences between an orange and an apple, you contrast the orange with the _____. (*apple*)

8. If you tell the differences between football and soccer, you contrast football with _____. (*soccer*)

9. Partner 2, contrast a dog and a cat. Tell your partner how these pets are different. __

10. Find Line 2. (Pause.) Read the word to yourself. (Pause.) What word? (*insist*)

11. Read the explanation with me. "If you speak very strongly about something, you <u>insist</u>."

12. If you tell your friend again and again that you want to go home, you _____. (*insist*)

13. If you tell your mother that you want ice cream and then you beg for ice cream, you _____. (*insist*)

14. Partner 1, ask your partner for a pencil. Insist that your partner give you a pencil. __ Partner 2, insist that your partner give you a piece of paper. __

ACTIVITY J: **Spelling Dictation** (See the *Student Book*, page 8.)

1.	complain	2.	imprint
3.	contrast	4.	inlaid

Activity Procedure: For each word, tell students the word, then have students say the parts of the word with you. Have them say the parts to themselves as they write the word. Then, have students compare their words with your word written on an overhead transparency or the board. Finally, have students cross out and rewrite any misspelled words.

Note:
- Distribute a piece of light cardboard to each of the students.

1. Find Activity J. Please cover up the rest of the page with your cardboard.

2. The first word is **complain**. What word? __ Fist in the air. Say the parts in **complain** with me. First part? (*com*) Next part? (*plain*) Say the parts slowly to yourself as you write the word. (Pause and monitor.)

3. (Write **complain** on the board or overhead transparency.) Check **complain**. If you misspelled it, cross it out and write it correctly.

4. The second word is **imprint**. What word? __ Fist in the air. Say the parts in **imprint** with me. First part? (*im*) Second part? (*print*) Say the parts slowly to yourself as you write the word. (Pause and monitor.)

5. (Write **imprint** on the board or overhead transparency.) Check **imprint**. If you misspelled it, cross it out and write it correctly.

6. (Repeat the procedures for the words **contrast** and **inlaid**.)

Lesson 3

Materials Needed

- Lesson 3 from the *Student Book*
- Overhead Transparency 3
- Washable overhead transparency pen
- Paper or cardboard to use when covering the overhead transparency
- Paper or cardboard for each student to use during spelling dictation

ACTIVITY A: **Oral Activity—Blending Word Parts Into Words**

> **Activity Procedure:** Say each word, pausing between the word parts, then have students blend the parts together and say the whole word.

1. Open your *Student Book* to Lesson 3.

2. Listen. I am going to say the parts of a word. You are going to say the whole word. (Say the word, pausing completely between the word parts.)
   pro gram mer. What word? __

3. (Repeat with the following examples.)

   reg u late

   con di tion al

   en er get ic

   un em ploy ment

   in de pen dent ly

ACTIVITY B: Vowel Combinations (See the *Student Book*, page 9.)

er (her)	ir (bird)	ur (turn)

1.	ir	ay	au	ur
2.	ai	ir	er	au

> **Activity Procedure:** Have students point to each new letter combination, tell them the sound as it is pronounced in the key word, and have students say the new sounds and the sounds from the previous lessons.

1. Find Activity B. We are going to learn some sounds. You may know some of them already.
2. Look at the box. Point to the letters **e - r**. The sound of these letters is usually /er/. What sound? __
3. Point to the letters **i - r**. The sound of these letters is usually /er/. What sound? __
4. Point to the letters **u - r**. The sound of these letters is usually /er/. What sound? __
5. Go back to the beginning of the line. Say the sounds again. What sound? __ Next sound? __ Next sound? __
6. Point to the first letters in Line 1. What sound? __ Next sound? __ Next sound? __ Next sound? __
7. (Repeat Step 6 for letters in Line 2.)

ACTIVITY C: Vowel Conversions (See the *Student Book*, page 9.)

o	a	i

> **Activity Procedure:** First tell students the new sound and have them repeat it. Then, tell students the name and have them repeat it. Have students practice saying the sound, then the name for each letter.

1. Find Activity C. When you are reading words and see these letters, first try the sound. If it doesn't make a real word, then try the name.
2. Point to the first letter. The sound is /ŏ/. What sound? __ The name is **o**. What name? __
3. Point to the next letter. What sound? __ What name? __
4. Point to the next letter. What sound? __ What name? __
5. First letter again. What sound? __ What name? __
6. Next letter. What sound? __ What name? __
7. Next letter. What sound? __ What name? __

ACTIVITY D: **Reading Parts of Real Words** (See the *Student Book*, page 9.)

1.	cur	tro*	vas	serv
2.	to*	surd	bliz	pris
3.	ver	dom	der	plaint
4.	turb	laun	vi*	strict

Activity Procedure: Have students say each word part to themselves, then aloud. Remind them to say the name when they see the asterisk.

Note:
- On word parts with an asterisk under the vowel, tell students to say the name. Ask: "What name?"

1. Find Activity D. We are going to read parts of real words. Most of these word parts are not real words by themselves.
2. Line 1. Read the first word part to yourself. Put your thumb up when you can say the part. __ What part? __
3. Next word part. Look at the vowel with the asterisk. What name? __ What part? __
4. Next word part. (Pause.) What part? __
5. Next word part. (Pause.) What part? __
6. (Repeat "What part?" or "What name? What part?" with all remaining word parts.)

Note:
- You may wish to provide additional practice by having students read a line to the group or to a partner.

ACTIVITY E: **Underlining Vowels in Words** (See the *Student Book*, page 10.)

1.	curtail	birthday	turn
2.	auto *	astronaut *	random
3.	launch	verdict	vitamin *
4.	birdbath	turban	whirlwind
5.	auburn	server	taunt

Activity Procedure: Have students underline the vowels and say the sounds. Next, have them say the word parts and the whole word.

 Use Overhead 3: Activity E

Note:
- An asterisk under the vowel of a word indicates that students should say the name.

1. Find Activity E. Listen. Each word part has one vowel sound. What does each word part have? __ Finding the vowels in a word helps us read the word.

2. Watch me find the vowels in these words. (Cover all lines on the overhead transparency except Line 1. On the transparency, underline the vowels in **curtail**. Point to the vowels.) What sound? __ What sound? __ How many vowel sounds? __ So, how many word parts? __

3. Watch again. (Underline the vowels in **birthday**. Point to the vowels.) What sound? __ What sound? __ How many vowel sounds? __ So, how many word parts? __

4. Watch one more. (Underline the vowel in **turn**. Point to the vowel.) What sound? __ How many vowel sounds? __ So, how many word parts? __

5. Now, you underline the vowels in the words in Line 1. (Pause.) Now underline the vowels in the rest of the words. Look up when you are done. __

6. (Show the rest of the overhead transparency.) Now check to see if you underlined all the vowels. Fix any mistakes. __

7. (When students are done checking, assist them in reading each word, beginning with the first word in Line 1. Touch the vowels in **curtail**.) What sound? __ What sound? __

   (Then loop under each word part in **cur tail**.) What part? __ What part? __

   (Run your finger under the whole word.) What word? __

8. (Repeat Step 7 with all words in Activity E.)

Note:
- You may wish to provide additional practice by having students read a line to the group or to a partner.

ACTIVITY F: **Oral Activity—Correcting Close Approximations Using Context**

> **Activity Procedure:** Pronounce the word incorrectly as shown. When saying the sentence, continue to mispronounce the word. Then, ask students to make the word into a real word.

1. Listen. Sometimes when we read a longer word, the word doesn't sound right. Let's see if you can change these words to make sense in the sentences.

2. Listen. I read the word "poi **sŏn**." Change the word to make sense in this sentence. "The king was warned that someone would try to poi **sŏn** him." What should the word be? __

3. (Repeat Step 2 with the following examples, stressing the bold word part.)

ath **lē** tic	The students who loved physical education were ath **lē** tic.
kĭnd ness	The boy carried the bags and was thanked for his **kĭnd** ness.
dis **crī** min ate	Many laws require that people not dis **crī** min ate against someone because of that person's race.
fĕm ale	The **fĕm** ale students performed the same on their math tests as the male students.

ACTIVITY G: **Prefixes and Suffixes** (See the *Student Book*, page 10.)

(be)long	be		(pre)vent	pre
(de)part	de		(pro)tect	pro
(re)turn	re			

Prefixes

1.	be	com	pro	ab	dis	de
2.	pro	re	mis	con	pre	be
3.	de	pre	com	ad	pro	re

Activity Procedure: Tell students the words, then the circled prefixes. Have students repeat the words and prefixes. Then, have students practice saying the new and previously learned prefixes.

1. Find Activity G. We are going to learn more prefixes. Do prefixes come at the beginning or at the end of words? __

2. Point to the first column in the box. The first word is **belong**. What word? __ Point to the circled prefix. The prefix is /be/. Say it. __

3. Point to the next word. The word is **depart**. What word? __ Point to the circled prefix. The prefix is /de/. Say it. __

4. Point to the next word. The word is **return**. What word? __ Point to the circled prefix. The prefix is /re/. Say it. __

5. Point to the third column. The first word is **prevent**. What word? __ The prefix is /pre/. Say it. __

6. (Repeat with **protect** and /pro/.)

7. Find the second column. It has prefixes only. Read the prefixes. What prefix? __ Next? __ Next? __

8. Find the last column. What prefix? __ Next? __

9. Go to Line 1 in the next box. Point to the first prefix. What prefix? __ Next? __ Next? __ Next? __ Next? __ Next? __

10. (Repeat Step 9 for prefixes in Lines 2 and 3.)

11. The parts of words you just learned come at the beginning of words. What are they called? __ In the next activity, you are going to circle all the prefixes you have learned.

ACTIVITY H: Circling Prefixes and Suffixes (See the *Student Book*, page 11.)

1.	prefer	disturb	canvas
2.	proclaim	betray	defraud
3.	behind	complaint	decay
4.	confirm	detail	reclaim
5.	absurd	prepay	restrain
6.	prohibit	distant	behold
7.	restrict	invalid	prison

Activity Procedure: Have students find prefixes and circle them. Then, assist students in checking their worksheets and reading the words, first part by part, then the whole word. Finally, time students for 10 seconds to see how many words they can read.

 Use Overhead 3: Activity H

1. Find Activity H. Circle all the prefixes you have learned in Activity G. Do prefixes come at the beginning or at the end of words? __ Remember, some words have no prefixes, and some words have one of the prefixes you have learned. Look up when you are done. __

2. (Show the overhead transparency.) Now check to see if you circled all the prefixes. Fix any mistakes. __

3. (When students are done checking, assist them in reading each word on the overhead transparency, beginning with the first word of Line 1.) Look up here. __

   (Loop under each word part in **pre fer**.) What part? __ What part? __

   (Run your finger under the whole word.) What word? __

4. (Repeat Step 3 with all words in Activity H.)

5. Get ready for a 10-second rapid read. Partner 1, you will be the first reader. Read as many words as you can until I say "Stop." Partner 2, count the words as your partner reads. Begin. (Time students for 10 seconds, and then say "Stop.")

6. Partner 2, hold up your fingers and show me how many words your partner read. (Look around the group.) Partner 2, your turn to read. Partner 1, count the words as your partner reads. Begin. (Time students for 10 seconds, and then say "Stop.")

7. Partner 1, hold up your fingers and show me how many words your partner read. (Look around the group.)

ACTIVITY I: **Vocabulary** (See the *Student Book*, page 11.)

a.	to claim again (Line 4, Activity H)	reclaim
b.	to pay before you get something (Line 5, Activity H)	prepay
c.	not valid or not true (Line 7, Activity H)	invalid

Special Vocabulary

1.   prefer—If you like something better than something else, you <u>prefer</u> that thing.

2.   absurd—When something is so untrue or so silly that we laugh at it, we could say it is <u>absurd</u>.

Activity Procedure: In the first part, read each definition and ask students to find the word that matches the meaning and write it in the space provided. In the second part, ask students to read each word silently and then read the word and explanation aloud with you. Give several more examples of how the word might be used. Finally, have students tell their assigned partners a particular application of the word.

Note:
 • Read this activity *carefully* before you teach because the wording changes in each lesson.

1.   Find Activity I. You are going to learn the meanings of words that have prefixes.

2.   Listen to the first definition, "to claim again." Find the word in Line 4 of Activity H and write it. (Pause and monitor.) What word means "to claim again"? (*reclaim*)

3.   Listen to the next definition, "to pay before you get something." Find the word in Line 5 and write it. (Pause and monitor.) What word means "to pay before you get something"? (*prepay*)

4.   Next definition. "Not valid or not true." Find the word in Line 7 and write it. (Pause and monitor.) What word means "not valid or not true"? (*invalid*)

5.   Find *Special Vocabulary*. Let's learn two vocabulary words. Find Line 1. (Pause.) Read the word to yourself. (Pause.) What word? (*prefer*)

6.   Read the explanation with me. "If you like something better than something else, you <u>prefer</u> that thing."

7.   If you like chocolate ice cream better than vanilla, which ice cream would you prefer? (*chocolate*)

8.   If you like playing baseball better than soccer, which sport would you prefer? (*baseball*)

9.   Partner 2, tell your partner some foods that you prefer. __

10.   Find Line 2. (Pause) Read the word to yourself. (Pause) What word? (*absurd*)

11. Read the explanation with me. "When something is so untrue or so silly that we laugh at it, we could say it is <u>absurd</u>."

12. If you saw a man in a gorilla suit driving a car down the freeway, it would be _____. (*absurd*)

13. If someone said that elephants could fly, you might say, "That's _____." (*absurd*)

14. Partner 1, tell your partner about something that would be absurd. __

ACTIVITY J: **Spelling Dictation** (See the *Student Book,* page 11.)

1.	defraud	2.	prohibit
3.	confirm	4.	prepay

Activity Procedure: For each word, tell students the word, then have students say the parts of the word with you. Have them say the parts to themselves as they write the word. Then, have students compare their words with your word and cross out and rewrite any misspelled words.

Note:
- Distribute a piece of light cardboard to each of the students.

1. Find Activity J. Please cover up the rest of the page with your cardboard.

2. The first word is **defraud**. What word? __ Fist in the air. Say the parts in **defraud** with me. First part? (*de*) Next part? (*fraud*) Say the parts slowly to yourself as you write the word. (Pause and monitor.)

3. (Write **defraud** on the board or overhead transparency.) Check **defraud**. If you misspelled it, cross it out and write it correctly.

4. The second word is **prohibit**. What word? __ Fist in the air. Say the parts in **prohibit** with me First part? (*pro*) Next part? (*hib*) Next part? (*it*) Say the parts slowly to yourself as you write the word. (Pause and monitor.)

5. (Write **prohibit** on the board or overhead transparency.) Check **prohibit**. If you misspelled it, cross it out and write it correctly.

6. (Repeat the procedures for the words **confirm** and **prepay**.)

Materials Needed

- Lesson 4 from the *Student Book*
- Overhead Transparency 4
- Washable overhead transparency pen
- Paper or cardboard to use when covering the overhead transparency
- Paper or cardboard for each student to use during spelling dictation

ACTIVITY A: **Oral Activity—Blending Word Parts Into Words**

> **Activity Procedure:** Say each word, pausing between the word parts, then have students blend the parts together and say the whole word.

1. Open your *Student Book* to Lesson 4.

2. Listen. I am going to say the parts of a word. You are going to say the whole word. (Say the word, pausing completely between the word parts.)
    mar vel ous. What word? __

3. (Repeat with the following examples.)

    un speak a ble

    ex plan a tion

    re con nec tion

    per form ance

    clas si fi ca tion

ACTIVITY B: **Vowel Combinations** (See the *Student Book*, page 12.)

ar (farm)		or (torn)	

1.	or	au	ar	ai
2.	ir	ar	ay	or

Activity Procedure: Have students point to each new letter combination, tell them the sound as it is pronounced in the key word, and have students say the new sounds and the sounds from the previous lessons.

1. Find Activity B.
2. Look at the box. Point to the letters **a - r**. The sound of these letters is usually /ar/. What sound? __
3. Point to the letters **o - r**. The sound of these letters is usually /or/. What sound? __
4. Go back to the beginning of the line. Say the sounds again. What sound? __ Next sound? __
5. Point to the first letters in Line 1. What sound? __ Next sound? __ Next sound? __ Next sound? __
6. (Repeat Step 5 for letters in Line 2.)

ACTIVITY C: **Vowel Conversions** (See the *Student Book*, page 12.)

a	o	i

Activity Procedure: Have students practice saying the sound, then the name for each letter.

1. Find Activity C. When you are reading words and see these letters, what should you try first, the sound or the name? __ If it doesn't make a real word, what should you try? __
2. Point to the first letter. What sound? __ What name? __
3. Point to the next letter. What sound? __ What name? __
4. Point to the next letter. What sound? __ What name? __
5. First letter again. What sound? __ What name? __
6. Next letter. What sound? __ What name? __
7. Next letter. What sound? __ What name? __

ACTIVITY D: **Reading Parts of Real Words** (See the *Student Book*, page 12.)

1.	gar	na *	hol	fraid
2.	lert	cos	po *	pert
3.	mer	bor	zard	ber
4.	tor	lin	ner	sorb

Activity Procedure: Have students say each word part to themselves, then aloud. Remind them to say the name when they see the asterisk.

Note:
- On word parts with an asterisk under the vowel, tell students to say the name. Ask: "What name?"

1. Find Activity D. We are going to read parts of real words. Most of these word parts are not real words by themselves.

2. Line 1. Read the first word part to yourself. Put your thumb up when you can say the part. __ What part? __

3. Next word part. Look at the vowel with the asterisk. What name? __ What part? __

4. Next word part. (Pause.) What part? __

5. Next word part. (Pause.) What part? __

6. (Repeat "What part?" or "What name? What part?" with all remaining word parts.)

Note:
- You may wish to provide additional practice by having students read a line to the group or to a partner.

Pre

Per

ACTIVITY E: **Underlining Vowels in Words** (See the *Student Book*, page 13.)

1.	blizzard	holiday	haunt
2.	mermaid	shortstop	partner
3.	northern	cargo *	hardship
4.	border	vermin	overhaul *
5.	garland	backyard	barbershop

Activity Procedure: Have students underline the vowels and say the sounds. Next, have them say the word parts and the whole word.

 Use Overhead 4: Activity E

Note:
- An asterisk under the vowel of a word indicates that students should say the name.

1. Find Activity E. Listen. Each word part has one vowel sound. What does each word part have? ___ Finding the vowels in a word helps us read the word.

2. Watch me find the vowels in these words. (Cover all lines on the overhead transparency except Line 1. On the transparency, underline the vowels in **blizzard**. Point to the vowels.) What sound? ___ What sound? ___ How many vowel sounds? ___ So, how many word parts? ___

3. Watch again. (Underline the vowels in **holiday**. Point to the vowels.) What sound? ___ What sound? ___ What sound? ___ How many vowel sounds? ___ So, how many word parts? ___

4. Watch one more. (Underline the vowel in **haunt**. Point to the vowel.) What sound? ___ How many vowel sounds? ___ So, how many word parts? ___

5. Now, you underline the vowels in the words in Line 1. (Pause.) Now underline the vowels in the rest of the words. Look up when you are done. ___

6. (Show the rest of the overhead transparency.) Now check to see if you underlined all the vowels. Fix any mistakes. ___

7. (When students are done checking, assist them in reading each word, beginning with the first word in Line 1. Touch the vowels in **blizzard**.) What sound? ___ What sound? ___

   (Then loop under each word part in **bliz zard**.) What part? ___ What part? ___

   (Run your finger under the whole word.) What word? ___

8. (Repeat Step 7 with all words in Activity E.)

Note:
- You may wish to provide additional practice by having students read a line to the group or to a partner.

ACTIVITY F: **Oral Activity—Correcting Close Approximations Using Context**

> **Activity Procedure:** Pronounce the word incorrectly as shown. When saying the sentence, continue to mispronounce the word. Then, ask students to make the word into a real word.

1. Listen. Change these words to make sense in the sentences.

2. Listen. I read the word "spec **tăt** ors." Change the word to make sense in this sentence. "We were spec **tăt** ors at the soccer game." What should the word be? __

3. (Repeat Step 2 with the following examples, stressing the bold word part.)

en er **gē** tic	All the soccer players seemed very en er **gē** tic.
ē lev **ă** tor	We took the ē lev **ă** tor to the sixteenth floor.
ex **pen** sīve	The beautiful sports car was very ex **pen** sīve.
happ **ī** ness	They were quite thankful and filled with much happ **ī** ness.

ACTIVITY G: **Prefixes and Suffixes** (See the *Student Book*, page 13.)

permit	per
unfair	un
above	a

Prefixes

1.	per	con	de	un	in	a
2.	con	a	dis	im	ad	pro
3.	pre	com	mis	per	ab	re
4.	un	con	be	per	com	a

Activity Procedure: Tell students the words, then the circled prefixes. Have students repeat the words and prefixes. Then, have students practice saying the new and previously learned prefixes.

1. Find Activity G. We are going to learn more prefixes. Where do we find prefixes? __

2. Point to the first column in the box. The first word is **permit**. What word? __ Point to the circled prefix. The prefix is /per/. Say it. __

3. Point to the next word. The word is **unfair**. What word? __ Point to the circled prefix. The prefix is /un/. Say it. __

4. Point to the next word. The word is **above**. What word? __ Point to the circled prefix. The prefix is /ŭ/. Say it. __

5. Find the second column. Read the prefixes. What prefix? __ Next? __ Next? __

6. Go to Line 1 in the next box. Point to the first prefix. What prefix? __ Next? __ Next? __ Next? __ Next? __ Next? __

7. (Repeat Step 6 for prefixes in Lines 2–4.)

8. The parts of words you just learned come at the beginning of words. What are they called? __ In the next activity, you are going to circle all the prefixes you have learned.

ACTIVITY H: **Circling Prefixes and Suffixes** (See the *Student Book*, page 14.)

1.	constrict	deprogram	cannon
2.	across	misinform	repay
3.	deform	unfit	unafraid
4.	absorb	perform	preserve
5.	perturb	impart	prefix
6.	record	alert	discard
7.	unchain	persist	prolong

Activity Procedure: Have students find prefixes and circle them. Then, assist students in checking their worksheets and reading the words, first part by part, then the whole word. Finally, time students for 10 seconds to see how many words they can read.

 Use Overhead 4: Activity H

1. Find Activity H. Some words have *no* prefixes, and some words have *one or more* prefixes. Look at the first word in Line 1. __ How many prefixes? __ Yes, one, so you will circle one prefix. Look at the second word. Start at the beginning of the word and look for prefixes. __ How many prefixes? __ Yes, two, so you will circle two prefixes. Look at the third word. __ How many prefixes? __ Yes, none, so you will not circle anything.

2. Go back to the first word in Line 1. Circle all the prefixes you have learned in Activity G. Remember, some words have no prefixes, and some words have one or more prefixes. Look up when you are done. __

3. (Show the overhead transparency.) Now check to see if you circled all the prefixes. Fix any mistakes. __

4. (When students are done checking, assist them in reading each word on the overhead transparency, beginning with the first word of Line 1.) Look up here. __

    (Loop under each word part in **con strict**.) What part? __ What part? __

    (Run your finger under the whole word.) What word? __

5. (Repeat Step 4 with all words in Activity H.)

6   Time for a 10-second rapid read. Partner 2, read first. Partner 1, count. (Time students for 10 seconds, and then say "Stop.")

7. Partner 1, show me how many words your partner read. (Look around the group.) Partner 1, your turn to read. Partner 2, count. (Time students for 10 seconds, and then say "Stop.")

8. Partner 2, show me how many words your partner read. (Look around the group.)

ACTIVITY I: **Vocabulary** (See the *Student Book,* page 14.)

a.	to give the wrong information (Line 2, Activity H)	__misinform__
b.	not fit or not healthy (Line 3, Activity H)	__unfit__
c.	to remove from chains (Line 7, Activity H)	__unchain__

Special Vocabulary

1.   persist—When you keep working on something or keep trying to do something, you <u>persist</u> at that thing.

2.   discard—When you throw something away, you <u>discard</u> it.

Activity Procedure: In the first part, read each definition and ask students to find the word that matches the meaning and write it in the space provided. In the second part, ask students to read each word silently and then read the word and explanation aloud with you. Give several more examples of how the word might be used. Finally, have students tell their assigned partners a particular application of the word.

Note:
• Read this activity *carefully* before you teach because the wording changes in each lesson.

1.   Find Activity I. You are going to learn the meanings of words that have prefixes.

2.   Listen to the first definition, "to give the wrong information." Find the word in Line 2 of Activity H and write it. (Pause and monitor.) What word means "to give the wrong information"? (*misinform*)

3.   Listen to the next definition, "not fit or not healthy." Find the word in Line 3 and write it. (Pause and monitor.) What word means "not fit or not healthy"? (*unfit*)

4.   Next definition. "To remove from chains." Find the word in Line 7 and write it. (Pause and monitor.) What word means "to remove from chains"? (*unchain*)

5.   Find *Special Vocabulary.* Let's learn two vocabulary words. Find Line 1. (Pause.) Read the word to yourself. (Pause.) What word? (*persist*)

6.   Read the explanation with me. "When you keep working on something or keep trying to do something, you <u>persist</u> at that thing."

7.   When you keep trying again and again to read a word, you _____. (*persist*)

8.   When you keep practicing and practicing a song on the piano, you _____. (*persist*)

9.   Partner 1, tell your partner one time when you decided to persist. __

10. Find Line 2. (Pause.) Read the word to yourself. (Pause.) What word? (*discard*)

11. Read the explanation with me. "When you throw something away, you <u>discard</u> it."

12. If you threw away a scrap of paper, you would _____. (*discard it*)

13. If you threw a box into a dumpster, you would _____. (*discard it*)

14. Partner 2, tell your partner some things that we discard in the classroom. __

ACTIVITY J: **Spelling Dictation** (See the *Student Book,* page 14.)

1. across	2. unafraid
3. misinform	4. persist

Activity Procedure: For each word, tell students the word, then have students say the parts of the word with you. Have them say the parts to themselves as they write the word. Then, have students compare their words with your word and cross out and rewrite any misspelled words.

Note:
- Distribute a piece of light cardboard to each of the students.

1. Find Activity J. Please cover up the rest of the page.

2. The first word is **across**. What word? __ Fist in the air. Say the parts in **across** with me. First part? (*a*) Next part? (*cross*) Say the parts in **across** slowly to yourself as you write the word. (Pause and monitor.)

3. (Write **across** on the board or overhead transparency.) Check **across**. If you misspelled it, cross it out and write it correctly.

4. The second word is **unafraid**. What word? __ Fist in the air. Say the parts in **unafraid** with me. First part? (*un*) Next part? (*a*) Next part? (*fraid*) Say the parts in **unafraid** slowly to yourself as you write the word. (Pause and monitor.)

5. (Write **unafraid** on the board or overhead transparency.) Check **unafraid**. If you misspelled it, cross it out and write it correctly.

6. (Repeat the procedures for the words **misinform** and **persist**.)

Lesson 5

Materials Needed

- Lesson 5 from the *Student Book*
- Overhead Transparency 5
- Washable overhead transparency pen
- Paper or cardboard to use when covering the overhead transparency
- Paper or cardboard for each student to use during spelling dictation

ACTIVITY A: **Oral Activity—Blending Word Parts Into Words**

> **Activity Procedure:** Say each word, pausing between the word parts, then have students blend the parts together and say the whole word. ·

1. Open your *Student Book* to Lesson 5.

2. Listen. I am going to say the parts of a word. You are going to say the whole word. (Say the word, pausing completely between the word parts.)
   ex ces sive. What word? __

3. (Repeat with the following examples.)

   num er ous

   un com fort able

   un pre vent able

   in con sis tent ly

   in ves ti ga tion

ACTIVITY B: **Vowel Combinations** (See the *Student Book,* page 15.)

a - e (make)	o - e (hope)	i - e (side)	e - e (Pete)	u - e (use)

1.	a - e	ai	au	or	e - e
2.	er	au	o - e	ar	ur
3.	i - e	u - e	ay	o - e	a - e

> **Activity Procedure:** Have students point to each new letter combination, tell them the sound as it is pronounced in the key word, and have students say the new sounds and the sounds from the previous lessons.

1. Find Activity B.

2. Look at the box. Point to the letters **a - e**. The sound of these letters is usually /ā/. What sound? __

3. Point to the letters **o - e**. The sound of these letters is usually /ō/. What sound? __

4. Point to the letters **i - e**. The sound of these letters is usually /ī/. What sound? __

5. Point to the letters **e - e**. The sound of these letters is usually /ē/. What sound? __

6. Point to the letters **u - e**. The sound of these letters is usually /ū/. What sound? __

7. Go back to the beginning of the line. Say the sounds again. What sound? __ Next sound? __ Next sound? __ Next sound? __ Next sound? __

8. Point to the first letters in Line 1. What sound? __ Next sound? __ Next sound? __ Next sound? __ Next sound? __

9. (Repeat Step 8 for letters in Lines 2 and 3.)

ACTIVITY C: **Vowel Conversions** (See the *Student Book,* page 15.)

u	i	a	o

> **Activity Procedure:** First tell students the sound and have them repeat it. Then, tell students the name and have them repeat it. Have students practice saying the sound, then the name for each letter.

1. Find Activity C. When you are reading words and see these letters, what should you try first, the sound or the name? ___ If it doesn't make a real word, what should you try? ___

2. Point to the first letter. The sound is /ŭ/. What sound? ___ The name is **u.** What name? ___

3. Point to the next letter. What sound? ___ What name? ___

4. Point to the next letter. What sound? ___ What name? ___

5. Point to the next letter. What sound? ___ What name? ___

6. First letter again. What sound? ___ What name? ___

7. Next letter. What sound? ___ What name? ___

8. (Repeat Step 7 for remaining letters.)

ACTIVITY D: **Reading Parts of Real Words** (See the *Student Book*, page 15.)

1.	treme	clude	do *	scribe
2.	tume	trate	gust	mur
3.	stile	pede	pau	lete
4.	struct	mote	larm	so *

> **Activity Procedure:** Have students say each word part to themselves, then aloud. Remind them to say the name when they see the asterisk.

Note:
- On word parts with an asterisk under the vowel, tell students to say the name. Ask: "What name?"

1. Find Activity D. We are going to read parts of real words. Most of these word parts are not real words by themselves.

2. Line 1. Read the first word part to yourself. Put your thumb up when you can say the part. __ What part? __

3. Next word part. (Pause.) What part? __

4. Next word part. Look at the vowel with the asterisk. What name? __ What part? __

5. Next word part. (Pause.) What part? __

6. (Repeat "What part?" or "What name? What part?" with all remaining word parts.)

Note:
- You may wish to provide additional practice by having students read a line to the group or to a partner.

ACTIVITY E: **Underlining Vowels in Words** (See the *Student Book,* page 16.)

1.	costume	timberline	turnstile
2.	stampede	autumn	backbone
3.	shipmate	maximum	sunstroke
4.	frustrate	marlin	murmur
5.	popcorn	tornado	obsolete
		* *	*

> **Activity Procedure:** Have students underline the vowels and say the sounds. Next, have them say the word parts and the whole word.

 Use Overhead 5: Activity E

Note:
- An asterisk under the vowel of a word indicates that students should say the name.

1. Find Activity E. Listen. What does each word part have? (*one vowel sound*)

2. Watch me find the vowels in these words. (Cover all lines on the overhead transparency except Line 1. On the transparency, underline the vowels in **costume**. Point to the vowels.) What sound? __ What sound? __ How many vowel sounds? __ So, how many word parts? __

3. Watch again. (Underline the vowels in **timberline**. Point to the vowels.) What sound? __ What sound? __ What sound? __ How many vowel sounds? __ So, how many word parts? __

4. Watch one more. (Underline the vowels in **turnstile**. Point to the vowels.) What sound? __ What sound? __ How many vowel sounds? __ So, how many word parts? __

5. Now, you underline the vowels in the words in Line 1. (Pause.) Now underline the vowels in the rest of the words. Look up when you are done. __

6. (Show the rest of the overhead transparency.) Now check to see if you underlined all the vowels. Fix any mistakes. __

7. (When students are done checking, assist them in reading each word, beginning with the first word in Line 1. Touch the vowels in **costume**.) What sound? __ What sound? __

   (Then loop under each word part in **cos tume**.) What part? __ What part? __

   (Run your finger under the whole word.) What word? __

8. (Repeat Step 7 with all words in Activity E.)

Note:
- You may wish to provide additional practice by having students read a line to the group or to a partner.

ACTIVITY F: Oral Activity—Correcting Close Approximations Using Context

> **Activity Procedure:** Pronounce the word incorrectly as shown. When saying the sentence, continue to mispronounce the word. Then, ask students to make the word into a real word.

1. Listen. Change these words to make sense in the sentences.

2. Listen. I read the word "prin **cī** păl." Change the word to make sense in this sentence. "The prin **cī** păl of the school began the day with announcements." What should the word be? __

3. (Repeat Step 2 with the following examples.)

nō vel ist	The **nō** vel ist has written 10 best-selling books.
nā tion al ity	Is the person's **nā** tion al ity German or Dutch?
con **tā** min ate	The oil spill will con **tā** min ate the ocean.
ex ā min **ă** tion	Another word for test is ex ā min **ă** tion.

ACTIVITY G: **Prefixes and Suffixes** (See the *Student Book,* page 16.)

(ex)port		ex
(en)list		en

Prefixes

1.	be	en	com	per	dis	ex
2.	con	un	im	de	ab	pre
3.	ex	re	com	in	mis	in
4.	a	com	en	ex	con	ad

Activity Procedure: Tell students the words, then the circled prefixes. Have students repeat the words and prefixes. Then, have students practice saying the new and previously learned prefixes.

1. Find Activity G. We are going to learn more prefixes.

2. Point to the first column in the box. The first word is **export**. What word? __ Point to the circled prefix. The prefix is /ex/. Say it. __

3. Point to the next word. The word is **enlist**. What word? __ Point to the circled prefix. The prefix is /en/. Say it. __

4. Find the second column. Read the prefixes. What prefix? __ Next? __

5. Go to Line 1 in the next box. Point to the first prefix. What prefix? __ Next? __ Next? __ Next? __ Next? __ Next? __

6. (Repeat Step 5 for prefixes in Lines 2–4.)

7. In the next activity, you are going to circle all the prefixes you have learned.

ACTIVITY H: **Circling Prefixes and Suffixes** (See the *Student Book*, page 17.)

1.	explain	disgust	reconstruct
2.	promote	unalike	berate
3.	combine	alarm	exact
4.	entire	readjust	impose
5.	enthrone	unpaid	misbehave
6.	prescribe	exclude	entail
7.	conclude	advise	extreme

Activity Procedure: Have students find prefixes and circle them. Then, assist students in checking their worksheets and reading the words, first part by part, then the whole word. Finally, time students for 10 seconds to see how many words they can read.

 Use Overhead 5: Activity H

1. Find Activity H. Remember, some words have no prefixes, and some words have one or more prefixes. Look at the first word in Line 1. __ How many prefixes? __ Yes, one, so you will circle one prefix. Look at the second word. __ How many prefixes? __ Yes, one, so you will circle one prefix. Look at the third word. Start at the beginning of the word and look for prefixes. __ How many prefixes? __ Yes, two, so you will circle two prefixes.

2. Go back to the first word in Line 1. Circle all the prefixes you have learned in Activity G. Be careful. Some words have no prefixes, and some words have one or more prefixes. Look up when you are done. __

3. (Show the overhead transparency.) Now check to see if you circled all the prefixes. Fix any mistakes. __

4. (When students are done checking, assist them in reading each word on the overhead transparency, beginning with the first word of Line 1.) Look up here. __

    (Loop under each word part in **ex plain**.) What part? __ What part? __

    (Run your finger under the whole word.) What word? __

5. (Repeat Step 4 with all words in Activity H.)

6. Time for a 10-second rapid read. Partner 1, read first. Partner 2, count. (Time students for 10 seconds, and then say "Stop.")

7. Partner 2, show me how many words your partner read. (Look around the group.) Partner 2, your turn to read. Partner 1, count. (Time students for 10 seconds, and then say "Stop.")

8. Partner 1, show me how many words your partner read. (Look around the group.)

ACTIVITY I: **Vocabulary** (See the *Student Book,* page 17.)

a.	to construct or build again (Line 1, Activity H)	**reconstruct**
b.	to adjust or change again (Line 4, Activity H)	**readjust**
c.	not paid (Line 5, Activity H)	**unpaid**

Special Vocabulary

1.   exclude—When you leave someone or something out of a group, you <u>exclude</u> them.

2.   entire—If you are talking about the whole group, and all the members of that group, you are talking about the <u>entire</u> group.

> **Activity Procedure:** In the first part, read each definition and ask students to find the word that matches the meaning and write it in the space provided. In the second part, ask students to read each word silently and then read the word and explanation aloud with you. Give several more examples of how the word might be used. Finally, have students tell their assigned partners a particular application of the word.

Note:
  • Read this activity *carefully* before you teach because the wording changes in each lesson.

1. Find Activity I.

2. Listen to the first definition, "to construct or build again." Find the word in Line 1 of Activity H and write it. (Pause and monitor.) What word means "to construct or build again"? (*reconstruct*)

3. Next definition. "To adjust or change again." Find the word in Line 4 and write it. (Pause and monitor.) What word means "to adjust or change again"? (*readjust*)

4. Next definition. "Not paid." Find the word in Line 5 and write it. (Pause and monitor.) What word means "not paid"? (*unpaid*)

5. Find *Special Vocabulary.* Let's learn two vocabulary words. Find Line 1. (Pause.) Read the word to yourself. (Pause.) What word? (*exclude*)

6. Read the explanation with me. "When you leave someone or something out of a group, you <u>exclude</u> them."

7. If second graders were not allowed on the playground, who would be excluded from the playground? __ (*second graders*)

8. If the soccer team would not let Pete play on the team, who would be excluded from the team? __ (*Pete*)

9. Partner 2, tell your partner who is excluded from being students in this class.

10. Find Line 2. (Pause.) Read the word to yourself. (Pause.) What word? (*entire*)

11. Read the explanation with me. "If you are talking about the whole group, and all the members of that group, you are talking about the <u>entire</u> group."

12. If you were talking about all the students in this class, you would be talking about the _____. (*entire class*)

13. If you were talking about all the animals in the zoo, you would be talking about the _____. (*entire zoo*)

ACTIVITY J: **Spelling Dictation** (See the *Student Book*, page 17.)

1. reconstruct	2. exclude
3. misbehave	4. enthrone

Activity Procedure: For each word, tell students the word, then have students say the parts of the word with you. Have them say the parts to themselves as they write the word. Then, have students compare their words with your word and cross out and rewrite any misspelled words.

Note:
• Distribute a piece of light cardboard to each of the students.

1. Find Activity J. Please cover up the rest of the page.

2. The first word is **reconstruct**. What word? __ Fist in the air. Say the parts in **reconstruct** with me. First part? __ Next part? __ Next part? __ Say the parts in **reconstruct** to yourself as you write the word. (Pause and monitor.)

3. (Write **reconstruct** on the board or overhead transparency.) Check **reconstruct**. If you misspelled it, cross it out and write it correctly.

4. The second word is **exclude**. What word? __ Fist in the air. Say the parts in **exclude** with me. First part? __ Next part? __ Say the parts in **exclude** to yourself as you write the word. (Pause and monitor.)

5. (Write **exclude** on the board or overhead transparency.) Check **exclude**. If you misspelled it, cross it out and write it correctly.

6. (Repeat the procedures for the words **misbehave** and **enthrone**.)

Lesson 6

Materials Needed

- Lesson 6 from the *Student Book*
- Overhead Transparency 6
- Washable overhead transparency pen
- Paper or cardboard to use when covering the overhead transparency
- Paper or cardboard for each student to use during spelling dictation

ACTIVITY A: **Oral Activity—Blending Word Parts Into Words**

> **Activity Procedure:** Say each word, pausing between the word parts, then have students blend the parts together and say the whole word.

1. Open your *Student Book* to Lesson 6.

2. Listen. (Say the word, pausing completely between the word parts.)
   es tim ate. What word? __

3. (Repeat with the following examples.)

   in struc tors

   un pre dict a ble

   ex pec ta tion

   ex cep tion al ly

   con tin u a tion

ACTIVITY B: **Vowel Combinations** (See the *Student Book,* page 18.)

oi (boil)			oy (boy)		

1.	au	oy	a - e	i - e	or
2.	oi	ar	ay	ai	oy
3.	o - e	er	ur	oi	ir

Activity Procedure: Have students point to each new letter combination, tell them the sound as it is pronounced in the key word, and have students say the new sounds and the sounds from the previous lessons.

1. Find Activity B.

2. Look at the box. Point to the letters **o - i**. The sound of these letters is usually /oy/. What sound? __

3. Point to the letters **o - y**. The sound of these letters is usually /oy/. What sound? __

4. Go back to the beginning of the line. Say the sounds again. What sound? __ Next sound? __

5. Point to the first letters in Line 1. What sound? __ Next sound? __ Next sound? __ Next sound? __ Next sound? __

6. (Repeat Step 5 for letters in Lines 2 and 3.)

ACTIVITY C: **Vowel Conversions** (See the *Student Book,* page 18.)

o	u	i	a

Activity Procedure: Have students practice saying the sound, then the name for each letter.

1. Find Activity C. When you are reading words and see these letters, what should you try first, the sound or the name? __ If it doesn't make a real word, what should you try? __

2. Point to the first letter. What sound? __ What name? __

3. Point to the next letter. What sound? __ What name? __

4. Point to the next letter. What sound? __ What name? __

5. Point to the next letter. What sound? __ What name? __

6. First letter again. What sound? __ What name? __

7. Next letter. What sound? __ What name? __

8. (Repeat Step 7 for remaining letters.)

ACTIVITY D: **Reading Word Parts** (See the *Student Book*, page 18.)

1.	moil	ster	mi *	tise
2.	plete	trude	trins	grad
3.	cor	gard	loi	crim
4.	frant	stroy	poi	cott

Activity Procedure: Have students say each word part to themselves, then aloud. Remind them to say the name when they see the asterisk.

Note:
- On word parts with an asterisk under the vowel, tell students to say the name. Ask: "What name?"

1.   Find Activity D. We are going to read parts of real words. Most of these word parts are not real words by themselves.

2.   Line 1. Read the first word part to yourself. Put your thumb up when you can say the part. __ What part? __

3.   Next word part. (Pause.) What part? __

4.   Next word part. Look at the vowel with the asterisk. What name? __ What part? __

5.   Next word part. (Pause.) What part? __

6.   (Repeat "What part?" with all remaining word parts.)

Note:
- You may wish to provide additional practice by having students read a line to the group or to a partner.

ACTIVITY E: **Underlining Vowels in Words** (See the *Student Book*, page 19.)

1.	turmoil	corduroy	boycott
2.	corrode	void	spoilsport
3.	barter	poison	joyride
4.	pauper	oyster	hoist
5.	loiter	launder	ordain

Activity Procedure: Have students underline the vowels. Then, have students say the sounds and the word parts to themselves. In this lesson, have them say only the whole word aloud.

 Use Overhead 6: Activity E

1. Find Activity E. Listen. What does each word part have? (*one vowel sound*)

2. Watch. (Cover all words on the overhead transparency except the first word. Underline the vowels in **turmoil**. Point to the vowels.) What sound? __ What sound? __ How many vowel sounds? __ So, how many word parts? __

3. Now, you underline the vowels in **turmoil**. (Pause.) Now underline the vowels in the rest of the words. Look up when you are done. __

4. (Show the rest of the overhead transparency.) Now check to see if you underlined all the vowels. Fix any mistakes. __

5. Look up here. (Pause.) Line 1. Read the first word to yourself. Put your thumb up when you can say a real word. __ What word? __

6. Next word. (Pause.) What word? __

7. Next word. (Pause.) What word? __

8. (Repeat Step 7 with all words in Activity E.)

Note:
- You may wish to provide additional practice by having students read a line to the group or to a partner.

ACTIVITY F: **Oral Activity—Correcting Close Approximations Using Context**

> **Activity Procedure:** Pronounce the word incorrectly as shown. When saying the sentence, continue to mispronounce the word. Then, ask students to make the word into a real word.

1. Listen. Change these words to make sense in the sentences.

2. Listen. I read the word "**fĭn** ăl." Change the word to make sense in this sentence. "Her decision about which car to buy was **fĭn** ăl." What should the word be? __

3. (Repeat Step 2 with the following examples.)

ar **gŭm** ĕnt	During the ar **gŭm** ĕnt, the boys and girls yelled at each other and refused to listen.
mar **vē** lous	The brilliant orange sunset was mar **vē** lous.
un **fort** ūn āte	Losing his new basketball was very un **fort** ūn āte.
in dĕp **end** ĕnt	The teenager longed to be in dĕp **end** ĕnt.

ACTIVITY G: **Prefixes and Suffixes** (See the *Student Book,* page 19.)

bird(s)	s	use(less)	less
runn(ing)	ing	kind(ness)	ness
land(ed)	ed	athlet(ic)	ic
regul(ate)	ate		

Prefixes					
1. ex	con	in	per	pro	pre
2. un	a	mis	en	com	re

Suffixes					
3. less	ing	ate	ness	ate	ic
4. ate	less	ness	ic	ing	less

> **Activity Procedure:** Tell students the words, then the circled suffixes. Have students repeat the words and suffixes. Then, have students practice saying the new and previously learned prefixes and suffixes.

1. Find Activity G. Now, we are going to learn about word parts we call suffixes. Suffixes always come at the end of words. Do suffixes come at the beginning or at the end of words? __

2. Point to the first column in the box. The first word is **birds**. What word? __ Point to the circled suffix. The suffix is /s/. Say it. __

3. Point to the next word. The word is **running**. What word? __ Point to the circled suffix. The suffix is /ing/. Say it. __

4. (Repeat with **landed** and /ed/, and **regulate** and /ate/.)

5. Point to the third column. The first word is **useless**. What word? __ The suffix is /less/. Say it. __

6. (Repeat with **kindness** and /ness/, and **athletic** and /ic/.)

7. Find the second column. It has suffixes only. Read the suffixes. What suffix? __ Next? __ Next? __ Next? __

8. Find the last column. What suffix? __ Next? __ Next? __

9. Find line 1. These are prefixes. Point to the first prefix. What prefix? __ Next? __ Next? __ Next? __ Next? __ Next? __

10. Line 2. Point to the first prefix. What prefix? __ Next? __ Next? __ Next? __ Next? __ Next? __

11. Find line 3. These are suffixes. Point to the first suffix. What suffix? __ Next? __ Next? __ Next? __ Next? __ Next? __

12. Line 4. Point to the first suffix. What suffix? __ Next? __ Next? __ Next? __ Next? __ Next? __

13. The parts of words you just learned come at the end of words. What are they called? __ In the next activity, you are going to circle these suffixes as well as all the prefixes you have learned.

ACTIVITY H: **Circling Prefixes and Suffixes** (See the *Student Book*, page 20.)

1.	extrinsic	hardness	hopelessness
2.	demanded	regardless	alarming
3.	dominates	relaxing	carelessness
4.	happiness	classic	captivates
5.	discriminate	frantic	rejoin
6.	graduate	destroy	fantastic
7.	softness	departed	completeness

Activity Procedure: Have students find prefixes and suffixes practiced in the previous activity and circle them. Then, assist students in checking their worksheets and reading the words, first part by part, then the whole word. Finally, time students for 10 seconds to see how many words they can read.

 Use Overhead 6: Activity H

1. Find Activity H. You already know how to look for prefixes at the beginning of words. Now we will also look for suffixes at the end of words. Some words have *no* suffixes at the end, and some words have *one or more* suffixes. Look at the first word in Line 1. __ How many suffixes? __ Yes, one, so you will circle one suffix. Look at the second word. __ How many suffixes? __ Yes, one, so you will circle one suffix. Look at the third word. Start at the end of the word and work backward to find all the suffixes. __ How many suffixes? __ Yes, two, so you will circle two suffixes.

2. Go back to the first word in Line 1. Circle all the prefixes *and* suffixes you have learned in Activity G. Remember, some words have no prefixes or suffixes, and some words have one or more prefixes or suffixes. Look up when you are done. __

3. (Show the overhead transparency.) Now check to see if you circled all the prefixes and suffixes. Fix any mistakes. __

4. (When students are done checking, assist them in reading each word on the overhead transparency, beginning with the first word of Line 1.) Look up here. __

    (Loop under each word part in **ex trins ic**.) What part? __ What part? __ What part? __

    (Run your finger under the whole word.) What word? __

5. (Repeat Step 4 with all words in Activity H.)

6. Time for a 10-second rapid read. Partner 2, read first. Partner 1, count. (Time students for 10 seconds, and then say "Stop.")

7. Partner 1, show me how many words your partner read. (Look around the group.) Partner 1, your turn to read. Partner 2, count. (Time students for 10 seconds, and then say "Stop.")

8. Partner 2, show me how many words your partner read. (Look around the group.)

ACTIVITY I: **Vocabulary** (See the *Student Book,* page 20.)

a.	the state of being without hope (Line 1, Activity H)	*hopelessness*
b.	the quality of being soft (Line 7, Activity H)	*softness*
c.	the condition of being complete (Line 7, Activity H)	*completeness*

Special Vocabulary

1.   discriminate—When people treat another person or group differently because of their race or religion, they <u>discriminate</u> against that person or group.

2.   destroy—When you wreck something or break it into pieces, you <u>destroy</u> it.

> **Activity Procedure:** In the first part, read each definition and ask students to find the word that matches the meaning and write it in the space provided. In the second part, ask students to read each word silently, and then read the word and explanation aloud with you. Give several more examples of how the word might be used. Finally, have students tell their assigned partners a particular application of the word.

Note:
- Read this activity *carefully* before you teach because the wording changes in each lesson.

1. Find Activity I. You are going to learn the meanings of words that have suffixes.

2. Listen to the first definition, "the state of being without hope." Find the word in Line 1 of Activity H and write it. (Pause and monitor.) What word means "the state of being without hope"? (*hopelessness*)

3. Listen to the next definition, "the quality of being soft." Find the word in Line 7 and write it. (Pause and monitor.) What word means "the quality of being soft"? (*softness*)

4. Next definition. "The condition of being complete." Find the word in Line 7 and write it. (Pause and monitor.) What word means "the condition of being complete"? (*completeness*)

5. Find *Special Vocabulary.* Let's learn two vocabulary words. Find Line 1. (Pause.) Read the word to yourself. (Pause.) What word? (*discriminate*)

6. Read the explanation with me. "When people treat another person or group differently because of their race or religion, they <u>discriminate</u> against that person or group."

7. If you are unkind to a person just because they are of a different race, then you _____. (*discriminate*)

8. If you are unkind to a person just because they have a different religion, then you _____. (*discriminate*)

9. If you don't let someone play on your soccer team just because they have a different skin color, you _____. (*discriminate*)

10. Find Line 2. (Pause.) Read the word to yourself. (Pause.) What word? (*destroy*)

11. Read the explanation with me. "When you wreck something or break it into pieces, you <u>destroy</u> it."

12. When you cut up a paper airplane, you _____. (*destroy it*)

13. When you drop a glass vase and break it, you _____. (*destroy it*)

14. Partner 1, tell your partner how you might destroy an eraser. __

ACTIVITY J: **Spelling Dictation** (See the *Student Book,* page 20.)

1.	carelessness	2.	discriminate
3.	classic	4.	completeness

Activity Procedure: For each word, tell students the word, then have students say the parts of the word with you. Have them say the parts to themselves as they write the word. Then, have students compare their words with your word and cross out and rewrite any misspelled words.

Note:
  • Distribute a piece of light cardboard to each of the students.

1. Find Activity J. Please cover up the rest of the page.

2. The first word is **carelessness**. What word? __ Fist in the air. Say the parts in **carelessness** with me. First part? __ Next part? __ Next part? __ Say the parts in **carelessness** to yourself as you write the word. (Pause and monitor.)

3. (Write **carelessness** on the board or overhead transparency.) Check **carelessness**. If you misspelled it, cross it out and write it correctly.

4. The second word is **discriminate**. What word? __ Fist in the air. Say the parts in **discriminate** with me. First part? __ Next part? __ Next part? __ Next part? __ Say the parts in **discriminate** to yourself as you write the word. (Pause and monitor.)

5. (Write **discriminate** on the board or overhead transparency.) Check **discriminate**. If you misspelled it, cross it out and write it correctly.

6. (Repeat the procedures for the words **classic** and **completeness**.)

Materials Needed

- Lesson 7 from the *Student Book*
- Overhead Transparency 7
- Washable overhead transparency pen

- Paper or cardboard to use when covering the overhead transparency
- Paper or cardboard for each student to use during spelling dictation

ACTIVITY A: **Oral Activity—Blending Word Parts Into Words**

> **Activity Procedure:** Say each word, pausing between the word parts, then have students blend the parts together and say the whole word.

1. Open your *Student Book* to Lesson 7.

2. Listen. (Say the word, pausing completely between the word parts.) gov ern ment. What word? __

3. (Repeat with the following examples.)

    in struc tion al

    com bin a tion

    in ex pen sive

    or gan i za tion

    in ves ti ga tor

ACTIVITY B: **Vowel Combinations** (See the *Student Book,* page 21.)

ee			
(deep)			

1.	ee	ar	au	ur	oy
2.	u - e	or	ee	o - e	i - e
3.	ir	oi	ai	ay	ee

> **Activity Procedure:** Have students point to the new letter combination, tell them the sound as it is pronounced in the key word, and have students say the new sounds and the sounds from the previous lessons.

1. Find Activity B.
2. Look at the box. Point to the letters **e - e**. The sound of these letters is usually /ē/. What sound? __
3. Say the sound again. What sound? __
4. Point to the first letters in Line 1. What sound? __ Next sound? __ Next sound? __ Next sound? __ Next sound? __
5. (Repeat Step 4 for letters in Lines 2 and 3.)

ACTIVITY C: **Vowel Conversions** (See the *Student Book,* page 21.)

e	o	a	u	i

> **Activity Procedure:** First tell students the sound and have them repeat it. Then, tell students the name and have students repeat it. Have students review saying the sound, then the name for each letter.

1. Find Activity C. When you are reading words and see these letters, what should you try first, the sound or the name? __ If it doesn't make a real word, what should you try? __
2. Point to the first letter. The sound is /ĕ/. What sound? __ The name is **e**. What name? __
3. Point to the next letter. What sound? __ What name? __
4. Point to the next letter. What sound? __ What name? __
5. Point to the next letter. What sound? __ What name? __
6. Point to the next letter. What sound? __ What name? __
7. First letter again. What sound? __ What name? __
8. Next letter. What sound? __ What name? __
9. (Repeat Step 8 for remaining letters.)

ACTIVITY D: **Reading Parts of Real Words** (See the *Student Book,* page 21.)

1.	slo	spect	sim	fif
	*			
2.	trode	auth	ston	duct
3.	pes	hudd	hend	lorn
4.	tex	blem	flor	fe
				*

Activity Procedure: Have students say each word part to themselves, then aloud. Remind them to say the name when they see the asterisk.

Note:
• On word parts with an asterisk under the vowel, tell students to say the name. Ask: "What name?"

1. Find Activity D. We are going to read parts of real words. Most of these word parts are not real words by themselves.

2. Line 1. Look at the vowel with the asterisk. What name? __ What part? __

3. Next word part. Thumb up when you are ready. __ What part? __

4. Next word part. (Pause.) What part? __

5. Next word part. (Pause.) What part? __

6. (Repeat "What part?" or "What name? What part?" with all remaining word parts.)

Note:
• You may wish to provide additional practice by having students read a line to the group or to a partner.

ACTIVITY E: **Underlining Vowels in Words** (See the *Student Book*, page 22.)

1.	streetcar	uniform *	fifteenth
2.	forget	textile	sweepstake
3.	freedom	forest	canteen
4.	female *	leftover *	forlorn
5.	penmanship	homeland	benefit

Activity Procedure: Have students underline the vowels. Then, have students say the sounds and the word parts to themselves. Have them say the whole word aloud.

 Use Overhead 7: Activity E

Note:
- An asterisk under the vowel of a word indicates that students should say the name.

1. Find Activity E. Listen. What does each word part have? (*one vowel sound*)

2. Watch. (Cover all words on the overhead transparency except the first word. Underline the vowels in **streetcar**. Point to the vowels.) What sound? __ What sound? __ How many vowel sounds? __ So, how many word parts? __

3. Now, you underline the vowels in **streetcar**. (Pause.) Now underline the vowels in the rest of the words. Look up when you are done. __

4. (Show the rest of the overhead transparency.) Now check to see if you underlined all the vowels. Fix any mistakes. __

5. Look up here. (Pause.) Line 1. Read the first word to yourself. Put your thumb up when you can say a real word. __ What word? __

6. Next word. (Pause.) What word? __

7. Next word. (Pause.) What word? __

8. (Repeat Step 7 with all words in Activity E.)

Note:
- You may wish to provide additional practice by having students read a line to the group or to a partner.

ACTIVITY F: **Oral Activity—Correcting Close Approximations Using Context**

> **Activity Procedure:** Pronounce the word incorrectly as shown. When saying the sentence, continue to mispronounce the word. Then, ask students to make the word into a real word.

1. Listen. Change these words to make sense in the sentences.

2. Listen. I read the word "ē lem **en** tary." Change the word to make sense in this sentence. "Do you attend an ē lem **en** tary school?" What should the word be? __

3. (Repeat Step 2 with the following examples.)

   hō **nĕst** y   Hō **nĕst** y is a quality that is important in a friendship.

   gŏv ern mĕnt   The **gŏv** ern mĕnt passes laws and makes sure that people follow them.

   dăn ger ous   Jumping off high places could be **dăn** ger ous.

   crăd le   The baby is sleeping in the **crăd** le.

ACTIVITY G: **Prefixes and Suffixes** (See the *Student Book,* page 22.)

selfish	ish	biggest	est
artist	ist	realism	ism

	Prefixes				
1.	ab	a	pre	en	con	com
2.	per	con	un	ex	ad	a

	Suffixes				
3.	ish	ate	ism	ness	est	ate
4.	ism	ic	ing	less	ish	ist

Activity Procedure: Tell students the words, then the circled suffixes. Have students repeat the words and suffixes. Then, have students practice saying the new and previously learned prefixes and suffixes.

1. Find Activity G. Now, we are going to learn more suffixes. Remember, suffixes always come at the end of words. Do suffixes come at the beginning or at the end of words? __

2. Point to the first column in the box. The first word is **selfish**. What word? __ Point to the circled suffix. The suffix is /ish/. Say it. __

3. Point to the next word. The word is **artist**. What word? __ Point to the circled suffix. The suffix is /ist/. Say it. __

4. Point to the third column. The first word is **biggest**. What word? __ The suffix is /est/. Say it. __

5. (Repeat with **realism** and /ism/.)

6. Find the second column. It has suffixes only. Read the suffixes. What suffix? __ Next? __

7. Find the last column. What suffix? __ Next? __

8. Point to the first prefix in Line 1. What prefix? __ Next? __ Next? __ Next? __ Next? __ Next? __

9. (Repeat Step 8 for prefixes in Line 2.)

10. Point to the first suffix in Line 3. What suffix? __ Next? __ Next? __ Next? __ Next? __ Next? __

11. (Repeat Step 10 for suffixes in Line 4.)

ACTIVITY H: **Circling Prefixes and Suffixes** (See the *Student Book*, page 23.)

1.	alarmist	vanish	astonishing
2.	punish	unselfish	interested
3.	pessimism	comprehends	famish
4.	respected	untrusting	heroism
5.	intrude	conducted	optimism
6.	humanist	advertise	smartest
7.	disarm	florist	blemish

Activity Procedure: Have students find prefixes and suffixes and circle them. Then, assist students in checking their worksheets and reading the words, first part by part, then the whole word. Finally, time students for 10 seconds to see how many words they can read.

 Use Overhead 7: Activity H

1. Find Activity H. Some words have *no* suffixes, and some words have *one or more* suffixes. Look at the first word in Line 1. ___ How many suffixes? ___ Yes, one, so you will circle one suffix. Look at the second word. ___ How many suffixes? ___ Yes, one, so you will circle one suffix. Look at the third word. Start at the end of the word and work backward to find all the suffixes. ___ How many suffixes? ___ Yes, two, so you will circle two suffixes.

2. Go back to the first word in Line 1. Circle all the prefixes and suffixes you have learned in Activity G. Remember, some words have no prefixes or suffixes, and some words have one or more prefixes or suffixes. Look up when you are done. ___

3. (Show the overhead transparency.) Now check to see if you circled all the prefixes and suffixes. Fix any mistakes. ___

4. (When students are done checking, assist them in reading each word on the overhead transparency, beginning with the first word of Line 1.) Look up here. ___

    (Loop under each word part in **a larm ist**.) What part? ___ What part? ___ What part? ___
    (Run your finger under the whole word.) What word? ___

5. (Repeat Step 4 with all words in Activity H.)

6. Time for a 10-second rapid read. Partner 1, read first. Partner 2, count. (Time students for 10 seconds, and then say "Stop.")

7. Partner 2, show me how many words your partner read. (Look around the group.) Partner 2, your turn to read. Partner 1, count. (Time students for 10 seconds, and then say "Stop.")

8. Partner 1, show me how many words your partner read. (Look around the group.)

ACTIVITY I: **Vocabulary** (See the *Student Book,* page 23.)

a.	not selfish (Line 2, Activity H)	__unselfish__
b.	the most smart (Line 6, Activity H)	__smartest__
c.	to remove arms or weapons (Line 7, Activity H)	__disarm__

Special Vocabulary

1.   optimism—When you expect the best results, you have <u>optimism</u>.

2.   pessimism—When you expect the worst results, you have <u>pessimism</u>.

> **Activity Procedure:** In the first part, read each definition and ask students to find the word that matches the meaning and write it in the space provided. In the second part, ask students to read each word silently, and then read the word and explanation aloud with you. Give several more examples of how the word might be used. Finally, have students tell their assigned partners a particular application of the word.

Note:
- Read this activity *carefully* before you teach because the wording changes in each lesson.

1. Find Activity I.

2. Listen to the first definition, "not selfish." Find the word in Line 2 of Activity H and write it. (Pause and monitor.) What word means "not selfish"? (*unselfish*)

3. Listen to the next definition, "the most smart." Find the word in Line 6 and write it. (Pause and monitor.) What word means "the most smart"? (*smartest*)

4. Next definition. "To remove arms or weapons." Find the word in Line 7 and write it. (Pause and monitor.) What word means "to remove arms or weapons"? (*disarm*)

5. Find *Special Vocabulary.* Find Line 1. (Pause.) Read the word to yourself. (Pause.) What word? (*optimism*)

6. Read the explanation with me. "When you expect the best results, you have <u>optimism</u>."

7. If it was raining on the day of your baseball game, but you thought the weather would surely clear up by game time, you would have _____. (*optimism*)

8. If some of your friends were ill, but you expected them to be well for your birthday party, you would have _____. (*optimism*)

9. Find Line 2. (Pause.) Read the word to yourself. (Pause.) What word? (*pessimism*)

10. Read the explanation with me. "When you expect the worst results, you have <u>pessimism</u>."

11. If it was raining on the day of your baseball game, and you thought the whole season would be rained out, you would have _____. (*pessimism*)

12. If some of your friends were ill, and you started thinking that no one would make it to your birthday party, you would have _____. (*pessimism*)

13. Tell me if you think this is an example of optimism or pessimism. You are sure that your team will never win a game. __ (*pessimism*)

14. Though your team has not won one of the last sixteen games, you are sure that it will win a game before the season is over. __ (*optimism*)

15. Though Marty has never turned in a report, the teacher is sure that he will turn one in this year. __ (*optimism*)

16. Though everyone in the class knows how to write wonderful reports, the teacher thinks that no one will turn in a good report. __ (*pessimism*)

ACTIVITY J: **Spelling Dictation** (See the *Student Book*, page 23.)

1.	unselfish	2.	advertise
3.	florist	4.	smartest

Activity Procedure: For each word, tell students the word, then have students say the parts of the word with you. Have them say the parts to themselves as they write the word. Then, have students compare their words with your word and cross out and rewrite any misspelled words.

Note:
- Distribute a piece of light cardboard to each of the students.

1. Find Activity J. Please cover up the rest of the page.

2. The first word is **unselfish**. What word? __ Fist in the air. Say the parts in **unselfish** with me. First part? __ Next part? __ Next part? __ Say the parts in **unselfish** to yourself as you write the word. (Pause and monitor.)

3. (Write **unselfish** on the board or overhead transparency.) Check **unselfish**. If you misspelled it, cross it out and write it correctly.

4. The second word is **advertise**. What word? __ Fist in the air. Say the parts in **advertise** with me. First part? __ Next part? __ Next part? __ Say the parts in **advertise** to yourself as you write the word. (Pause and monitor.)

5. (Write **advertise** on the board or overhead transparency.) Check **advertise**. If you misspelled it, cross it out and write it correctly.

6. (Repeat the procedures for the words **florist** and **smartest**.)

Lesson 8

Materials Needed

- Lesson 8 from the *Student Book*
- Overhead Transparency 8
- Washable overhead transparency pen
- Paper or cardboard to use when covering the overhead transparency
- Paper or cardboard for each student to use during spelling dictation

ACTIVITY A: **Oral Activity—Blending Word Parts Into Words**

> **Activity Procedure:** Say each word, pausing between the word parts, then have students blend the parts together and say the whole word.

1. Open your *Student Book* to Lesson 8.

2. Listen. (Say the word, pausing completely between the word parts.)
    pre vent able. What word? __

3. (Repeat with the following examples.)

    in vi ta tion

    un men tion a ble

    ac com plish ment

    con ver sa tion al

    dis sat is fac tion

ACTIVITY B: **Vowel Combinations** (See the *Student Book*, page 24.)

oa (boat)			ou (loud)	

1.	oa	oi	au	ou	i - e
2.	ee	or	oy	ay	oa
3.	ou	er	ar	a - e	ai

The Other Sound of C

cent	city	cycle
space	civil	cyclone
cellar	pencil	fancy

Activity Procedure: Have students point to each new letter combination, tell them the sound as it is pronounced in the key word, and have students say the new sounds and the sounds from the previous lessons. Then introduce the rule that when the letter **c** is followed by **e**, **i**, or **y**, the sound is /sss/. Have students read the words.

1. Find Activity B.

2. Look at the box. Point to the letters **o - a**. The sound of these letters is usually /ō/. What sound? __

3. Point to the letters **o - u**. The sound of these letters is usually /ou/. What sound? __

4. Go back to the beginning of the line. Say the sounds again. What sound? __ Next sound? __

5. Point to the first letters in Line 1. What sound? __ Next sound? __ Next sound? __ Next sound? __ Next sound? __

6. (Repeat Step 5 for letters in Lines 2 and 3.)

7. Find the box labeled "The Other Sound of C." __ The letter **c** has more than one sound. When **c** is followed by the letters **e**, **i**, or **y**, the sound of the letter **c** is /sss/. Look at the first word. Is the **c** followed by **e**, **i**, or **y**? __ Sound out the word using the sound /sss/. __ What word? (*cent*) Now, sound out the two words below "cent." Put your thumb up when you can read the two words. __ First word. What word? (*space*) Next word. What word? (*cellar*)

8. Go to the next column and look at the first word. __ Is the **c** followed by **e**, **i**, or **y**? __ Sound out the word using the sound /sss/. __ What word? (*city*) Now, sound out the two words below "city." Put your thumb up when you can read the two words. __ First word. What word? (*civil*) Next word. What word? (*pencil*)

9. Go to the next column and look at the first word. __ Is the **c** followed by **e**, **i**, or **y**? __ Sound out the word using the sound /sss/. __ What word? (*cycle*) Now, sound out the two words below "cycle." Put your thumb up when you can read the two words. __ First word. What word? (*cyclone*) Next word. What word? (*fancy*)

ACTIVITY C: **Vowel Conversions** (See the *Student Book,* page 24.)

a	i	o	u	e

> **Activity Procedure:** Have students review saying the sound, then the name for each letter.

1. Find Activity C. When you are reading words and see these letters, what should you try first, the sound or the name? __ If it doesn't make a real word, what should you try? __

2. Point to the first letter. What sound? __ What name? __

3. Point to the next letter. What sound? __ What name? __

4. Point to the next letter. What sound? __ What name? __

5. Point to the next letter. What sound? __ What name? __

6. Point to the next letter. What sound? __ What name? __

7. First letter again. What sound? __ What name? __

8. Next letter. What sound? __ What name? __

9. (Repeat Step 8 for remaining letters.)

ACTIVITY D: **Reading Parts of Real Words** (See the *Student Book,* page 25.)

1.	cide	pa *	cen	ploy
2.	cess	sid	cit	fau
3.	loy	plode	spec	sir
4.	thir	sus	lec	pi *

Activity Procedure: Have students say each word part to themselves, then aloud. Remind them to say the name when they see the asterisk.

Note:
- On word parts with an asterisk under the vowel, tell students to say the name. Ask: "What name?"

1. Find Activity D. We are going to read parts of real words.

2. Line 1. Read the first word part to yourself. Put your thumb up when you can say the part. What part? __

3. Next word part. Look at the vowel with the asterisk. What name? __ What part? __

4. Next word part. (Pause.) What part? __

5. Next word part. (Pause.) What part? __

6. (Repeat "What part?" or "What name? What part?" with all remaining word parts.)

Note:
- You may wish to provide additional practice by having students read a line to the group or to a partner.

ACTIVITY E: **Underlining Vowels in Words** (See the *Student Book,* page 25.)

1.	southwestern	cloudburst	seventeen
2.	carload	railroad	coach
3.	roadside	electrode	playground
4.	faucet	spellbound	northwestern
5.	coatrack	greenhouse	census

Activity Procedure: Have students underline the vowels. Then, have students say the sounds and the word parts to themselves. Have them say the whole word aloud.

Use Overhead 8: Activity E

1. Find Activity E. Listen. What does each word part have? (*one vowel sound*)

2. Watch. (Cover all words on the overhead transparency except the first word. Underline the vowels in **southwestern**. Point to the vowels.) What sound? __ What sound? __ What sound? __ How many vowel sounds? __ So, how many word parts? __

3. Now, you underline the vowels in **southwestern**. (Pause.) Now underline the vowels in the rest of the words. Look up when you are done. __

4. (Show the rest of the overhead transparency.) Now check to see if you underlined all the vowels. Fix any mistakes. __

5. Look up here. (Pause.) Line 1. Read the first word to yourself. Put your thumb up when you can say a real word. __ What word? __

6. Next word. (Pause.) What word? __

7. Next word. (Pause.) What word? __

8. (Repeat Step 7 with all words in Activity E.)

Note:
• You may wish to provide additional practice by having students read a line to the group or to a partner.

ACTIVITY F: **Oral Activity—Correcting Close Approximations Using Context**

> **Activity Procedure:** Pronounce the word incorrectly as shown. When
> saying the sentence, continue to mispronounce the word. Then, ask students
> to make the word into a real word.

1. Make these words into real words. Listen. I read the word "med ī căl." Change the
    word to make sense in this sentence. "The doctor keeps med ī căl records on each
    patient." What should the word be? __

2. (Repeat with the following examples.)

    con **trī** bu tion   Mr. and Mrs. Lee gave a $50 con **trī** bu tion to the club.

    in vī **tă** tion   The children received an in vī **tă** tion to a birthday party.

    dĭg **es** tīve   Our dĭg **es** tīve system allows us to get energy from the food
                               we eat.

ACTIVITY G: **Prefixes and Suffixes** (See the *Student Book,* page 26.)

careful	ful	farmer	er
final	al	inventor	or

Prefixes					
1. com	de	en	mis	per	con
2. ex	a	pro	pre	com	im

Suffixes					
3. ful	ist	er	est	or	al
4. al	or	ate	ful	ic	ism

Activity Procedure: Tell students the words, then the circled suffixes. Have students repeat the words and suffixes. Then, have students practice saying the new and previously learned prefixes and suffixes.

1. Find Activity G. Now, we are going to learn more suffixes. Do suffixes come at the beginning or at the end of words? __

2. Point to the first column in the box. The first word is **careful**. What word? __ Point to the circled suffix. The suffix is /ful/. Say it. __

3. (Repeat for **final** and /al/.)

4. Point to the third column. The first word is **farmer**. What word? __ The suffix is /er/. Say it. __

5. (Repeat with **inventor** and /or/.)

6. Find the second column. It has suffixes only. Read the suffixes. What suffix? __ Next? __

7. Find the last column. What suffix? __ Next? __

8. Point to the first prefix in Line 1. What prefix? __ Next? __ Next? __ Next? __ Next? __ Next? __

9. (Repeat Step 8 for prefixes in Line 2.)

10. Point to the first suffix in Line 3. What suffix? __ Next? __ Next? __ Next? __ Next? __ Next? __

11. (Repeat Step 10 for suffixes in Line 4.)

ACTIVITY H: **Circling Prefixes and Suffixes** (See the *Student Book*, page 26.)

1.	loyalist	employer	percent
2.	consider	sailor	proposal
3.	author	consumers	respectful
4.	advertiser	personal	historical
5.	arrival	explode	cinder
6.	spectator	ungrateful	unfortunate
7.	untruthful	abnormal	successful

> **Activity Procedure:** Have students find prefixes and suffixes and circle them. Then, assist students in checking their worksheets and reading the words, first part by part, then the whole word. Finally, time students for 10 seconds to see how many words they can read.

 Use Overhead 8: Activity H

1. Find Activity H. Some words have no suffixes, and some words have one or more suffixes. Look at the first word in Line 1. Start at the end of the word and work backward to find all the suffixes. __ How many suffixes? __ Yes, two, so you will circle two suffixes. Look at the second word. __ How many suffixes? __ Yes, one, so you will circle one suffix. Look at the third word. __ How many suffixes? __ Yes, none, so you will not circle anything at the end of the word.

2. Go back to the first word in Line 1. Circle all the prefixes and suffixes you have learned in Activity G. Remember, some words have no prefixes or suffixes, and some words have one or more prefixes or suffixes. Look up when you are done. __

3. (Show the overhead transparency.) Now check to see if you circled all the prefixes and suffixes. Fix any mistakes. __

4. (When students are done checking, assist them in reading each word on the overhead transparency, beginning with the first word of Line 1.) Look up here __

    (Loop under each word part in **loy al ist**.) What part? __ What part? __ What part? __

    (Run your finger under the whole word.) What word? __

5. (Repeat Step 4 with all words in Activity H.)

6. Time for a 10-second rapid read. Partner 2, read first. Partner 1, count. (Time students for 10 seconds, and then say "Stop.")

7. Partner 1, show me how many words your partner read. (Look around the group.) Partner 1, your turn to read. Partner 2, count. (Time students for 10 seconds, and then say "Stop.")

8. Partner 2, show me how many words your partner read. (Look around the group.)

Note:
- The strategy students are learning in this program is a flexible strategy. This means that some words could have a word part either circled or underlined and still lead to a close approximation of the word's pronunciation. For example, in the word **historical**, students could either circle the "or" as a word part they have learned or underline the "or" as a vowel sound they have learned. When you loop, it might look like this **histor**i**cal** or like this **histor**i**cal**.

ACTIVITY I: **Vocabulary** (See the *Student Book*, page 27.)

a.	being full of respect (Line 3, Activity H)	respectful
b.	relating to a particular person (Line 4, Activity H)	personal
c.	being full of success (Line 7, Activity H)	successful

Special Vocabulary

1.   unfortunate—When you are not lucky, you are <u>unfortunate</u>.

2.   spectator—When you watch a sporting event, a parade, or a play, you are a <u>spectator</u>.

> **Activity Procedure:** In the first part, read each definition and ask students to find the word that matches the meaning and write it in the space provided. In the second part, ask students to read each word silently, and then read the word and explanation aloud with you. Give several more examples of how the word might be used. Finally, have students tell their assigned partners a particular application of the word.

Note:
- Read this activity *carefully* before you teach because the wording changes in each lesson.

1. Find Activity I.

2. Listen to the first definition, "being full of respect." Find the word in Line 3 of Activity H and write it. (Pause and monitor.) What word means "being full of respect"? (*respectful*)

3. Listen to the next definition, "relating to a particular person." Find the word in Line 4 and write it. (Pause and monitor.) What word means "relating to a particular person"? (*personal*)

4. Next definition. "Being full of success." Find the word in Line 7 and write it. (Pause and monitor.) What word means "being full of success"? (*successful*)

5. Find *Special Vocabulary*. Find Line 1. (Pause.) Read the word to yourself. (Pause.) What word? (*unfortunate*)

6. Read the explanation with me. "When you are not lucky, you are <u>unfortunate</u>."

7. If a hurricane destroyed your house, you would be very _____. (*unfortunate*)

8. If you slipped and broke your arm, that would be _____. (*unfortunate*)

9. Partner 1, tell your partner one unfortunate thing that has happened to you. __

10. Find Line 2. (Pause.) Read the word to yourself. (Pause.) What word? (*spectator*)

11. Read the explanation with me. "When you watch a sporting event, a parade, or a play, you are a <u>spectator</u>."

12. If you watched a basketball game, you would be a _____. (*spectator*)

13. If you watched a parade but were not in the parade, you would be a _____. (*spectator*)

14. Partner 2, tell your partner when you have been a spectator. __

ACTIVITY J: **Spelling Dictation** (See the *Student Book*, page 27.)

1.	personal	2.	consider
3.	respectful	4.	author

Activity Procedure: For each word, tell students the word, then have students say the parts of the word with you. Have them say the parts to themselves as they write the word. Then, have students compare their words with your word and cross out and rewrite any misspelled words.

Note:
- Distribute a piece of light cardboard to each of the students.

1. Find Activity J. Please cover up the rest of the page.

2. The first word is **personal**. What word? __ Fist in the air. Say the parts in **personal** with me. First part? __ Next part? __ Next part? __ Say the parts in **personal** to yourself as you write the word. (Pause and monitor.)

3. (Write **personal** on the board or overhead transparency.) Check **personal**. If you misspelled it, cross it out and write it correctly.

4. The second word is **consider**. What word? __ Fist in the air. Say the parts in **consider** with me. First part? __ Next part? __ Next part? __ Say the parts in **consider** to yourself as you write the word. (Pause and monitor.)

5. (Write **consider** on the board or overhead transparency.) Check **consider**. If you misspelled it, cross it out and write it correctly.

6. (Repeat the procedures for the words **respectful** and **author**.)

Lesson 9

Materials Needed

- Lesson 9 from the *Student Book*
- Overhead Transparency 9
- Washable overhead transparency pen
- Paper or cardboard to use when covering the overhead transparency
- Paper or cardboard for each student to use during spelling dictation

ACTIVITY A: **Oral Activity—Blending Word Parts Into Words**

> **Activity Procedure:** Say each word, pausing between the word parts, then have students blend the parts together and say the whole word.

1. Open your *Student Book* to Lesson 9.

2. Listen. (Say the word, pausing completely between the word parts.) dem on stra tion. What word? __

3. (Repeat with the following examples.)

   un man age a ble

   en vi ron ment

   mis in for ma tion

   ex ter mi na tor

   re or gan i za tion

ACTIVITY B: **Vowel Combinations** (See the *Student Book*, page 28.)

ow
(low) (down)

1.	oa	ow	au	ay	oy
2.	ow	er	a - e	oi	or
3.	ou	ee	ai	ow	ar

The Other Sound of C		
cent	city	cycle
price	citrus	lacy
center	decide	cyclops

Activity Procedure: In this lesson, students learn that sometimes a letter combination has two sounds. They learn that when they see this letter combination in a word or word part, they should try the first sound they have learned. If the word doesn't sound right, they should try the second sound they have learned. Have students point to the new letter combination. Tell them the sound as it is pronounced in the first key word. Then, tell students that if they try this sound and the word doesn't sound right, to try a second sound. Tell them the sound, then have them practice what they would say first and what they would say second. Have students say the new sounds and the sounds from the previous lessons. Whenever they come to a box around a letter combination, they should say both sounds. Then review the rule that when the letter **c** is followed by **e**, **i**, or **y**, the sound is /sss/. Have students read the words.

1. Find Activity B. We are going to learn two sounds for these letters.

2. Look at the box. Point to the letters **o - w**. The sound of these letters is usually /ō/ as in "low." What sound? __ If the word doesn't sound right, try /ou/ as in "down." What sound? __

3. Let's review. What sound would you try first? (/ō/) What sound would you try next? (/ou/)

Note:
 • Whenever you come to letters in a box, ask "What sound would you try first? What sound would you try next?"

4. Point to the first letters in Line 1. What sound? __ Boxed letters. What sound would you try first? __ What sound would you try next? __ Next sound? __ Next sound? __ Next sound? __

5. (Continue Step 4 for letters in Lines 2 and 3.)

6. Find the box labeled "The Other Sound of C." __ Remember, the letter **c** has more than one sound. When **c** is followed by the letters **e**, **i**, or **y**, the sound of the letter **c** is /sss/. Look at the first word. Is the **c** followed by **e**, **i**, or **y**? __ Sound out the word using the sound /sss/. __ What word? (*cent*) Now, sound out the two words below "cent." Put your thumb up when you can read the two words. __ First word. What word? (*price*) Next word. What word? (*center*)

7. Go to the next column and look at the first word. __ Is the **c** followed by **e**, **i**, or **y**? __ Sound out the word using the sound /sss/. __ What word? (*city*) Now, sound out the two words below "city." Put your thumb up when you can read the two words. __ First word. What word? (*citrus*) Next word. What word? (*decide*)

8. Go to the next column and look at the first word. __ Is the **c** followed by **e**, **i**, or **y**? __ Sound out the word using the sound /sss/. __ What word? (*cycle*) Now, sound out the two words below "cycle." Put your thumb up when you can read the two words. __ First word. What word? (*lacy*) Next word. What word? (*cyclops*)

ACTIVITY C: **Vowel Conversions** (See the *Student Book,* page 28.)

a	e	o	i	u

> **Activity Procedure:** Have students review saying the sound, then the name for each letter.

1. Find Activity C. When you are reading words and see these letters, what should you try first, the sound or the name? __ If it doesn't make a real word, what should you try? __

2. Point to the first letter. What sound? __ What name? __

3. Point to the next letter. What sound? __ What name? __

4. Point to the next letter. What sound? __ What name? __

5. Point to the next letter. What sound? __ What name? __

6. Point to the next letter. What sound? __ What name? __

7. First letter again. What sound? __ What name? __

8. Next letter. What sound? __ What name? __

9. (Repeat Step 8 for remaining letters.)

ACTIVITY D: **Reading Parts of Real Words** (See the *Student Book,* page 29.)

1.	dow	te *	gret	gre *
2.	ceed	cel	plow	sence
3.	laud	flow	har	strugg
4.	semb	civ	mar	cer

Activity Procedure: In this lesson, you no longer wait for students to say the word part to themselves. Have students say each word part aloud. Remind them to say the name when they see the asterisk. Remind them to say both sounds when they see a box.

Notes:
- On word parts with an asterisk under the vowel, tell students to say the name. Ask: "What name?"
- Whenever you come to a word part in a box, ask "What sound would you try first? What part? What sound would you try next? What part?"

1. Find Activity D. We are going to read parts of real words.

2. Line 1. What sound would you try first? (/ō/) What part? (/dō/) What sound would you try next? (/ou/) What part? (/dou/)

3. Next word part. What name? __ What part? __

4. Next word part. What part? __

5. Next word part. What name? __ What part? __

6. (For each remaining word part, ask "What part?" or "What sound would you try first? What part? What sound would you try next? What part?")

Note:
- You may wish to provide additional practice by having students read a line to the group or to a partner.

ACTIVITY E: **Underlining Vowels in Words** (See the *Student Book,* page 29.)

1.	pillow	chowder	roadway
2.	succeed	elbow	cinch
3.	flowerpot	willow	outgrow
4.	snowplow	embrace	sundown
5.	thirteenth	shallow	windowpane

Activity Procedure: Have students underline the vowels. Then, have students say the sounds and the word parts to themselves. Have them say the whole word aloud. Remind them to try both sounds when they see an **ow** in the word.

 Use Overhead 9: Activity E

1. Find Activity E. Listen. What does each word part have? (*one vowel sound*)

2. Watch. (Cover all words on the overhead transparency except the first word. Underline the vowels in **pi̱llo̱w**. Point to the vowels.) What sound? __ What sound? __ How many vowel sounds? __ So, how many word parts? __

3. Now, you underline the vowels in **pillow**. (Pause.) Now underline the vowels in the rest of the words. Look up when you are done. __

4. (Show the rest of the overhead transparency.) Now check to see if you underlined all the vowels. Fix any mistakes. __

5. Look up here. (Pause.) Line 1. Read the first word to yourself. You may have to try both sounds for **ow**. Put your thumb up when you can say a real word. __ What word?

6. Next word. (Pause.) What word? __

7. Next word. (Pause.) What word? __

8. (Repeat Step 7 with all words in Activity E.)

Note:
- You may wish to provide additional practice by having students read a line to the group or to a partner.

ACTIVITY F: **Oral Activity—Correcting Close Approximations Using Context**

> **Activity Procedure:** Pronounce the word incorrectly as shown. When saying the sentence, continue to mispronounce the word. Then, ask students to make the word into a real word.

1. Make these words into real words. Listen. I read the word "**shā** llow." Change the word to make sense in this sentence. "The river was quite **shā** llow." What should the word be? __

2. (Repeat with the following examples.)

    pō pu **lă** tion   The city's **pō** pu **lă** tion is more than 50,000.

    in ex **pen** sīve   The dinner at the take-out restaurant was in ex **pen** sīve.

    tour **nā** ment   Fourteen teams played in the basketball tour **nā** ment.

ACTIVITY G: **Prefixes and Suffixes** (See the *Student Book,* page 30.)

courage	age
cradle	le

Prefixes

1.	mis	be	pro	un	com	dis
2.	con	ex	pro	per	a	con

Suffixes

3.	age	ful	ist	al	or	le
4.	less	le	ate	age	est	ism

Activity Procedure: Tell students the words, then the circled suffixes. Have students repeat the words and suffixes. Then, have students practice saying the new and previously learned prefixes and suffixes.

1. Find Activity G. Now, we are going to learn more suffixes. Where do we find suffixes? __

2. Point to the first column in the box. The first word is **courage**. What word? __ Point to the circled suffix. The suffix is /age/. Say it. __

3. (Repeat for **cradle** and /le/.)

4. Find the second column. Read the suffixes. What suffix? __ Next? __

5. Point to the first prefix in Line 1. What prefix? __ Next? __ Next? __ Next? __ Next? __ Next? __

6. (Repeat Step 5 for prefixes in Line 2.)

7. Point to the first suffix in Line 3. What suffix? __ Next? __ Next? __ Next? __ Next? __ Next? __

8. (Repeat Step 7 for suffixes in Line 4.)

ACTIVITY H: **Circling Prefixes and Suffixes** (See the *Student Book*, page 30.)

1.	manage	computers	struggle
2.	reconsider	priceless	programmer
3.	mishandle	absence	regretful
4.	successor	bemoan	mileage
5.	elevator	harvested	huddle
6.	barbarism	unfaithful	shortage
7.	resemble	sausage	entertainers

Activity Procedure: Have students find prefixes and suffixes and circle them. Then, assist students in checking their worksheets and reading the words, first part by part, then the whole word. Finally, time students for 10 seconds to see how many words they can read.

 Use Overhead 9: Activity H

1. Find Activity H. Circle all the prefixes and suffixes you have learned in Activity G. Remember, some words have no prefixes or suffixes, and some words have one or more prefixes or suffixes. When you look for suffixes, remember to start at the end of the word and work backward. Look up when you are done. __

2. (Show the overhead transparency.) Now check to see if you circled all the prefixes or suffixes. Fix any mistakes. __

3. (When students are done checking, assist them in reading each word on the overhead transparency, beginning with the first word of Line 1.) Look up here. __

   (Loop under each word part in **man age**.) What part? __ What part? __

   (Run your finger under the whole word.) What word? __

4. (Repeat Step 3 with all words in Activity H.)

5. Time for a 10-second rapid read. Partner 1, read first. Partner 2, count. (Time students for 10 seconds, and then say "Stop.")

6. Partner 2, show me how many words your partner read. (Look around the group.) Partner 2, your turn to read. Partner 1, count. (Time students for 10 seconds, and then say "Stop.")

7. Partner 1, show me how many words your partner read. (Look around the group.)

ACTIVITY I: **Vocabulary** (See the *Student Book,* page 31.)

a.   a person who programs computers (Line 2, Activity H) __programmer__

b.   not faithful or not loyal (Line 6, Activity H) __unfaithful__

c.   people who entertain others (Line 7, Activity H) __entertainers__

Special Vocabulary

1.   reconsider—If you carefully think about an idea again, you <u>reconsider</u> the idea.

2.   resemble—If you look like or act like another person, you <u>resemble</u> that person.

Activity Procedure: In the first part, read each definition and ask students to find the word that matches the meaning and write it in the space provided. In the second part, ask students to read each word silently, and then read the word and explanation aloud with you. Give several more examples of how the word might be used. Finally, have students tell their assigned partners a particular application of the word.

Note:
- Read this activity *carefully* before you teach because the wording changes in each lesson.

1. Find Activity I.

2. Listen to the first definition, "a person who programs computers." Find the word in Line 2 and write it. (Pause and monitor.) What word means "a person who programs computers"? (*programmer*)

3. Listen to the next definition, "not faithful or not loyal." Find the word in Line 6 and write it. (Pause and monitor.) What word means "not faithful or not loyal"? (*unfaithful*)

4. Next definition. "People who entertain others." Find the word in Line 7 and write it. (Pause and monitor.) What word means "people who entertain others"? (*entertainers*)

5. Find *Special Vocabulary.* Find Line 1. (Pause.) Read the word to yourself. (Pause.) What word? (*reconsider*)

6. Read the explanation with me. "If you carefully think about an idea again, you <u>reconsider</u> the idea."

7. When your parents ask you to carefully think about an idea again, you _____. (*reconsider it*)

8. If you read an idea in a book that you have thought about once before and you carefully think about it again, you _____. (*reconsider it*)

9. Find Line 2. (Pause.) Read the word to yourself. (Pause.) What word? (*resemble*)

10. Read the explanation with me. "If you look like or act like another person, you <u>resemble</u> that person."

11. If Thomas looks like his twin, Charles, then Thomas would resemble _____. (*Charles*)

12. If Margaret looked very much like her mother, then Margaret would resemble her _____. (*mother*)

13. Partner 2, tell your partner whom you most resemble. __

14. Partner 1, tell your partner whom you most resemble. __

ACTIVITY J: **Spelling Dictation** (See the *Student Book,* page 31.)

1. manage	2. mishandle
3. reconsider	4. entertainers

Activity Procedure: For each word, tell students the word, then have students say the parts of the word with you. Have them say the parts to themselves as they write the word. Then, have students compare their words with your word and cross out and rewrite any misspelled words.

Note:
• Distribute a piece of light cardboard to each of the students.

1. Find Activity J. Please cover up the rest of the page.

2. The first word is **manage**. What word? __. Fist in the air. Say the parts in **manage** with me. First part? __ Next part? __ Say the parts in **manage** to yourself as you write the word. (Pause and monitor.)

3. (Write **manage** on the board or overhead transparency.) Check **manage**. If you misspelled it, cross it out and write it correctly.

4. The second word is **mishandle**. What word? __. Fist in the air. Say the parts in **mishandle** with me. First part? __ Next part? __ Next part? __ Say the parts in **mishandle** to yourself as you write the word. (Pause and monitor.)

5. (Write **mishandle** on the board or overhead transparency.) Check **mishandle**. If you misspelled it, cross it out and write it correctly.

6. (Repeat the procedures for the words **reconsider** and **entertainers**.)

Lesson 10

Materials Needed

- Lesson 10 from the *Student Book*
- Overhead Transparency 10
- Washable overhead transparency pen
- Paper or cardboard to use when covering the overhead transparency
- Paper or cardboard for each student to use during spelling dictation

ACTIVITY A: **Oral Activity—Blending Word Parts Into Words**

> **Activity Procedure:** Say each word, pausing between the word parts, then have students blend the parts together and say the whole word.

1. Open your *Student Book* to Lesson 10.

2. Listen. (Say the word, pausing completely between the word parts.)
    im per son al. What word? __

3. (Repeat with the following examples.)

    gov ern ment al

    un der stand a ble

    in struc tion al ly

    in for ma tion al

    ad min is tra tion

ACTIVITY B: **Vowel Combinations** (See the *Student Book*, page 32.)

	ow (low) (down)				

1.	ow		oa		ow		ir		ar
2.	oi		or		au		ay		ou
3.	ou		ow		ur		ai		oy

The Other Sound of G

gentle	gist	gypsy
gem	giraffe	energy
change	magic	gym

Activity Procedure: In this lesson, students review the two sounds of the letter combination introduced in the previous lesson. Have students point to the letter combination. Tell them the first sound. Then, tell students that if they try this sound and the word doesn't sound right, to try a second sound. Tell them the sound, then have them practice what they would say first and what they would say second. Have students say the new sounds and the sounds from the previous lessons. Whenever they come to a box around a letter combination, they should say both sounds. Then introduce the rule that when the letter **g** is followed by **e**, **i**, or **y**, the sound is /j/. Have students read the words.

1. Find Activity B. We are going to review a difficult sound.

2. Look at the box. Point to the letters **o - w**. The sound of these letters is usually /ō/. What sound? __ If the word doesn't sound right, try /ou/. What sound? __

3. Let's review. What sound would you try first? (/ō/) What sound would you try next? (/ou/)

Note:
• Whenever you come to letters in a box, ask "What sound would you try first? What sound would you try next?"

4. Point to the boxed letters in Line 1. What sound would you try first? __ What sound would you try next? __ Next sound? __ Boxed letters. What sound would you try first? __ What sound would you try next? __ Next sound? __ Next sound? __

5. (Continue Step 4 for letters in Lines 2 and 3.)

6. Find the box labeled "The Other Sound of G." __ The letter **g** has more than one sound. When **g** is followed by the letters **e**, **i**, or **y**, the sound of the letter **g** is /j /. Look at the first word. Is the **g** followed by **e**, **i**, or **y**? __ Sound out the word using the sound /j/. __ What word? (*gentle*) Now, sound out the two words below "gentle." Put your thumb up when you can read the two words. __ First word. What word? (*gem*) Next word. What word? (*change*)

7. Go to the next column and look at the first word. __ Is the **g** followed by **e**, **i**, or **y**? __ Sound out the word using the sound /j/. __ What word? (*gist*) Now, sound out the two words below "gist." Put your thumb up when you can read the two words. __ First word. What word? (*giraffe*) Next word. What word? (*magic*)

8. Go to the next column and look at the first word. __ Is the **g** followed by **e**, **i**, or **y**? __ Sound out the word using the sound /j/. __ What word? (*gypsy*) Now, sound out the two words below "gypsy." Put your thumb up when you can read the two words. __ First word. What word? (*energy*) Next word. What word? (*gym*)

ACTIVITY C: **Vowel Conversions** (See the *Student Book*, page 32.)

u	a	e	o	i

Activity Procedure: Have students review saying the sound, then the name for each letter.

1. Find Activity C. When you are reading words and see these letters, what should you try first, the sound or the name? __ If it doesn't make a real word, what should you try? __

2. Point to the first letter. What sound? __ What name? __

3. Point to the next letter. What sound? __ What name? __

4. Point to the next letter. What sound? __ What name? __

5. Point to the next letter. What sound? __ What name? __

6. Point to the next letter. What sound? __ What name? __

7. First letter again. What sound? __ What name? __

8. Next letter. What sound? __ What name? __

9. (Repeat Step 8 for remaining letters.)

ACTIVITY D: **Reading Parts of Real Words** (See the *Student Book*, page 33.)

1.	blow	il	loin	ple *
2.	gen	pow	shad	germ
3.	sault	gant	mo *	tec
4.	show	blige	nov	cau

Activity Procedure: Have students say each word part aloud. Remind them to say the name when they see the asterisk. Remind them to say both sounds when they see a box.

Notes:
- On word parts with an asterisk under the vowel, tell students to say the name. Ask: "What name?"
- Whenever you come to a word part in a box, ask "What sound would you try first? What part? What sound would you try next? What part?"

1. Find Activity D. We are going to read parts of real words.
2. Line 1. What sound would you try first? (/ō/) What part? (/blō/) What sound would you try next? (/ou/) What part? (/blou/)
3. Next word part. What part? __
4. Next word part. What part? __
5. Next word part. What name? __ What part? __
6. (For each remaining word part, ask "What part?" or "What sound would you try first? What part? What sound would you try next? What part?" or "What name? What part?")

Note:
- You may wish to provide additional practice by having students read a line to the group or to a partner.

ACTIVITY E: **Underlining Vowels in Words** (See the *Student Book,* page 33.)

1.	rainbow	margin	township
2.	shadow	lifeboat	oblige
3.	boatload	germfree	downtown
4.	snowflake	outgrowth	downhill
5.	sirloin	cowboy	marshmallow

Activity Procedure: Have students underline the vowels. Then, have students say the sounds and the word parts to themselves. Have them say the whole word aloud. Remind them to say both sounds when they see an **ow** in the word.

 Use Overhead 10: Activity E

1. Find Activity E. Listen. What does each word part have? (*one vowel sound*)

2. Watch. (Cover all words on the overhead transparency except the first word. Underline the vowels in **ra̲i̲nbo̲w̲**. Point to the vowels.) What sound? __ What sound? __ How many vowel sounds? __ So, how many word parts? __

3. Now, you underline the vowels in **rainbow**. (Pause.) Now underline the vowels in the rest of the words. Look up when you are done. __

4. (Show the rest of the overhead transparency.) Now check to see if you underlined all the vowels. Fix any mistakes. __

5. Look up here. (Pause.) Line 1. Read the first word to yourself. You may have to try both sounds for **ow**. Put your thumb up when you can say a real word. __ What word? __

6. Next word. (Pause.) What word? __

7. Next word. (Pause.) What word? __

8. (Repeat Step 7 with all words in Activity E.)

Note:
• You may wish to provide additional practice by having students read a line to the group or to a partner.

ACTIVITY F: **Oral Activity—Correcting Close Approximations Using Context**

> **Activity Procedure:** Pronounce the word incorrectly as shown. When saying the sentence, continue to mispronounce the word. Then, ask students to make the word into a real word.

1. Make these real words. Listen. I read the word "ĭn **crēd** ible." Change the word to make sense in this sentence. "He could make a CD; his singing voice is quite ĭn **crēd** ible." What should the word be? __

2. (Repeat with the following examples.)

    cŏm **par** i sŏn   The cŏm **par** i sŏn of the two cars favored one style.

    in for **mă** tion   I need a lot of in for **mă** tion about Venezuela if I am to write a report about it.

    com **mŭn** ī cate   We could com **mŭn** ī cate by phone or e-mail.

ACTIVITY G: **Prefixes and Suffixes** (See the *Student Book,* page 34.)

action	tion		attentive	tive
discussion	sion		expensive	sive

Prefixes

1.	ex	com	re	im	a	con
2.	un	pro	ab	de	com	en

Suffixes

3.	tion	age	or	sive	le	sion
4.	tive	sion	ful	al	tion	tive

Activity Procedure: Tell students the words, then the circled suffixes. Have students repeat the words and suffixes. Then, have students practice saying the new and previously learned prefixes and suffixes.

1. Find Activity G. We are going to learn more suffixes.

2. Point to the first column in the box. The first word is **action**. What word? __ Point to the circled suffix. The suffix is /tion/. Say it. __

3. (Repeat for **discussion** and /sion/.)

4. Point to the third column. The first word is **attentive**. What word? __ The suffix is /tive/. Say it. __

5. (Repeat with **expensive** and /sive/.)

6. Find the second column. It has suffixes only. Read the suffixes. What suffix? __ Next? __

7. Find the last column. What suffix? __ Next? __

8. Point to the first prefix in Line 1. What prefix? __ Next? __ Next? __ Next? __ Next? __ Next? __

9. (Repeat Step 8 for prefixes in Line 2.)

10. Point to the first suffix in Line 3. What suffix? __ Next? __ Next? __ Next? __ Next? __ Next? __

11. (Repeat Step 10 for suffixes in Line 4.)

ACTIVITY H: **Circling Prefixes and Suffixes** (See the *Student Book*, page 34.)

1.	expansive	protection	permissive
2.	novelist	repulsive	civilization
3.	percussionist	gigantic	invasion
4.	postage	expression	caution
5.	refusal	completion	regenerate
6.	conditional	effective	demonstrations
7.	unintentional	panelist	professional

Activity Procedure: Have students find prefixes and suffixes and circle them. Then, assist students in checking their worksheets and reading the words, first part by part, then the whole word. Finally, time students for 10 seconds to see how many words they can read.

 Use Overhead 10: Activity H

1.   Find Activity H. Circle all the prefixes and suffixes. Remember, some words have no prefixes or suffixes, and some words have one or more prefixes or suffixes. When you look for suffixes, remember to start at the end of the word and work backward. Look up when you are done. __

2.   (Show the overhead transparency.) Now check to see if you circled all the prefixes and suffixes. Fix any mistakes. __

3.   (When students are done checking, assist them in reading each word on the overhead transparency, beginning with the first word of Line 1.) Look up here. __

     (Loop under each word part in **ex pan sive**.) What part? __ What part? __ What part? __

     (Run your finger under the whole word.) What word? __

4.   (Repeat Step 3 with all words in Activity H.)

5.   Time for a 10-second rapid read. Partner 2, read first. Partner 1, count. (Time students for 10 seconds, and then say "Stop.")

6.   Partner 1, show me how many words your partner read. (Look around the group.) Partner 1, your turn to read. Partner 2, count. (Time students for 10 seconds, and then say "Stop.")

7.   Partner 2, show me how many words your partner read. (Look around the group.)

ACTIVITY I: **Vocabulary** (See the *Student Book,* page 35.)

a.	the act of protecting from harm (Line 1, Activity H)	**protection**
b.	the act of expressing oneself (Line 4, Activity H)	**expression**
c.	the act of refusing (Line 5, Activity H)	**refusal**

Special Vocabulary

1.   repulsive—When you really dislike something or are really bothered by it, it would be <u>repulsive</u>.

2.   permissive—If parents gave their children too much freedom, the parents would be <u>permissive</u>.

Activity Procedure: In the first part, read each definition and ask students to find the word that matches the meaning and write it in the space provided. In the second part, ask students to read each word silently, and then read the word and explanation aloud with you. Give several more examples of how the word might be used. Finally, have students tell their assigned partners a particular application of the word.

Note:
• Read this activity *carefully* before you teach because the wording changes in each lesson.

1.   Find Activity I.

2.   Listen to the first definition, "the act of protecting from harm." Find the word in Line 1 and write it. (Pause and monitor.) What word means "the act of protecting from harm"? (*protection*)

3.   Listen to the next definition, "the act of expressing oneself." Find the word in Line 4 and write it. (Pause and monitor.) What word means "the act of expressing oneself"? (*expression*)

4.   Next definition. "The act of refusing." Find the word in Line 5 and write it. (Pause and monitor.) What word means "the act of refusing"? (*refusal*)

5.   Find *Special Vocabulary.* Find Line 1. (Pause.) Read the word to yourself. (Pause.) What word? (*repulsive*)

6.   Read the explanation with me. "When you really dislike something or are really bothered by it, it would be <u>repulsive</u>."

7.   Most people would find eating live worms _____. (*repulsive*)

8.   Many people would find touching spiders _____. (*repulsive*)

9.   Partner 1, tell your partner one thing that is repulsive to you. __

10. Find Line 2. Read the word to yourself. (Pause.) What word? (*permissive*)

11. Read the explanation with me. "If parents gave their children too much freedom, the parents would be <u>permissive</u>."

12. If parents let their small child do anything they wanted, the parents would be _____. (*permissive*)

13. If a pet owner let the puppy do whatever the puppy wanted, the pet owner would be _____. (*permissive*)

14. Tell me if this is permissive. The mother let the toddler throw food around the room. Is this permissive? __ (*Yes*)

15. The mother stopped the toddler from throwing food around the room. Is this permissive? __ (*No*)

ACTIVITY J: **Spelling Dictation** (See the *Student Book,* page 35.)

1.	protection	2.	permissive
3.	expansive	4.	unintentional

Activity Procedure: For each word, tell students the word, then have students say the parts of the word with you. Have them say the parts to themselves as they write the word. Then, have students compare their words with your word and cross out and rewrite any misspelled words.

Note:
- Distribute a piece of light cardboard to each of the students.

1. Find Activity J. Please cover up the rest of the page.

2. The first word is **protection**. What word? __ Fist in the air. Say the parts in **protection** with me. First part? __ Next part? __ Next part? __ Say the parts in **protection** to yourself as you write the word. (Pause and monitor.)

3. (Write **protection** on the board or overhead transparency.) Check **protection**. If you misspelled it, cross it out and write it correctly.

4. The second word is **permissive**. What word? __ Fist in the air. Say the parts in **permissive** with me. First part? __ Next part? __ Next part? __ Say the parts in **permissive** to yourself as you write the word. (Pause and monitor.)

5. (Write **permissive** on the board or overhead transparency.) Check **permissive**. If you misspelled it, cross it out and write it correctly.

6. (Repeat the procedures for the words **expansive** and **unintentional**.)

Lesson 11

Materials Needed

- Lesson 11 from the *Student Book*
- Overhead Transparency 11
- Washable overhead transparency pen
- Paper or cardboard to use when covering the overhead transparency
- Paper or cardboard for each student to use during spelling dictation

ACTIVITY A: **Oral Activity—Blending Word Parts Into Words**

> **Activity Procedure:** Say each word, pausing between the word parts, then have students blend the parts together and say the whole word.

1. Open your *Student Book* to Lesson 11.
2. Listen. (Say the word, pausing completely between the word parts.)
   tre men dous ly. What word? __
3. (Repeat with the following examples.)

   at trac tive ness

   su per in ten dent

   in stru men tal ist

   ex a min a tion

   pre cip i ta tion

ACTIVITY B: **Vowel Combinations** (See the *Student Book,* page 36.)

oo
(moon) (book)

1.	oo	au	oi	ow	ar
2.	oa	e - e	ou	oo	ai
3.	oy	oo	ee	ur	ow

The Other Sound of G

gentle	gist	gypsy
gerbil	ginger	trilogy
urgent	engineer	gymnast

Activity Procedure: In this lesson, students learn the two sounds of a new letter combination. Have students point to the new letter combination. Tell them the sound as it is pronounced in the first key word. Then, tell students that if they try this sound and the word doesn't sound right, to try a second sound. Tell them the sound, then have them practice what they would say first and what they would say second. Have students say the new sounds and the sounds from the previous lessons. Remind them to say both sounds when they see a box. Then review the rule that when the letter **g** is followed by **e, i,** or **y,** the sound is /j/. Have students read the words.

1. Find Activity B. We are going to learn two sounds for these letters.

2. Look at the box. Point to the letters **o - o.** The sound of these letters is usually /o͞o/ as in "moon." What sound? __ If the word doesn't sound right, try /o͝o/ as in "book." What sound? __

3. Let's review. What sound would you try first? (/o͞o/) What sound would you try next? (/o͝o/)

Note:
  • Whenever you come to letters in a box, ask "What sound would you try first? What sound would you try next?"

4. Point to the boxed letters in Line 1. What sound would you try first? __ What sound would you try next? __ Next sound? __ Next sound? __ Boxed letters. What sound would you try first? __ What sound would you try next? __ Next sound? __

5. (Continue Step 4 for letters in Lines 2 and 3.)

6. Find the box labeled "The Other Sound of G." __ Remember, the letter **g** has more than one sound. When **g** is followed by the letters **e**, **i**, or **y**, the sound of the letter **g** is /j /. Look at the first word. Is the **g** followed by **e**, **i**, or **y**? __ Sound out the word using the sound /j/. __ What word? (*gentle*) Now, sound out the two words below "gentle." Put your thumb up when you can read the two words. __ First word. What word? (*gerbil*) Next word. What word? (*urgent*)

7. Go to the next column and look at the first word. __ Is the **g** followed by **e**, **i**, or **y**? __ Sound out the word using the sound /j/. __ What word? (*gist*) Now, sound out the two words below "gist." Put your thumb up when you can read the two words. __ First word. What word? (*ginger*) Next word. What word? (*engineer*)

8. Go to the next column and look at the first word. __ Is the **g** followed by **e**, **i**, or **y**? __ Sound out the word using the sound /j/. __ What word? (*gypsy*) Now, sound out the two words below "gypsy." Put your thumb up when you can read the two words. __ First word. What word? (*trilogy*) Next word. What word? (*gymnast*)

ACTIVITY C: **Vowel Conversions** (See the *Student Book,* page 36.)

e	u	i	a	o

Activity Procedure: Have students review saying the sound, then the name for each letter.

1. Find Activity C. When you see these letters, what should you try first, the sound or the name? __ If it doesn't make a real word, what should you try? __

2. Point to the first letter. What sound? __ What name? __

3. Point to the next letter. What sound? __ What name? __

4. Point to the next letter. What sound? __ What name? __

5. Point to the next letter. What sound? __ What name? __

6. Point to the next letter. What sound? __ What name? __

7. First letter again. What sound? __ What name? __

8. Next letter. What sound? __ What name? __

9. (Repeat Step 8 for remaining letters.)

ACTIVITY D: **Reading Parts of Real Words** (See the *Student Book*, page 37.)

1.	hood	vol	jur	foot
2.	fec	tam	plex	lar
3.	co *	va *	crow	bil
4.	roon	pend	toon	gree

Activity Procedure: Have students say each word part aloud. Remind them to say the name when they see the asterisk. Remind them to say both sounds when they see a box.

Notes:
- On word parts with an asterisk under the vowel, tell students to say the name. Ask: "What name?"
- Whenever you come to a word part in a box, ask "What sound would you try first? What part? What sound would you try next? What part?"

1. Find Activity D. We are going to read parts of real words.

2. Line 1. What sound would you try first? (/o͞o/) What part? (/ho͞od/) What sound would you try next? (/o͝o/) What part? (/ho͝od/)

3. Next word part. What part? __

4. Next word part. What part? __

5. Next word part. What sound would you try first? (/o͞o/) What part? (/fo͞ot/) What sound would you try next? (/o͝o/) What part? (/fo͝ot/)

6. (For each remaining word part, ask "What part?" or "What sound would you try first? What part? What sound would you try next? What part?" or "What name? What part?")

Note:
- You may wish to provide additional practice by having students read a line to the group or to a partner.

ACTIVITY E: **Underlining Vowels in Words** (See the *Student Book*, page 37.)

1.	cartoon	toothpick	igloo
2.	footprint	monsoon	riverbank
3.	cookbook	shampoo	showboat
4.	sagebrush	fishhook	loophole
5.	woodshed	macaroon	boomerang

Activity Procedure: Have students underline the vowels. Then, have students say the sounds and the word parts to themselves. Have them say the whole word aloud. Remind them to try both sounds for some vowels.

 Use Overhead 11: Activity E

1. Find Activity E. Listen. What does each word part have? (*one vowel sound*)

2. Watch. (Cover all words on the overhead transparency except the first word. Underline the vowels in **cartoon**. Point to the vowels.) What sound? __ What sound? __ How many vowels? __ So, how many word parts? __

3. Now, you underline the vowels in **cartoon**. (Pause.) Now underline the vowels in the rest of the words. Look up when you are done. __

4. (Show the rest of the overhead transparency.) Now check to see if you underlined all the vowels. Fix any mistakes. __

5. Look up here. (Pause.) Line 1. Read the first word to yourself. You may have to try both sounds for some vowels. Put your thumb up when you can say a real word. __ What word? __

6. Next word. (Pause.) What word? __

7. Next word. (Pause.) What word? __

8. (Repeat Step 7 with all words in Activity E.)

Note:
  • You may wish to provide additional practice by having students read a line to the group or to a partner.

ACTIVITY F: **Oral Activity—Correcting Close Approximations Using Context**

> **Activity Procedure:** Pronounce the word incorrectly as shown. When saying the sentence, continue to mispronounce the word. Then, ask students to make the word into a real word.

1. Make these real words. Listen. I read the word "es tī **mă** tion." Change the word to make sense in this sentence. "Paul's es tī **mă** tion of the number of marbles in the jar was very close to the correct answer." What should the word be? __

2. (Repeat with the following examples.)

    děp art měnt   We will shop at the **děp** art měnt store.

    op er **ă** tor   The telephone op er **ă** tor came on the line.

    dis **ăp** pear ănce   The police have no information about the child's dis **ăp** pear ănce.

ACTIVITY G: **Prefixes and Suffixes** (See the *Student Book,* page 38.)

thir**sty**	y		mission**ary**	ary
safe**ly**	ly		odd**ity**	ity

Prefixes						
1.	in	com	pro	a	ex	dis
2.	a	pre	en	un	con	per

Suffixes						
3.	sion	ary	ate	ly	le	sive
4.	y	ism	ary	age	ity	al

Activity Procedure: Tell students the words, then the circled suffixes.
Have students repeat the words and suffixes. Then, have students practice
saying the new and previously learned prefixes and suffixes.

1. Find Activity G. We are going to learn more suffixes.

2. Point to the first column in the box. The first word is **thirsty**. What word? __ Point to the circled suffix. The suffix is /y/. Say it. __

3. (Repeat for **safely** and /ly/.)

4. Point to the third column. The first word is **missionary**. What word? __ The suffix is /ary/. Say it. __

5. (Repeat with **oddity** and /ity/.)

6. Find the second column. It has suffixes only. Read the suffixes. What suffix? __ Next? __

7. Find the last column. What suffix? __ Next? __

8. Point to the first prefix in Line 1. What prefix? __ Next? __ Next? __ Next? __ Next? __ Next? __

9. (Repeat Step 8 for prefixes in Line 2.)

10. Point to the first suffix in Line 3. What suffix? __ Next? __ Next? __ Next? __ Next? __ Next? __

11. (Repeat Step 10 for suffixes in Line 4.)

REWARDS Intermediate Teacher's Guide

ACTIVITY H: **Circling Prefixes and Suffixes** (See the *Student Book*, page 38.)

1.	precaution	dictionary	celery
2.	injury	dismissal	belabor
3.	disability	absurdity	complexity
4.	grocery	energetic	voluntary
5.	nationally	similarity	relatively
6.	adhesive	disloyal	perfectionist
7.	personality	intensive	contaminate

> **Activity Procedure:** Have students find prefixes and suffixes and circle them. Then, assist students in checking their worksheets and reading the words, first part by part, then the whole word. Finally, time students for 10 seconds to see how many words they can read.

Use Overhead 11: Activity H

1. Find Activity H. Circle all the prefixes and suffixes. Remember, some words have no prefixes or suffixes, and some words have one or more prefixes and suffixes. Look up when you are done. __

2. (Show the overhead transparency.) Now check to see if you circled all the prefixes and suffixes. Fix any mistakes. __

3. (When students are done checking, assist them in reading each word on the overhead transparency, beginning with the first word of Line 1.) Look up here. __

    (Loop under each word part in **pre cau tion**.) What part? __   What part? __   What part? __

    (Run your finger under the whole word.) What word? __

4. (Repeat Step 3 with all words in Activity H.)

5. Time for a 10-second rapid read. Partner 1, read first. Partner 2, count. (Time students for 10 seconds, and then say "Stop.")

6. Partner 2, show me how many words your partner read. (Look around the group.) Partner 2, your turn to read. Partner 1, count. (Time students for 10 seconds, and then say "Stop.")

7. Partner 1, show me how many words your partner read. (Look around the group.)

Note:
*   For some words, students may identify prefixes one of two ways. Whichever way they choose, circling the prefix will still lead to a close approximation of the word's pronunciation. For example, when circling prefixes for the word **disability** and then looping, the word might look like this  or like this disability.

ACTIVITY I: **Vocabulary** (See the *Student Book,* page 39.)

a.	caution taken before doing something (Line 1, Activity H)	precaution
b.	not loyal (Line 6, Activity H)	disloyal
c.	a person who wants perfection (Line 6, Activity H)	perfectionist

Special Vocabulary

1.   contaminate—If we pollute or make something unclean, we <u>contaminate</u> it.

2.   voluntary—When you do something that you don't have to do but just want to do it, it would be a <u>voluntary</u> act.

Activity Procedure: In the first part, read each definition and ask students to find the word that matches the meaning and write it in the space provided. In the second part, ask students to read each word silently, and then read the word and explanation aloud with you. Give several more examples of how the word might be used. Finally, have students tell their assigned partners a particular application of the word.

1.   Find Activity I.

2.   Listen to the first definition, "caution taken before doing something." Find the word in Line 1 and write it. (Pause and monitor.) What word means "caution taken before doing something"? (*precaution*)

3.   Listen to the next definition, "not loyal." Find the word in Line 6 and write it. (Pause and monitor.) What word means "not loyal"? (*disloyal*)

4.   Next definition. "A person who wants perfection." Find the word in Line 6 and write it. (Pause and monitor.) What word means "a person who wants perfection"? (*perfectionist*)

5.   Find *Special Vocabulary.* Find Line 1. (Pause). Read the word to yourself. (Pause.) What word? (*contaminate*)

6.   Read the explanation with me. "If we pollute or make something unclean, we <u>contaminate</u> it."

7.   When oil spills into the ocean, what will be contaminated? __ (*the ocean*)

8.   When heavy smoke from a forest fire blows into the air, what will be contaminated? __ (*the air*)

9.   Partner 1, tell your partner some things that could get contaminated. __

10.   Find Line 2. Read the word to yourself. (Pause.) What word? (*voluntary*)

11.   Read the explanation with me. "When you do something that you don't have to do but just want to do it, it would be a <u>voluntary</u> act."

12. If you helped your partner without the teacher even asking, that act would be
    _____. (*voluntary*)

13. If you picked up trash on the playground without the principal asking, that act
    would be _____. (voluntary)

14. Tell me if this act is voluntary. Sara's mother says she must take care of her brother
    every day after school. Is that act voluntary? __ (*No*)

15. Sara knows that her mother needs to shop, so she says she will play with her
    brother while her mother shops. Is that act voluntary? __ (*Yes*)

ACTIVITY J: **Spelling Dictation** (See the *Student Book*, page 39.)

1.	perfectionist	2.	grocery
3.	nationally	4.	similarity

> **Activity Procedure:** For each word, tell students the word, then have
> students say the parts of the word with you. Have them say the parts to
> themselves as they write the word. Then, have students compare their
> words with your word and cross out and rewrite any misspelled words.

Note:
- Distribute a piece of light cardboard to each of the students.

1. Find Activity J. Please cover up the rest of the page.

2. The first word is **perfectionist**. What word? __ Fist in the air. Say the parts in
   perfectionist with me. First part? __ Next part? __ Next part? __ Next part? __ Say
   the parts in **perfectionist** to yourself as you write the word. (*Pause and monitor.*)

3. (Write **perfectionist** on the board or overhead transparency.) Check **perfectionist**.
   If you misspelled it, cross it out and write it correctly.

4. The second word is **grocery**. What word? __ Fist in the air. Say the parts in
   grocery with me. First part? __ Next part? __ Next part? __ Say the parts in
   grocery to yourself as you write the word. (*Pause and monitor.*)

5. (Write **grocery** on the board or overhead transparency.) Check **grocery**. If you
   misspelled it, cross it out and write it correctly.

6. (Repeat the procedures for the words **nationally** and **similarity**.)

Lesson 12

Materials Needed

- Lesson 12 from the *Student Book*
- Overhead Transparency 12
- Washable overhead transparency pen
- Paper or cardboard to use when covering the overhead transparency
- Paper or cardboard for each student to use during spelling dictation

ACTIVITY A: **Oral Activity—Blending Word Parts Into Words**

Activity Procedure: Say each word, pausing between the word parts, then have students blend the parts together and say the whole word.

1. Open your *Student Book* to Lesson 12.

2. Listen. (Say the word, pausing completely between the word parts.)
   gen er os i ty. What word? __

3. (Repeat with the following examples.)

   dis ap pear ance

   rev o lu tion ar y

   ex cep tion al i ty

   de ter min a tion

   dis or gan i za tion

ACTIVITY B: **Vowel Combinations** (See the *Student Book*, page 40.)

oo
(moon) (book)

1.	ai	oo	ay	er	ow
2.	ar	oi	ee	oo	oy
3.	ow	or	au	ir	oo

Activity Procedure: In this lesson, students review the two sounds of the letter combination introduced in the previous lesson. Have students point to the letter combination. Tell them the first sound. Then, tell students that if they try this sound and the word doesn't sound right, to try a second sound. Tell them the sound, then have them practice what they would say first and what they would say second. Have students say the new sounds and the sounds from the previous lessons. Remind them to say both sounds when they see a box.

1.   Find Activity B. We are going to review a difficult sound.

2.   Look at the box. Point to the letters **o - o**. The sound of these letters is usually /o͞o/. What sound? __ If the word doesn't sound right, try /o͝o/. What sound? __

3.   Let's review. What sound would you try first? (/o͞o/) What sound would you try next? (/o͝o/)

Note:
 • Whenever you come to letters in a box, ask "What sound would you try first? What sound would you try next?"

4.   Point to the first letters in Line 1. What sound? __ Boxed letters. What sound would you try first? __ What sound would you try next? __ Next sound? __ Next sound? __ Boxed letters. What sound would you try first? __ What sound would you try next? __

5.   (Continue Step 4 for letters in Lines 2 and 3.)

ACTIVITY C: **Vowel Conversions** (See the *Student Book,* page 40.)

o	a	u	e	i

> **Activity Procedure:** Have students review saying the sound, then the name for each letter.

1. Find Activity C. When you see these letters, what should you try first, the sound or the name? __ If it doesn't make a real word, what should you try? __

2. Point to the first letter. What sound? __ What name? __

3. Point to the next letter. What sound? __ What name? __

4. Point to the next letter. What sound? __ What name? __

5. Point to the next letter. What sound? __ What name? __

6. Point to the next letter. What sound? __ What name? __

7. First letter again. What sound? __ What name? __

8. Next letter. What sound? __ What name? __

9. (Repeat Step 8 for remaining letters.)

ACTIVITY D: **Reading Parts of Real Words** (See the *Student Book*, page 40.)

1.	roof	chow	scrap	dif
2.	cite	kan	doc	fir
3.	rac	aut	room	ges
4.	struc	coon	fect	pli *

Activity Procedure: Have students say each word part aloud. Remind them to say the name when they see the asterisk. Remind them to say both sounds when they see a box.

Notes:
- On word parts with an asterisk under the vowel, tell students to say the name. Ask: "What name?"
- Whenever you come to a word part in a box, ask "What sound would you try first? What part? What sound would you try next? What part?"

1. Find Activity D. We are going to read parts of real words.

2. Line 1. What sound would you try first? (/ōō/) What part? (/rōof/) What sound would you try next? (/ŏŏ/) What part? (/rŏŏf/)

3. Next word part. What sound would you try first? (/ō/) What part? (/chō/) What sound would you try next? (/ou/) What part? (/chou/)

4. Next word part. What part? ___

5. Next word part. What part? ___

6. (For each remaining word part, ask "What part?" or "What sound would you try first? What part? What sound would you try next? What part?" or "What name? What part?")

Note:
- You may wish to provide additional practice by having students read a line to the group or to a partner.

ACTIVITY E: Underlining Vowels in Words (See the *Student Book*, page 41.)

1.	raccoon	scapegoat	uproot
2.	outlook	fluke	boyhood
3.	rooftop	scrapbook	firstborn
4.	balloon	classroom	girlhood
5.	toothbrush	kangaroo	schoolyard

Activity Procedure: Have students underline the vowels. Then, have students say the sounds and the word parts to themselves. Have them say the whole word aloud. Remind them to try both sounds for some vowels.

 Use Overhead 12: Activity E

1. Find Activity E. Listen. What does each word part have? (*one vowel sound*)

2. Watch. (Cover all words on the overhead transparency except the first word. Underline the vowels in **raccoon**. Point to the vowels.) What sound? __ What sound? __ How many vowels? __ So, how many word parts? __

3. Now you underline the vowels in **raccoon**. (Pause.) Now underline the vowels in the rest of the words. Look up when you are done. __

4. (Show the rest of the overhead transparency.) Now check to see if you underlined all the vowels. Fix any mistakes. __

5. Look up here. (Pause.) Line 1. Read the first word to yourself. You may have to try both sounds for some vowels. Put your thumb up when you can say a real word. __ What word? __

6. Next word. (Pause.) What word? __

7. Next word. (Pause.) What word? __

8. (Repeat Step 7 with all words in Activity E.)

Note:
• You may wish to provide additional practice by having students read a line to the group or to a partner.

ACTIVITY F: **Oral Activity—Correcting Close Approximations Using Context**

> **Activity Procedure:** Pronounce the word incorrectly as shown. When saying the sentence, continue to mispronounce the word. Then, ask students to make the word into a real word.

1. Make these real words. Listen. I read the word "ed u **că** tion." Change the word to make sense in this sentence. "You can go to college to further your ed u **că** tion." What should the word be? __

2. (Repeat with the following examples.)

in **ten** sīve   The exercise program was very in **ten** sīve.

ex plăn **ă** tion   The teacher gave a clear ex plăn **ă** tion of how to write an essay.

lēa ther   His coat and boots were made of **lēa** ther.

ACTIVITY G: **Prefixes and Suffixes** (See the *Student Book*, page 41.)

dorm(ant)	ant
persist(ent)	ent
argum(ent)	ment

Prefixes						
1.	dis	pro	ex	ad	en	com
2.	pre	con	a	in	per	re

Suffixes						
3.	ant	ity	ly	age	tive	ment
4.	ary	le	ent	y	tion	ant

Activity Procedure: Tell students the words, then the circled suffixes. Have students repeat the words and suffixes. Then, have students practice saying the new and previously learned prefixes and suffixes.

1. Find Activity G. We are going to learn more suffixes.

2. Point to the first column in the box. The first word is **dormant**. What word? __ Point to the circled suffix. The suffix is /ant/. Say it. __

3. (Repeat for **persistent** and /ent/, and **argument** and /ment/.)

4. Find the second column. Read the suffixes. What suffix? __ Next? __ Next? __

5. Point to the first prefix in Line 1. What prefix? __ Next? __ Next? __ Next? __ Next? __ Next? __

6. (Repeat Step 5 for prefixes in Line 2.)

7. Point to the first suffix in Line 3. What suffix? __ Next? __ Next? __ Next? __ Next? __ Next? __

8. (Repeat Step 7 for suffixes in Line 4.)

ACTIVITY H: **Circling Prefixes and Suffixes** (See the *Student Book*, page 42.)

1.	complimentary	continent	racism
2.	different	documentary	challenging
3.	servant	passage	suggestive
4.	cartoonist	permanent	assistant
5.	excitement	princely	examination
6.	independently	enjoyment	entertainment
7.	disinfectant	unemployment	construction

Activity Procedure: Have students find prefixes and suffixes and circle them. Then, assist students in checking their worksheets and reading the words, first part by part, then the whole word. Finally, time students for 10 seconds to see how many words they can read.

 Use Overhead 12: Activity H

1. Find Activity H. Circle all the prefixes and suffixes. Remember, some words have no prefixes or suffixes, and some words have one or more prefixes or suffixes. Look up when you are done. __

2. (Show the overhead transparency.) Now check to see if you circled all the prefixes and suffixes. Fix any mistakes. __

3. (When students are done checking, assist them in reading each word on the overhead transparency, beginning with the first word of Line 1.) Look up here. __

    (Loop under each word part in **com pli ment ary**.) What part? __   What part? __ What part? __   What part? __

    (Run your finger under the whole word.) What word? __

4. (Repeat Step 3 with all words in Activity H.)

5. Time for a 10-second rapid read. Partner 2, read first. Partner 1, count. (Time students for 10 seconds, and then say "Stop.")

6. Partner 1, show me how many words your partner read. (Look around the group.) Partner 1, your turn to read. Partner 2, count. (Time students for 10 seconds, and then say "Stop.")

7. Partner 2, show me how many words your partner read. (Look around the group.)

ACTIVITY I: **Vocabulary** (See the *Student Book,* page 42.)

a.	a person who serves (Line 3, Activity H)	**servant**
b.	a person who assists or helps (Line 4, Activity H)	**assistant**
c.	the act of enjoying (Line 6, Activity H)	**enjoyment**

Special Vocabulary

1.   permanent—If something is meant to last forever without changing, it is <u>permanent</u>.

2.   examination—Another word for test is <u>examination</u>.

> **Activity Procedure:** In the first part, read each definition and ask students to find the word that matches the meaning and write it in the space provided. In the second part, ask students to read each word silently, and then read the word and explanation aloud with you. Give several more examples of how the word might be used. Finally, have students tell their assigned partners a particular application of the word.

1.   Find Activity I.

2.   Listen to the first definition, "a person who serves." Find the word in Line 3 and write it. (Pause and monitor.) What word means "a person who serves"? (*servant*)

3.   Listen to the next definition, "a person who assists or helps." Find the word in Line 4 and write it. (Pause and monitor.) What word means "a person who assists or helps"? (*assistant*)

4.   Next definition. "The act of enjoying." Find the word in Line 6 and write it. (Pause and monitor.) What word means "the act of enjoying"? (*enjoyment*)

5.   Find *Special Vocabulary.* Find Line 1. (Pause.) Read the word to yourself. (Pause.) What word? (*permanent*)

6.   Read the explanation with me. "If something is meant to last forever without changing, it is <u>permanent</u>."

7.   If a statue were made of stone and cement, the artist would expect the statue to be _____. (*permanent*)

8.   If a farmer puts up a metal fence set in concrete, he is hoping that the fence will be _____. (*permanent*)

9.   Tell me if this is permanent. The ink will not come off the shirt. Is the ink permanent? ___ (*Yes*)

10. The ink washes off the shirt. Is the ink permanent? ___ (*No*)

11. Find Line 2. (Pause.) Read the word to yourself. (Pause.) What word? (*examination*)

12. Read the explanation with me. "Another word for test is <u>examination</u>."

13. A big math test could be called a math _____. (examination)

14. A spelling test could be called a spelling _____. (examination)

ACTIVITY J: **Spelling Dictation** (See the *Student Book,* page 42.)

1. permanent	2. enjoyment
3. complimentary	4. servant

Activity Procedure: For each word, tell students the word, then have students say the parts of the word with you. Have them say the parts to themselves as they write the word. Then, have students compare their words with your word and cross out and rewrite any misspelled words.

Note:
• Distribute a piece of light cardboard to each of the students.

1. Find Activity J. Please cover up the rest of the page.

2. The first word is **permanent**. What word? __ Fist in the air. Say the parts in **permanent** with me. First part? __ Next part? __ Next part? __ Say the parts in **permanent** to yourself as you write the word. (Pause and monitor.)

3. (Write **permanent** on the board or overhead transparency.) Check **permanent**. If you misspelled it, cross it out and write it correctly.

4. The second word is **enjoyment**. What word? __ Fist in the air. Say the parts in **enjoyment** with me. First part? __ Next part? __ Next part? __ Say the parts in **enjoyment** to yourself as you write the word. (Pause and monitor.)

5. (Write **enjoyment** on the board or overhead transparency.) Check **enjoyment**. If you misspelled it, cross it out and write it correctly.

6. (Repeat the procedures for the words **complimentary** and **servant**.)

Lesson 13

Materials Needed

- Lesson 13 from the *Student Book*
- Overhead Transparency 13
- Washable overhead transparency pen
- Paper or cardboard to use when covering the overhead transparency
- Paper or cardboard for each student to use during spelling dictation

ACTIVITY A: **Oral Activity—Blending Word Parts Into Words**

> **Activity Procedure:** Say each word, pausing between the word parts, then have students blend the parts together and say the whole word.

1. Open your *Student Book* to Lesson 13.

2. Listen. (Say the word, pausing completely between the word parts.) re dun dant ly. What word? __

3. (Repeat with the following examples.)

   re pro duc tion

   con di tion al ly

   im prac ti cal i ty

   un in ten tion al ly

   ed u ca tion al ly

ACTIVITY B: **Vowel Combinations** (See the *Student Book,* page 43.)

ea				
(meat) (thread)				

1.	au	ea	oo	oy	ai
2.	ow	ir	ou	or	oo
3.	a - e	oa	ea	i - e	ay
4.	ea	ee	ar	oo	oi

Activity Procedure: In this lesson, students learn the two sounds of a new letter combination. Have students point to the new letter combination. Tell them the sound as it is pronounced in the first key word. Then, tell students that if they try this sound and the word doesn't sound right, to try a second sound. Tell them the sound, then have them practice what they would say first and what they would say second. Have students say the new sounds and the sounds from the previous lessons. Remind them to say both sounds when they see a box.

1. Find Activity B. We are going to learn two sounds for these letters.

2. Look at the box. Point to the letters **e - a**. The sound of these letters is usually /ē/ as in "meat." What sound? __ If the word doesn't sound right, try /ĕ/ as in "thread." What sound? __

3. Let's review. What sound would you try first? (/ē/) What sound would you try next? (/ĕ/)

Note:
  • Whenever you come to letters in a box, ask "What sound would you try first? What sound would you try next?"

4. Point to the first letters in Line 1. What sound? __ Boxed letters. What sound would you try first? __ What sound would you try next? __ Boxed letters. What sound would you try first? __ What sound would you try next? __ Next sound? __ Next sound? __

5. (Continue Step 4 for letters in Lines 2–4.)

ACTIVITY C: **Vowel Conversions** (See the *Student Book*, page 43.)

i	o	e	a	u

> **Activity Procedure:** Have students review saying the sound, then the name for each letter.

1. Find Activity C. When you are reading words and see these letters, what should you try first, the sound or the name? __ If it doesn't make a real word, what should you try? __

2. Point to the first letter. What sound? __ What name? __

3. Point to the next letter. What sound? __ What name? __

4. Point to the next letter. What sound? __ What name? __

5. Point to the next letter. What sound? __ What name? __

6. Point to the next letter. What sound? __ What name? __

7. First letter again. What sound? __ What name? __

8. Next letter. What sound? __ What name? __

9. (Repeat Step 8 for remaining letters.)

ACTIVITY D: **Reading Parts of Real Words** (See the *Student Book,* page 44.)

1.	mead	fa *	steam	tend
2.	trow	ger	fid	gent
3.	mitt	meal	proof	tol
4.	port	nif	net	stead

Activity Procedure: Have students say each word part aloud. Remind them to say the name when they see the asterisk. Remind them to say both sounds when they see a box.

Notes:
- On word parts with an asterisk under the vowel, tell students to say the name. Ask: "What name?"
- Whenever you come to a word part in a box, ask "What sound would you try first? What part? What sound would you try next? What part?"

1. Find Activity D. We are going to read parts of real words.

2. Line 1. What sound would you try first? (/ē/) What part? (/mēd/) What sound would you try next? (/ĕ/) What part? (/mĕd/)

3. Next word part. What name? __ What part? __

4. Next word part. What sound would you try first? (/ē/) What part? (/stēm/) What sound would you try next? (/ĕ/) What part? (/stĕm/)

5. Next word part. What part? __

6. (For each remaining word part, ask "What part?" or "What sound would you try first? What part? What sound would you try next? What part?")

Note:
- You may wish to provide additional practice by having students read a line to the group or to a partner.

ACTIVITY E: **Underlining Vowels in Words** (See the *Student Book,* page 44.)

1.	steamboat	bedroom	streambed
2.	meadow	peanut	widespread
3.	showdown	streamline	meant
4.	seashell	headstrong	meantime
5.	oatmeal	daydream	gingerbread

Activity Procedure: Have students underline the vowels. Then, have students say the sounds and the word parts to themselves. Have them say the whole word aloud. Remind them to try both sounds for some vowels.

 Use Overhead 13: Activity E

1. Find Activity E. Listen. What does each word part have? (*one vowel sound*)

2. Watch. (Cover all words on the overhead transparency except the first word. Underline the vowels in **steamboat**. Point to the vowels.) What sound? __ What sound? __ How many vowels? __ So, how many word parts? __

3. Now, you underline the vowels in **steamboat**. (Pause.) Now underline the vowels in the rest of the words. Look up when you are done. __

4. (Show the rest of the overhead transparency.) Now check to see if you underlined all the vowels. Fix any mistakes. __

5. Look up here. (Pause.) Line 1. Read the first word to yourself. You may have to try both sounds for some vowels. Put your thumb up when you can say a real word. __ What word? __

6. Next word. (Pause.) What word? __

7. Next word. (Pause.) What word? __

8. (Repeat Step 7 with all words in Activity E.)

Note:
• You may wish to provide additional practice by having students read a line to the group or to a partner.

ACTIVITY F: **Oral Activity—Correcting Close Approximations Using Context**

> **Activity Procedure:** Pronounce the word incorrectly as shown. When saying the sentence, continue to mispronounce the word. Then, ask students to make the word into a real word.

1. Make these real words. Listen. I read the word "dē **sper** āte." Change the word to make sense in this sentence. "After the hurricane, the people were dē **sper** āte for food." What should the word be? __

2. (Repeat with the following examples.)

fas cin **ăt** ing   When something is really interesting, we say it is fas cin **ăt** ing.

prē par **ă** tion   The dinner took a great deal of prē par **ă** tion.

vĭ **o** lence   Fighting or any other type of vĭ **o** lence is not allowed in schools.

ACTIVITY G: **Prefixes and Suffixes** (See the *Student Book,* page 45.)

disturb(ance)	ance
influ(ence)	ence

Prefixes					
1. a	con	en	pro	mis	re
2. ex	im	per	ab	pre	com

Suffixes					
3. ity	ance	ism	ment	sive	ence
4. ant	ary	ance	ate	ence	ly

Activity Procedure: Tell students the words, then the circled suffixes. Have students repeat the words and suffixes. Then, have students practice saying the new and previously learned prefixes and suffixes.

1. Find Activity G. We are going to learn more suffixes.

2. Point to the first column in the box. The first word is **disturbance**. What word? __ Point to the circled suffix. The suffix is /ance/. Say it. __

3. (Repeat for **influence** and /ence/.)

4. Find the second column. Read the suffixes. What suffix? __ Next? __

5. Point to the first prefix in Line 1. What prefix? __ Next? __ Next? __ Next? __ Next? __ Next? __

6. (Repeat Step 5 for prefixes in Line 2.)

7. Point to the first suffix in Line 3. What suffix? __ Next? __ Next? __ Next? __ Next? __ Next? __

8. (Repeat Step 7 for suffixes in Line 4.)

ACTIVITY H: **Circling Prefixes and Suffixes** (See the *Student Book*, page 45.)

1.	explanation	difference	dependence
2.	importance	fictional	refinance
3.	gently	endurance	baggage
4.	powerfully	confectionary	attendance
5.	admittance	intolerant	magnetism
6.	maintenance	misunderstand	confidence
7.	significance	performance	consistent

Activity Procedure: Have students find prefixes and suffixes and circle them. Then, assist students in checking their worksheets and reading the words, first part by part, then the whole word. Finally, time students for 10 seconds to see how many words they can read.

 Use Overhead 13: Activity H

1. Find Activity H. Circle all the prefixes and suffixes. Remember, some words have no prefixes or suffixes, and some words have one or more prefixes or suffixes. Look up when you are done. __

2. (Show the overhead transparency.) Now check to see if you circled all the prefixes and suffixes. Fix any mistakes. __

3. (When students are done checking, assist them in reading each word on the overhead transparency, beginning with the first word of Line 1.) Look up here. __

    (Loop under each word part in **ex pla na tion**.) What part? __ What part? __ What part? __ What part? __

    (Run your finger under the whole word.) What word? __

4. (Repeat Step 3 with all words in Activity H.)

5. Time for a 10-second rapid read. Partner 1, read first. Partner 2, count. (Time students for 10 seconds, and then say "Stop.")

6. Partner 2, show me how many words your partner read. (Look around the group.) Partner 2, your turn to read. Partner 1, count. (Time students for 10 seconds, and then say "Stop.")

7. Partner 1, show me how many words your partner read. (Look around the group.)

ACTIVITY I: **Vocabulary** (See the *Student Book*, page 46.)

---

a.   in a manner that is powerful (Line 4, Activity H) __powerfully__

b.   not tolerant; not willing to accept differences (Line 5, Activity H)
__intolerant__

c.   thinking or acting in the same way again and again (Line 7, Activity H)
__consistent__

Special Vocabulary

1.   dependence—When someone has to do something for us, we have
__dependence__ on that person.

2.   endurance—When you can do something for a very long time, you have
__endurance__.

Activity Procedure: In the first part, read each definition and ask students to find the word that matches the meaning and write it in the space provided. In the second part, ask students to read each word silently, and then read the word and explanation aloud with you. Give several more examples of how the word might be used. Finally, have students tell their assigned partners a particular application of the word.

1. Find Activity I.

2. Listen to the first definition, "in a manner that is powerful." Find the word in Line 4 and write it. (Pause and monitor.) What word means "in a manner that is powerful"? (*powerfully*)

3. Listen to the next definition, "not tolerant; not willing to accept differences." Find the word in Line 5 and write it. (Pause and monitor.) What word means "not tolerant; not willing to accept differences"? (*intolerant*)

4. Next definition. "Thinking or acting in the same way again and again." Find the word in Line 7 and write it. (Pause and monitor.) What word means "thinking or acting in the same way again and again"? (*consistent*)

5. Find the *Special Vocabulary*. Find Line 1. (Pause.) Read the word to yourself. (Pause.) What word? (*dependence*)

6. Read the explanation with me. "When someone must do something for us, we have __dependence__ on that person."

7. A baby cannot feed himself, so his mother feeds him. This is an example of _____. (*dependence*)

8. A pet dog must get its food from its owner. This is an example of _____. (*dependence*)

9. Tell me if this is dependence. The mother puts the baby bottle in the baby's mouth because the baby cannot do it. Is this dependence? __ (*Yes*)

10. The mother hands the teenager a bottle of water after he finishes the long run. Is this dependence? __ (*No*)

11. Find Line 2. (Pause) Read the word to yourself. (Pause.) What word? (*endurance*)

12. Read the explanation with me. "When you can do something for a very long time, you have <u>endurance</u>."

13. If you worked on a project for five hours, and you didn't stop working at all, you would be showing _____. (*endurance*)

14. Belinda walks home seven miles every day. Is she showing endurance? __ (*Yes*)

ACTIVITY J: **Spelling Dictation** (See the *Student Book,* page 46.)

1. endurance	2. fictional
3. powerfully	4. dependence

> **Activity Procedure:** For each word, tell students the word, then have students say the parts of the word with you. Have them say the parts to themselves as they write the word. Then, have students compare their words with your word and cross out and rewrite any misspelled words.

Note:
- Distribute a piece of light cardboard to each of the students.

1. Find Activity J. Please cover up the rest of the page.

2. The first word is **endurance**. What word? __ Fist in the air. Say the parts in **endurance** with me. First part? __ Next part? __ Next part? __ Say the parts in **endurance** to yourself as you write the word. (Pause and monitor.)

3. (Write **endurance** on the board or overhead transparency.) Check **endurance**. If you misspelled it, cross it out and write it correctly.

4. The second word is **fictional**. What word? __ Fist in the air. Say the parts in **fictional** with me. First part? __ Next part? __ Next part? __ Say the parts in **fictional** to yourself as you write the word. (Pause and monitor.)

5. (Write **fictional** on the board or overhead transparency.) Check **fictional**. If you misspelled it, cross it out and write it correctly.

6. (Repeat the procedures for the words **powerfully** and **dependence**.)

Lesson 14

Materials Needed

- Lesson 14 from the *Student Book*
- Overhead Transparency 14
- Washable overhead transparency pen
- Paper or cardboard to use when covering the overhead transparency
- Paper or cardboard for each student to use during spelling dictation

---

ACTIVITY A: **Oral Activity—Blending Word Parts Into Words**

> **Activity Procedure:** Say each word, pausing between the word parts, then have students blend the parts together and say the whole word.

1. Open your *Student Book* to Lesson 14.

2. Listen. (Say the word, pausing completely between the word parts.)
   mem or i al. What word? __

3. (Repeat with the following examples.)

   pro duc tive ness

   in con sist ent ly

   un ex pect ed ness

   in ter na tion al ly

   en vi ron ment al ly

ACTIVITY B: **Vowel Combinations** (See the *Student Book*, page 47.)

ea
(meat) (thread)

1.	ow	oa	ea	au	or
2.	ee	ar	er	o - e	oo
3.	ea	ou	oy	ay	au
4.	ow	ai	ir	oi	ea

> **Activity Procedure:** In this lesson, students review the two sounds of the new letter combination learned in the previous lesson. Have students point to the letter combination. Tell them the first sound. Then, tell students that if they try this sound and the word doesn't sound right, to try a second sound. Tell them the sound, then have them practice what they would say first and what they would say second. Have students say the new sounds and the sounds from the previous lessons. Remind them to say both sounds when they see a box.

1.   Find Activity B. We are going to review a difficult sound.

2.   Look at the box. Point to the letters **e - a**. The sound of these letters is usually /ē/. What sound? __ If the word doesn't sound right, try /ĕ/. What sound? __

3.   Let's review. What sound would you try first? (/ē/) What sound would you try next? (/ĕ/)

Note:
- Whenever you come to letters in a box, ask "What sound would you try first? What sound would you try next?"

4.   Point to the boxed letters in Line 1. What sound would you try first? __ What sound would you try next? __ Next sound? __ Boxed letters. What sound would you try first? __ What sound would you try next? __ Next sound? __ Next sound? __

5.   (Continue Step 4 for letters in Lines 2–4.)

ACTIVITY C: **Vowel Conversions** (See the *Student Book,* page 47.)

u	o	a	i	e

> **Activity Procedure:** Have students review saying the sound, then the name for each letter.

1. Find Activity C. When you are reading words and see these letters, what should you try first, the sound or the name? __ If it doesn't make a real word, what should you try? __

2. Point to the first letter. What sound? __ What name? __

3. Point to the next letter. What sound? __ What name? __

4. Point to the next letter. What sound? __ What name? __

5. Point to the next letter. What sound? __ What name? __

6. Point to the next letter. What sound? __ What name? __

7. First letter again. What sound? __ What name? __

8. Next letter. What sound? __ What name? __

9. (Repeat Step 8 for remaining letters.)

ACTIVITY D: **Reading Parts of Real Words** (See the *Student Book*, page 48.)

1.	thread	ca *	vel	break
2.	par	boon	tre *	fac
3.	tra *	phan	read	ven
4.	ves	clu *	ket	fes

Activity Procedure: Have students say each word part aloud. Remind them to say the name when they see the asterisk. Remind them to say both sounds when they see a box.

Notes:
- On word parts with an asterisk under the vowel, tell students to say the name. Ask: "What name?"
- Whenever you come to a word part in a box, ask "What sound would you try first? What part? What sound would you try next? What part?"

1. Find Activity D. We are going to read parts of real words.

2. Line 1. What sound would you try first? (/ē/) What part? (/thrēd/) What sound would you try next? (/ĕ/) What part? (/thrĕd/)

3. Next word part. What name? __ What part? __

4. Next word part. What part? __

5. Next word part. What sound would you try first? (/ē/) What part? (/brēk/) What sound would you try next? (/ĕ/) What part? (/brĕk/)

6. (For each remaining word part, ask "What part?" or "What sound would you try first? What part? What sound would you try next? What part?" or "What name? What part?")

Note:
- You may wish to provide additional practice by having students read a line to the group or to a partner.

ACTIVITY E: **Underlining Vowels in Words** (See the *Student Book,* page 48.)

1.	peacock	threadbare	steamship
2.	breakfast	gemstone	moonbeam
3.	footpath	soybean	letterhead
4.	health	seamstress	sweatshirt
5.	seaweed	proofread	southeastern

Activity Procedure: Have students underline the vowels. Then, have students say the sounds and the word parts to themselves. Have them say the whole word aloud.

 Use Overhead 14: Activity E

1. Find Activity E. Listen. What does each word part have? (*one vowel sound*)

2. Watch. (Cover all words on the overhead transparency except the first word. Underline the vowels in **peacock**. Point to the vowels.) What sound? __ What sound? __ How many vowel sounds? __ So, how many word parts? __

3. Now, you underline the vowels in **peacock**. (Pause.) Now underline the vowels in the rest of the words. Look up when you are done. __

4. (Show the rest of the overhead transparency.) Now check to see if you underlined all the vowels. Fix any mistakes. __

5. Look up here. (Pause.) Line 1. Read the first word to yourself. You may have to try both sounds for some vowels. Put your thumb up when you can say a real word. __ What word? __

6. Next word. (Pause.) What word? __

7. Next word. (Pause.) What word? __

8. (Repeat Step 7 with all words in Activity E.)

Note:
• You may wish to provide additional practice by having students read a line to the group or to a partner.

ACTIVITY F: **Oral Activity—Correcting Close Approximations Using Context**

> **Activity Procedure:** Pronounce the word incorrectly as shown. When saying the sentence, continue to mispronounce the word. Then, ask students to make the word into a real word.

1. Make these real words. Listen. I read the word "**pŏst** āge." Change the word to make sense in this sentence. "Remember to put the right **pŏst** āge on the letter." What should the word be? __

2. (Repeat with the following examples.)

    re vers **īble**   He can wear either side because his jacket is re vers **īble**.

    ă dor **āble**   The kitten was so ă dor **āble**, we wanted to take it home.

    tor **pĕd** ō   The submarine fired a tor **pĕd** ō at the enemy ship.

ACTIVITY G: **Prefixes and Suffixes** (See the *Student Book,* page 49.)

fam(ous)	ous
pic(ture)	ture

Prefixes						
1.	com	pre	mis	pro	im	per
2.	re	dis	con	dis	a	dis

Suffixes						
3.	ous	ity	ary	ence	or	ture
4.	tion	ance	age	er	ture	ous

Activity Procedure: Tell students the words, then the circled suffixes. Have students repeat the words and suffixes. Then, have students practice saying the new and previously learned prefixes and suffixes.

1.   Find Activity G. We are going to learn more suffixes.

2.   Point to the first column in the box. The first word is **famous**. What word? __ Point to the circled suffix. The suffix is /ous/. Say it. __

3.   (Repeat for **picture** and /ture/.)

4.   Find the second column. Read the suffixes. What suffix? __ Next? __

5.   Point to the first prefix in Line 1. What prefix? __ Next? __ Next? __ Next? __ Next? __ Next? __

6.   (Repeat Step 5 for prefixes in Line 2.)

7.   Point to the first suffix in Line 3. What suffix? __ Next? __ Next? __ Next? __ Next? __ Next? __

8.   (Repeat Step 7 for suffixes in Line 4.)

ACTIVITY H: **Circling Prefixes and Suffixes** (See the *Student Book*, page 49.)

1.	marvelous	continuous	healthy
2.	inactive	literature	orphanage
3.	enormous	tremendous	absorbent
4.	departure	instructors	elementary
5.	excessive	conformity	vulture
6.	adventure	ineffective	confession
7.	investigation	inconclusive	identification

Activity Procedure: Have students find prefixes and suffixes and circle them. Then, assist students in checking their worksheets and reading the words, first part by part, then the whole word. Finally, time students for 10 seconds to see how many words they can read.

 Use Overhead 14: Activity H

1. Find Activity H. Circle all the prefixes and suffixes. Remember, some words have no prefixes or suffixes, and some words have one or more prefixes or suffixes. Look up when you are done. __

2. (Show the overhead transparency.) Now check to see if you circled all the prefixes and suffixes. Fix any mistakes. __

3. (When students are done checking, assist them in reading each word on the overhead transparency, beginning with the first word of Line 1.) Look up here. __

    (Loop under each word part in **mar vel ous**.) What part? __ What part? __ What part? __

    (Run your finger under the whole word.) What word? __

4. (Repeat Step 3 with all words in Activity H.)

5. Time for a 10-second rapid read. Partner 2, read first. Partner 1, count. (Time students for 10 seconds, and then say "Stop.")

6. Partner 1, show me how many words your partner read. (Look around the group.) Partner 1, your turn to read. Partner 2, count. (Time students for 10 seconds, and then say "Stop.")

7. Partner 2, show me how many words your partner read. (Look around the group.)

ACTIVITY I: **Vocabulary** (See the *Student Book,* page 50.)

a.	given to excess or beyond what is necessary (Line 5, Activity H)	__excessive__
b.	not effective because it doesn't work (Line 6, Activity H)	__ineffective__
c.	not having a conclusion or clear result (Line 7, Activity H)	__inconclusive__

Special Vocabulary

1.   continuous—If something just keeps on going without stopping, it is <u>continuous</u>.

2.   investigation—When we really want to know something and we search for information about it, we are involved in an <u>investigation</u>.

Activity Procedure: In the first part, read each definition and ask students to find the word that matches the meaning and write it in the space provided. In the second part, ask students to read each word silently, and then read the word and explanation aloud with you. Give several more examples of how the word might be used. Finally, have students tell their assigned partner a particular application of the word.

1.   Find Activity I.

2.   Listen to the first definition, "given to excess or beyond what is necessary." Find the word in Line 5 and write it. (Pause and monitor.) What word means "given to excess or beyond what is necessary"? (*excessive*)

3.   Listen to the next definition, "not effective because it doesn't work." Find the word in Line 6 and write it. (Pause and monitor.) What word means "not effective because it doesn't work"? (*ineffective*)

4.   Next definition. "Not having a conclusion or clear result." Find the word in Line 7 and write it. (Pause and monitor.) What word means "not having a conclusion or clear result"? (*inconclusive*)

5.   Find the *Special Vocabulary.* Find Line 1. (Pause.) Read the word to yourself. (Pause.) What word? (*continuous*)

6.   Read the explanation with me. "If something just keeps on going without stopping, it is <u>continuous</u>."

7.   If the clock kept on ticking day after day, month after month, year after year, the ticking would be _____. (*continuous*)

8.   If you finished a book and got a new book and then another book and another book, your reading would be _____. (*continuous*)

9.   Tell me if this is continuous. Breathing. __ (*Yes*) Moving your arms. __ (*No*)

10. Find Line 2. (Pause.) Read the word to yourself. (Pause.) What word? (*investigation*)

11. Read the explanation with me. "When we really want to know something and we search for information about it, we are involved in an <u>investigation</u>."

12. If you studied the minerals in rocks, you would be involved in an _____. (*investigation*)

13. If you went online and learned everything about lunar eclipses, you would be doing an _____. (*investigation*)

14. Partner 2, tell your partner a topic that you would like to do an investigation into.

15. Partner 1, tell your partner a topic that you would like to do an investigation into.

ACTIVITY J: **Spelling Dictation** (See the *Student Book,* page 50.)

1. investigation	2. adventure
3. departure	4. tremendous

Activity Procedure: For each word, tell students the word, then have students say the parts of the word with you. Have them say the parts to themselves as they write the word. Then, have students compare their words with your word and cross out and rewrite any misspelled words.

Note:
- Distribute a piece of light cardboard to each of the students.

1. Find Activity J. Please cover up the rest of the page.

2. The first word is **investigation**. What word? __ Fist in the air. Say the parts in **investigation** with me. First part? __ Next part? __ Next part? __ Next part? __ Next part? __ Say the parts in **investigation** to yourself as you write the word. (Pause and monitor.)

3. (Write **investigation** on the board or overhead transparency.) Check **investigation**. If you misspelled it, cross it out and write it correctly.

4. The second word is **adventure**. What word? __ Fist in the air. Say the parts in **adventure** with me. First part? __ Next part? __ Next part? __ Say the parts in **adventure** to yourself as you write the word. (Pause and monitor.)

5. (Write **adventure** on the board or overhead transparency.) Check **adventure**. If you misspelled it, cross it out and write it correctly.

6. (Repeat the procedures for the words **departure** and **tremendous**.)

Lesson 15

Materials Needed

- Lesson 15 from the *Student Book*
- Overhead Transparency 15
- Washable overhead transparency pen
- Paper or cardboard to use when covering the overhead transparency
- Paper or cardboard for each student to use during spelling dictation

ACTIVITY A: **Oral Activity—Blending Word Parts Into Words**

> **Activity Procedure:** Say each word, pausing between the word parts, then have students blend the parts together and say the whole word.

1. Open your *Student Book* to Lesson 15.

2. Listen. (Say the word, pausing completely between the word parts.)
   un pre vent a ble. What word? __

3. (Repeat with the following examples.)

   con tra dic tion

   in de struc ti ble

   ad min is tra tive

   i den ti fi ca tion

   de vel op ment al ly

ACTIVITY B: **Vowel Combinations** (See the *Student Book,* page 51.)

ea
(meat) (thread)

1.	☐ea	☐oo	oi	oa	ou
2.	or	au	ir	i - e	☐ow
3.	ee	a - e	ay	☐ea	er
4.	ur	☐ea	ai	oy	☐oo

Activity Procedure: In this lesson, students review the two sounds of the new letter combination learned in the previous two lessons. Have students point to the letter combination. Tell them the first sound. Then, tell students that if they try this sound and the word doesn't sound right, to try a second sound. Tell them the sound, then have them practice what they would say first and what they would say second. Have students say the new sounds and the sounds from the previous lessons. Remind them to say both sounds when they see a box.

1. Find Activity B. We are going to review a difficult sound.

2. Look at the box. Point to the letters **e - a**. The sound of these letters is usually /ē/. What sound? __ If the word doesn't sound right, try /ĕ/. What sound? __

3. Let's review. What sound would you try first? (/ē/) What sound would you try next? (/ĕ/)

Note:
 • Whenever you come to letters in a box, ask "What sound would you try first? What sound would you try next?"

4. Point to the boxed letters in Line 1. What sound would you try first? __ What sound would you try next? __ Boxed letters. What sound would you try first? __ What sound would you try next? __ Next sound? __ Next sound? __ Next sound? __

5. (Continue Step 4 for letters in Lines 2–4.)

ACTIVITY C: **Vowel Conversions** (See the *Student Book,* page 51.)

e	u	i	a	o

> **Activity Procedure:** Have students review saying the sound, then the name for each letter.

1. Find Activity C. When you are reading words and see these letters, what should you try first, the sound or the name? __ If it doesn't make a real word, what should you try? __

2. Point to the first letter. What sound? __ What name? __

3. Point to the next letter. What sound? __ What name? __

4. Point to the next letter. What sound? __ What name? __

5. Point to the next letter. What sound? __ What name? __

6. Point to the next letter. What sound? __ What name? __

7. First letter again. What sound? __ What name? __

8. Next letter. What sound? __ What name? __

9. (Repeat Step 8 for remaining letters.)

ACTIVITY D: **Reading Parts of Real Words** (See the *Student Book,* page 52.)

1.	round	sur	team	foil
2.	norm	scrip	tinc	flex
3.	poss	tin	cred	place
4.	fort	spons	vail	speak

Activity Procedure: Have students say each word part aloud. Remind them to say both sounds when they see a box.

Note:
- Whenever you come to a word in a box, ask "What sound would you try first? What part? What sound would you try next? What part?"

1. Find Activity D. We are going to read parts of real words.

2. Line 1. What part? __

3. Next word part. What part? __

4. Next word part. What sound would you try first? (/ē/) What part? (/tēm/) What sound would you try next? (/ĕ/) What part? (/tĕm/)

5. Next word part. What part? __

6. (For each remaining word part, ask "What part?" or "What sound would you try first? What part? What sound would you try next? What part?")

Note:
- You may wish to provide additional practice by having students read a line to the group or to a partner.

ACTIVITY E: **Underlining Vowels in Words** (See the *Student Book,* page 52.)

1.	teammate	headdress	marketplace
2.	monorail ＊	tinfoil	reason
3.	seasick	surround	baboon
4.	bedspread	torpedo ＊ ＊	downstream
5.	bookcase	footstool	sunbeam

> **Activity Procedure:** Have students underline the vowels. Then, have students say the sounds and the word parts to themselves. Have them say the whole word aloud. Remind them to try both sounds for some vowels.

 Use Overhead 15: Activity E

Note:
- An asterisk under the vowel of a word indicates that students should say the name.

1. Find Activity E. Listen. What does each word part have? (*one vowel sound*)

2. Watch. (Cover all words on the overhead transparency except the first word. Underline the vowels in **teammate**. Point to the vowels.) What sound? __ What sound? __ How many vowel sounds? __ So, how many word parts? __

3. Now, you underline the vowels in **teammate**. (Pause.) Now underline the vowels in the rest of the words. Look up when you are done. __

4. (Show the rest of the overhead transparency.) Now check to see if you underlined all the vowels. Fix any mistakes. __

5. Look up here. (Pause.) Line 1. Read the first word to yourself. You may have to try both sounds for some vowels. Put your thumb up when you can say a real word. __ What word? __

6. Next word. (Pause.) What word? __

7. Next word. (Pause.) What word? __

8. (Repeat Step 7 with all words in Activity E.)

Note:
- You may wish to provide additional practice by having students read a line to the group or to a partner.

ACTIVITY F: **Oral Activity—Correcting Close Approximations Using Context**

> **Activity Procedure:** Pronounce the word incorrectly as shown. When saying the sentence, continue to mispronounce the word. Then, ask students to make the word into a real word.

1. Make these real words. Listen. I read the word "gen er ōs ity." Change the word to make sense in this sentence. "Because of Mrs. Swenson's gen er ōs ity, the library will be able to purchase many new books." What should the word be? __

2. (Repeat with the following examples.)

dis **ăg** ree ment	The dis **ăg** ree ment resulted from the boys having different ideas.
pŏll **ŭ** tion	The river was dirty and full of pŏll **ŭ** tion.
med **ī** cīne	The doctor prescribed med **ī** cīne for the sick child.

ACTIVITY G: **Prefixes and Suffixes** (See the *Student Book*, page 53.)

comfort(able)	able
revers(ible)	ible
memor(ize)	ize

Prefixes

1.	ex	pro	con	im	mis	per
2.	un	a	ab	com	in	en

Suffixes

3.	ize	able	ence	ous	ment	ible
4.	able	ance	ture	ant	ize	ary

> **Activity Procedure:** Tell students the words, then the circled suffixes. Have students repeat the words and suffixes. Then, have students practice saying the new and previously learned prefixes and suffixes.

1. Find Activity G. We are going to learn more suffixes.

2. Point to the first column in the box. The first word is **comfortable**. What word? __ Point to the circled suffix. The suffix is /able/. Say it. __

3. (Repeat for **reversible** and /ible/, and **memorize** and /ize/.)

4. Find the second column. Read the suffixes. What suffix? __ Next? __ Next? __

5. Point to the first prefix in Line 1. What prefix? __ Next? __ Next? __ Next? __ Next? __ Next? __

6. (Repeat Step 5 for prefixes in Line 2.)

7. Point to the first suffix in Line 3. What suffix? __ Next? __ Next? __ Next? __ Next? __ Next? __

8. (Repeat Step 7 for suffixes in Line 4.)

ACTIVITY H: **Circling Prefixes and Suffixes** (See the *Student Book*, page 53.)

1.	inconsistently	impossible	responsible
2.	predictable	available	civilize
3.	drinkable	normalize	descriptive
4.	laminate	inflexible	preventable
5.	incapable	incredible	legalize
6.	misunderstanding	enjoyable	sterilize
7.	department	reproduction	unconventional

Activity Procedure: Have students find prefixes and suffixes and circle them. Then, assist students in checking their worksheets and reading the words, first part by part, then the whole word. Finally, time students for 10 seconds to see how many words they can read.

 Use Overhead 15: Activity H

1. Find Activity H. Circle all the prefixes and suffixes. Remember, some words have no prefixes or suffixes, and some words have one or more prefixes or suffixes. Look up when you are done. __

2. (Show the overhead transparency.) Now check to see if you circled all the prefixes and suffixes. Fix any mistakes. __

3. (When students are done checking, assist them in reading each word on the overhead transparency, beginning with the first word of Line 1.) Look up here. __

    (Loop under each word part in **in con sist ent ly**.) What part? __ What part? __ What part? __ What part? __ What part? __

    (Run your finger under the whole word.) What word? __

4. (Repeat Step 3 with all words in Activity H.)

5. Time for a 10-second rapid read. Partner 1, read first. Partner 2, count. (Time students for 10 seconds, and then say "Stop.")

6. Partner 2, show me how many words your partner read. (Look around the group.) Partner 2, your turn to read. Partner 1, count. (Time students for 10 seconds, and then say "Stop.")

7. Partner 1, show me how many words your partner read. (Look around the group.)

ACTIVITY I: **Vocabulary** (See the *Student Book,* page 54.)

a.	not possible (Line 1, Activity H) __impossible__
b.	able to be predicted or told ahead of time (Line 2, Activity H) __predictable__
c.	a wrong understanding (Line 6, Activity H) __misunderstanding__

Special Vocabulary

1.   inconsistently—If you are not acting consistently or in the same way each time, you are behaving <u>inconsistently</u>.

2.   available—If you can get something or use something, it is <u>available</u>.

> **Activity Procedure:** In the first part, read each definition and ask students to find the word that matches the meaning and write it in the space provided. In the second part, ask students to read each word silently, and then read the word and explanation aloud with you. Give several more examples of how the word might be used. Finally, have students tell their assigned partners a particular application of the word.

1. Find Activity I.

2. Listen to the first definition, "not possible." Find the word in Line 1 and write it. (Pause and monitor.) What word means "not possible"? (*impossible*)

3. Listen to the next definition, "able to be predicted or told ahead of time." Find the word in Line 2 and write it. (Pause and monitor.) What word means "able to be predicted or told ahead of time"? (*predictable*)

4. Next definition. "A wrong understanding." Find the word in Line 6 and write it. (Pause and monitor.) What word means "a wrong understanding"? (*misunderstanding*)

5. Find the *Special Vocabulary.* Find Line 1. (Pause.) Read the word to yourself. (Pause.) What word? (*inconsistently*)

6. Read the explanation with me. "If you are not acting consistently or in the same way each time, you are behaving <u>inconsistently</u>."

7. If an artist sometimes created large sculptures and sometimes painted small stones, that artist would be acting _____. (*inconsistently*)

8. If you sometimes obeyed your parents' rules and sometimes you didn't, you would be acting _____. (*inconsistently*)

9. Tell me if this is an example of behaving inconsistently. On Mondays and Tuesdays, you greet the teacher when you enter the room; the rest of the week you say nothing. Are you behaving inconsistently? __ (*Yes*) Every day of the week, the teacher teaches you how to read. Is the teacher behaving inconsistently? __ (*No*)

10. Find Line 2. (Pause) Read the word to yourself. (Pause.) What word? (*available*)

11. Read the explanation with me. "If you can get something or use something, it is <u>available</u>."

12. If we had library books on a table in our room, the books would be _____.
     (*available*)

13. If we had a box of pens that everyone could use, the pens would be _____.
     (*available*)

14. Partner 1, tell your partner three things that are available for use in the classroom.

15. Partner 2, tell your partner some other things that are available for use in the
     classroom.

ACTIVITY J: **Spelling Dictation** (See the *Student Book*, page 54.)

1.	inconsistently	2.	normalize
3.	enjoyable	4.	impossible

> **Activity Procedure:** For each word, tell students the word, then have
> students say the parts of the word with you. Have them say the parts to
> themselves as they write the word. Then, have students compare their
> words with your word and cross out and rewrite any misspelled words.

Note:
   • Distribute a piece of light cardboard to each of the students.

1. Find Activity J. Please cover up the rest of the page.

2. The first word is **inconsistently**. What word? __ Fist in the air. Say the parts in
    inconsistently with me. First part? __ Next part? __ Next part? __ Next part? __
    Next part? __ Say the parts in **inconsistently** to yourself as you write the word.
    (Pause and monitor.)

3. (Write **inconsistently** on the board or overhead transparency.) Check
    inconsistently. If you misspelled it, cross it out and write it correctly.

4. The second word is **normalize**. What word? __ Fist in the air. Say the parts in
    normalize with me. First part? __ Next part? __ Next part? __ Say the parts in
    normalize to yourself as you write the word. (Pause and monitor.)

5. (Write **normalize** on the board or overhead transparency.) Check **normalize**. If you
    misspelled it, cross it out and write it correctly.

6. (Repeat the procedures for the words **enjoyable** and **impossible**.)

Transition Notes:
   • By completing Lessons 1–15, your students have finished learning the preskills needed to attack longer
     words. In the next set of lessons, Lessons 16–25, students will use those preskills to figure out longer words.
     They will read these words in lists, in sentences, and in grade-level passages.
   • A word of warning: Lessons 16–25 may take longer to complete, depending on how fluent your students
     are with using the preskills to figure out longer words. Your students may also find these lessons to be more
     difficult than the lessons they just completed.
   • Remember that the strategy they have learned is a flexible strategy. This means that some words could
     be segmented into word parts in more than one way yet still lead to a close approximation of the word's
     pronunciation.

Lesson 16

Materials Needed

- Lesson 16 from the *Student Book*
- Overhead Transparencies 16 and 17
- Washable overhead transparency pen
- Paper or cardboard to use when covering the overhead transparencies
- Paper or cardboard for each student to use during spelling dictation

ACTIVITY A: **Vowel Combinations Review** (See the *Student Book*, page 55.)

1.	au	er	ea	oa	e - e
2.	oi	ur	oy	ee	i - e
3.	ow	ay	u - e	oo	or

> **Activity Procedure:** In this activity, students review letter combinations learned in the first 15 lessons. Have students say the sounds. When the letter combination has a box around it, ask students to tell you both sounds.

Note:

- Whenever you come to letters in a box, ask "What sound would you try first? What sound would you try next?"

1. Find Activity A. Let's review vowel combinations.

2. Point to the first letters in Line 1. What sound? __ Next sound? __ Boxed letters. What sound would you try first? __ What sound would you try next? __ Next sound? __ Next sound? __

3. (Continue Step 2 for letters in Lines 2 and 3.)

ACTIVITY B: **Vowel Conversions Review** (See the *Student Book*, page 55.)

o	i	e	u	a

> **Activity Procedure:** Have students review saying the sound, then the name for each letter.

1. Find Activity B. When you are reading words and see these letters, what should you try first, the sound or the name? __ If it doesn't make a real word, what should you try? __

2. Point to the first letter. What sound? __ What name? __

3. Next letter. What sound? __ What name? __

4. Next letter. What sound? __ What name? __

5. Next letter. What sound? __ What name? __

6. Next letter. What sound? __ What name? __

ACTIVITY C: **Prefixes and Suffixes Review** (See the *Student Book*, page 55.)

Prefixes				
1.	per	a	con	en	be
2.	mis	in	com	un	pro

Suffixes				
3.	ance	tion	y	ture	ible
4.	able	ist	ity	ness	le
5.	ly	ment	ous	al	ent

> **Activity Procedure:** Have students review saying prefixes and suffixes aloud.

1. Find Activity C.

2. Point to the first prefix in Line 1. What prefix? __ Next? __ Next? __ Next? __ Next? __

3. (Repeat Step 2 for prefixes in Line 2.)

4. Point to the first suffix in Line 3. What suffix? __ Next? __ Next? __ Next? __ Next? __

5. (Repeat Step 4 for suffixes in Lines 4 and 5.)

ACTIVITY D: **Strategy Instruction** (See the *Student Book*, page 56.)

1.	prevention	description
2.	estimate	unlucky
3.	excellence	redundant
4.	appearance	adversity
5.	community	enormity
6.	remainder	prediction

Activity Procedure: In this activity, students practice using all the skills learned in the first 15 lessons for figuring out longer words. First, use two words to show students how to use the strategy. Then, work with students to apply the strategy to the remaining words. Ask students if the word has any prefixes or suffixes, then circle them. Underline the vowels and have students say the sounds. Finally, have students say the word, first part by part, and then as a whole word.

 Use Overhead 16: Activity D

Note:
- Read this activity *carefully* before you teach, because the wording changes in each lesson.

1. Find Activity D.

2. Today we are going to learn a strategy for figuring out longer words. The *REWARDS* strategy uses all the skills you have learned in the first 15 lessons.

3. Look up here. Watch me use the strategy. (Point to the word **prevention**.)

4. First, I circle prefixes and suffixes. (Circle **pre** and **tion**. Point to each affix and ask…) What prefix? __ What suffix? __

5. Next, I underline the vowels in the rest of the word. (Underline **e** in **ven**. Point to the vowel and ask…) What sound? __

6. Next, I say the parts in the word. (Loop under each part and say the parts.)
    pre ven tion

7. Next, we say the whole word. It must be a real word. What word? __

8. (Repeat Steps 4–7 with **description**.)

9. Let's read some more words.

10. (Point to the first word in Line 2.) Does the word have a prefix? __ (If the answer is yes, circle the prefix and ask…) What prefix? __

11. Does the word have a suffix? ___ (If the answer is yes, circle the suffix and ask...) What suffix? ___

12. (Underline the vowels in the rest of the word and ask...) What sound? ___

13. Say the word by parts. (Loop under each part and ask...) What part? ___ What part? ___ What part? ___

14. (Run your finger under the whole word.) What word? ___

15. (Repeat Steps 10–14 with each remaining word in Activity D.)

Note:
- You may wish to provide additional practice by having students read a line to the group or to a partner.

ACTIVITY E: **Strategy Practice** (See the *Student Book*, page 56.)

1.	helplessness	distinction
2.	projector	numerous
3.	consultant	connection

> **Activity Procedure:** In this activity, students practice using the strategy themselves for figuring out longer words. Have students circle prefixes and suffixes and underline the vowels. Assist students in checking their work, then reading each word, first part by part, and then as a whole word.

 Use Overhead 16: Activity E

1. Find Activity E.

2. Now it's your turn. For each word, circle prefixes and suffixes and underline the vowels in the rest of the word. Look up when you are done. ___

3. (Show the overhead transparency.) Now check and fix any mistakes. ___

4. (When students are done checking, assist them in reading each word on the overhead transparency, beginning with the first word in Line 1.) Look up here. ___

   (Loop under each word part in **help less ness**.) What part? ___ What part? ___ What part? ___

   (Run your finger under the whole word.) What word? ___

5. (Repeat Step 4 with all words in Activity E.)

Note:
- You may wish to provide additional practice by having students read a line to the group or to a partner.

ACTIVITY F: **Word Families** (See the *Student Book*, page 57.)

A	B
prevent—to keep from happening	connect—to join or fasten together
prevents	connected
prevented	connecting
preventing	connection
prevention	reconnect
preventable	reconnecting
unpreventable	reconnection

Activity Procedure: In this activity, students focus on the relationships among words created by adding various prefixes and/or suffixes to a common root word. Tell students the meaning of the first word in Column A. Have students read words in the first column to themselves, and then twice with the teacher. Then, have students read Column A to their partners. Repeat these procedures for the words in Column B, with opposite partners reading.

excellant

Use Overhead 17: Activity F

1. Find Activity F.

2. Find Column A. These words belong to the same word family. The first word is <u>prevent</u>. Prevent means "to keep from happening." Prefixes and suffixes were added to make new words that have similar meanings to the word <u>prevent</u>. Say each word in Column A to yourself until I say "Stop." __

3. Now let's read the words together. Touch under the first word and read each word with me. (Read the list of words with students.)

4. Let's read those words together again. Touch under the first word and read with me. (Read the list of words with students.)

5. Touch under the first word in Column A again. Partner 1, read the list to your partner. Look up when you are done. __ (Monitor partner reading.)

6. Find Column B. These words belong to the same word family. The first word is <u>connect</u>. Connect means "to join or fasten together." Prefixes and suffixes were added to make new words that have similar meanings to the word <u>connect</u>. Say each word in Column B to yourself until I say "Stop." __

7. (Repeat Steps 3–5 with words in Column B. In Step 5, have Partner 2 read.)

ACTIVITY G: **Spelling Dictation** (See the *Student Book,* page 57.)

1.	prevention	2.	excellence
3.	community	4.	numerous

Activity Procedure: For each word, tell students the word, then have students say the parts of the word with you. Have them say the parts to themselves as they write the word. Then, have students compare their words with your word and cross out and rewrite any misspelled words.

Note:
- Distribute a piece of light cardboard to each of the students.

1. Find Activity G. Please cover up the rest of the page.

2. The first word is **prevention**. What word? __ Fist in the air. Say the parts in **prevention** with me. First part? __ Next part? __ Next part? __ Say the parts in **prevention** to yourself as you write the word. (*Pause and monitor.*)

3. (Write **prevention** on the board or overhead transparency.) Check **prevention**. If you misspelled it, cross it out and write it correctly.

4. The second word is **excellence**. What word? __ Fist in the air. Say the parts in **excellence** with me. First part? __ Next part? __ Next part? __ Say the parts in **excellence** to yourself as you write the word. (*Pause and monitor.*)

5. (Write **excellence** on the board or overhead transparency.) Check **excellence**. If you misspelled it, cross it out and write it correctly.

6. (Repeat the procedures for the words **community** and **numerous**.)

ACTIVITY H: **Vocabulary** (See the *Student Book,* page 57.)

a.	not lucky (Activity D)	___unlucky___
b.	the result of predicting or making a guess (Activity D)	___prediction___
c.	the result of being connected (Activity E)	___connection___

Special Vocabulary

1.   adversity—When you have many things go wrong in your life or you have many problems, you experience <u>adversity</u>.

2.   estimate—If you guess an amount or number, you <u>estimate</u>.

> **Activity Procedure:** In the first part, read each definition and ask students to find the word that matches the meaning and write it in the space provided. In the second part, ask students to read each word silently, and then read the word and explanation aloud with you. Give several more examples of how the word might be used. Finally, have students tell their assigned partner a particular application of the word.

1. Find Activity H.

2. Listen to the first definition, "not lucky." Look back at the words in Activity D. Find the word and write it. (Pause and monitor.) What word means "not lucky"? (*unlucky*)

3. Listen to the next definition, "the result of predicting or making a guess." Look back at the words in Activity D. Find the word and write it. (Pause and monitor.) What word means "the result of predicting or making a guess"? (*prediction*)

4. Next definition. "The result of being connected." Look back at the words in Activity E. Find the word and write it. (Pause and monitor.) What word means "the result of being connected"? (*connection*)

5. Find the *Special Vocabulary.* Find Line 1. (Pause.) Read the word to yourself. (Pause.) What word? (*adversity*)

6. Read the explanation with me. "When you have many things go wrong in your life or you have many problems, you experience <u>adversity</u>."

7. If a woman became very ill, and then lost her job, she would experience _____. (*adversity*)

8. If an earthquake destroyed your home, your family would experience _____. (*adversity*)

9. Tell me if this person would experience adversity. Jamul lost his pencil. Would he experience adversity? __ (*No*) Jamul's house and school were destroyed by a tornado. Would he experience adversity? __ (*Yes*)

10. Find Line 2. (Pause.) Read the word to yourself. (Pause.) What word? (*estimate*)

11. Read the explanation with me. "If you guess an amount or number, you <u>estimate</u>."

12. In order to guess how many pieces of candy are in a bowl, you would _____. (*estimate*)

13. If you were looking around a room filled with people and wanting to guess the number of people, you would _____. (*estimate*)

14. Partner 2, look around the room and estimate the number of children sitting in the classroom. Don't count, estimate.

15. Partner 1, look around the room and estimate the number of books in the classroom. Don't count, estimate.

ACTIVITY I: **Sentence Reading** (See the *Student Book*, page 58.)

1.   The consultant will help the people plan for the rock star's appearance.

2.   The community felt great helplessness in the face of adversity.

3.   The description of the art gallery made it sound quite marvelous.

4.   The police department was awarded a medal of distinction for excellence in crime prevention.

5.   The projector did not work because the connection was poor.

6.   The students needed to estimate the remainder for the division problems.

7.   The teacher laminated the remainder of the pictures so they would not be ruined.

8.   The passage repeated the main points several times, making the last two pages very redundant.

9.   The unlucky children were very upset with the enormity of the impossible task.

10.   Numerous events in the community were halted because of the adversity.

Activity Procedure: In this activity, students use the strategy for figuring out longer words in the context of sentences that contain words they have already practiced. Have students read a sentence to themselves. Then, choose from several options of having students read the sentence together, to partners, or individually to the class.

1. Find Sentence 1 in Activity I. These sentences include words that we practiced today. Read the first sentence to yourself. When you can read all of the words in the sentence, put your thumb up. __

2. (When students can read the sentence, use one of the following options:

    a. Ask the students to read the sentence together, i.e., choral reading.

    b. Have students read the sentence to their partners. Then, call on one student to read the sentence to the group.

    c. Ask one student to read the sentence to the group.)

3. (Repeat these procedures with the remaining sentences. Be sure that you give ample thinking time for each sentence.)

Materials Needed

- Lesson 17 from the *Student Book*
- Overhead Transparencies 18 and 19
- Washable overhead transparency pen
- Paper or cardboard to use when covering the overhead transparencies
- Paper or cardboard for each student to use during spelling dictation

ACTIVITY A: **Vowel Combinations Review** (See the *Student Book*, page 59.)

1.	ir	or	oa	oo	ay
2.	u - e	ai	ar	ou	oy
3.	i - e	ow	ea	ur	oi

Activity Procedure: Have students review saying the sounds for letter combinations. When the letter combination has a box around it, ask students to tell you both sounds.

Note:
- Whenever you come to letters in a box, ask "What sound would you try first? What sound would you try next?"

1. Find Activity A. Let's review vowel combinations.

2. Point to the first letters in Line 1. What sound? __ Next sound? __ Next sound? __ Boxed letters. What sound would you try first? __ What sound would you try next? __ Next sound? __

3. (Continue Step 2 for letters in Lines 2 and 3.)

ACTIVITY B: **Vowel Conversions Review** (See the *Student Book*, page 59.)

a	e	u	o	i

> **Activity Procedure:** Have students review saying the sound, then the name for each letter.

1. Activity B. When you are reading words and see these letters, what should you try first, the name or the sound? __ If it doesn't make a real word, what should you try? __

2. Point to the first letter. What sound? __ What name? __

3. Next letter. What sound? __ What name? __

4. Next letter. What sound? __ What name? __

5. Next letter. What sound? __ What name? __

6. Next letter. What sound? __ What name? __

ACTIVITY C: **Prefixes and Suffixes Review** (See the *Student Book*, page 59.)

Prefixes				
1.	dis	ad	im	pre	ex
2.	de	re	ab	com	a

Suffixes				
3.	less	ic	ing	ate	ish
4.	est	ary	ism	ful	or
5.	age	sion	ence	ent	ize

> **Activity Procedure:** Have students review saying prefixes and suffixes aloud.

1. Find Activity C.

2. Point to the first prefix in Line 1. What prefix? __ Next? __ Next? __ Next? __ Next? __

3. (Repeat Step 2 for prefixes in Line 2.)

4. Point to the first suffix in Line 3. What suffix? __ Next? __ Next? __ Next? __ Next? __

5. (Repeat Step 4 for suffixes in Lines 4 and 5.)

ACTIVITY D: **Strategy Instruction** (See the *Student Book,* page 60.)

1.	temporary	perfection
2.	complaining	beginner
3.	suddenness	reduction
4.	pollution	productive
5.	observant	propeller
6.	extinction	mismanage

Activity Procedure: First, use two words to show students how to use the strategy for figuring out longer words. Then, work with students to apply the strategy to the remaining words. For each word, ask students if the word has any prefixes or suffixes, then circle them. Underline the vowels and have students say the sounds. Finally, have students say the word, first part by part, and then as a whole word.

 Use Overhead 18: Activity D

1. Find Activity D.

2. Today we are going to practice the *REWARDS* strategy for figuring out longer words.

3. Look up here. Watch me use the strategy. (Point to the word **temporary**.)

4. First, I circle prefixes and suffixes. (Work backward and circle **ary** and **or**. Point to each suffix and ask...) What suffix? __   What suffix? __

5. Next, I underline the vowels in the rest of the word. (Underline **e** in **temp**. Point to the vowel and ask...) What sound? __

6. Next, I say the parts in the word. (Loop under each part and say the parts.)
   temp or ary

7. Next, we say the whole word. It must be a real word. What word? __

8. (Repeat Steps 4–7 with **perfection**.)

9. Let's read some more words.

10. (Point to the first word in Line 2.) Does the word have a prefix? __ (If the answer is yes, circle the prefix and ask...) What prefix? __

11. Does the word have a suffix? __ (If the answer is yes, circle the suffix and ask...) What suffix? __

12. (Underline the vowels in the rest of the word and ask...) What sound? __

13. Say the word by parts. (Loop under each part and ask...) What part? __ What part? __ What part? __

14. (Run your finger under the whole word.) What word? __

15. (Repeat Steps 10–14 with each remaining word in Activity D.)

Note:
   • You may wish to provide additional practice by having students read a line to the group or to a partner.

ACTIVITY E: **Strategy Practice** (See the *Student Book*, page 60.)

1.	convertible	ignorance
2.	refreshments	amazingly
3.	unpredictable	promotion

Activity Procedure: Have students circle prefixes and suffixes and underline the vowels. Assist students in checking their work, then reading each word, first part by part, and then as a whole word.

 Use Overhead 18: Activity E

1. Find Activity E.

2. Now it's your turn. For each word, circle prefixes and suffixes and underline the vowels in the rest of the word. Look up when you are done. __

3. (Show the overhead transparency.) Now check and fix any mistakes. __

4. (When students are done checking, assist them in reading each word on the overhead transparency, beginning with the first word in Line 1.) Look up here. __

   (Loop under each word part in **con vert ible**.) What part? __ What part? __ What part? __

   (Run your finger under the whole word.) What word? __

5. (Repeat Step 4 with all words in Activity E.)

Note:
   • You may wish to provide additional practice by having students read a line to the group or to a partner.

ACTIVITY F: **Word Families** (See the *Student Book,* page 61.)

A	B
predict—to tell about something before it happens	produce—to make something
predicts	production
predicted	productive
predicting	productivity
predictor	productiveness
prediction	reproduce
unpredictable	reproduction

Activity Procedure: Tell students the meaning of the first word in Column A. Have students read words in the first column to themselves, and then twice with the teacher. Then, have students read Column A to their partners. Repeat these procedures for the words in Column B, with opposite partners reading.

 Use Overhead 19: Activity F

1.   Find Activity F.

2.   Find Column A. These words belong to the same word family. The first word is <u>predict</u>. Predict means "to tell about something before it happens." Prefixes and suffixes were added to make new words that have similar meanings to the word <u>predict</u>. Say each word in Column A to yourself until I say "Stop." __

3.   Now let's read the words together. Touch under the first word and read each word with me. (Read the list of words with students.)

4.   Let's read those words together again. Touch under the first word and read with me. (Read the list of words with students.)

5.   Touch under the first word in Column A again. Partner 2, read the list to your partner. Look up when you are done. __ (Monitor partner reading.)

6.   Find the Column B word family. The first word is <u>produce</u>. Produce means "to make something." The words in Column B have similar meanings to the word <u>produce</u>. Say each word in Column B to yourself until I say "Stop." __

7.   (Repeat Steps 3–5 with words in Column B. In Step 5, have Partner 1 read.)

ACTIVITY G: **Spelling Dictation** (See the *Student Book,* page 61.)

1.	beginner	2.	perfection
3.	complaining	4.	convertible

Activity Procedure: For each word, tell students the word, then have students say the parts of the word with you. Have them say the parts to themselves as they write the word. Then, have students compare their words with your word and cross out and rewrite any misspelled words.

Note:
- Distribute a piece of light cardboard to each of the students.

1. Find Activity G.

2. The first word is **beginner**. What word? ___ Fist in the air. Say the parts of **beginner** with me. First part? ___ Next part? ___ Next part? ___ Say the parts in **beginner** to yourself as you write the word. (Pause and monitor.)

3. (Write **beginner** on the board or overhead transparency.) Check **beginner**. If you misspelled it, cross it out and write it correctly.

4. The second word is **perfection**. What word? ___ Fist in the air. Say the parts of **perfection** with me. First part? ___ Next part? ___ Next part? ___ Say the parts in **perfection** to yourself as you write the word. (Pause and monitor.)

5. (Write **perfection** on the board or overhead transparency.) Check **perfection**. If you misspelled it, cross it out and write it correctly.

6. (Repeat the procedures for the words **complaining** and **convertible**.)

ACTIVITY H: **Vocabulary** (See the *Student Book*, page 62.)

a.	a person who is beginning something new (Activity D)	_beginner_
b.	the state of being perfect (Activity D)	_perfection_
c.	not able to be predicted (Activity E)	_unpredictable_

Special Vocabulary

1.   productive—Someone who is <u>productive</u> is very successful at making or growing something.

2.   promotion—When a person has a job and gets an even better job in the same company, that person gets a <u>promotion</u>.

1.   Find Activity H.

2.   Listen to the first definition, "a person who is beginning something new." Look back at the words in Activity D. Find the word and write it. (Pause and monitor.) What word means "a person who is beginning something new"? (*beginner*)

3.   Listen to the next definition, "the state of being perfect." Look back at the words in Activity D. Find the word and write it. (Pause and monitor.) What word means "the state of being perfect"? (*perfection*)

4.   Next definition. "Not able to be predicted." Look back at the words in Activity E. Find the word and write it. (Pause and monitor.) What word means "not able to be predicted"? (*unpredictable*)

5.   Find the *Special Vocabulary*. Find Line 1. (Pause.) Read the word to yourself. (Pause.) What word? (*productive*)

6.   Read the explanation with me. "Someone who is <u>productive</u> is very successful at making or growing something."

7.   If factory workers were very efficient at making paper, you would say that the factory workers were _____. (*productive*)

8.   If the cooks in a restaurant were able to make excellent food very quickly, you would say that the cooks were _____. (*productive*)

9.   Farm workers grew corn and were very productive. Ones, tell your partner what you would know about the farm workers. __

10. During the writing period, Thomas was very productive. Twos, tell your partner what you would know about Thomas. __

11. Find Line 2. (Pause.) Read the word to yourself. (Pause.) What word? (*promotion*)

12. Read the explanation with me. "When a person has a job and gets an even better job in the same company, the person gets a <u>promotion</u>."

13. Mr. Marino went from a line worker in the factory to a floor supervisor. He got a _____. (*promotion*)

14. Miss Jensen went from being a waitress in the restaurant to being the manager. She got a _____. (*promotion*)

15. Partner 2, tell your partner some reasons that a person might get a promotion. __

ACTIVITY I: **Sentence Reading** (See the *Student Book*, page 63.)

1.	He polished the convertible to perfection until it was sleek and shiny.
2.	The propeller on the boat stopped with great suddenness.
3.	The beginner was discouraged and began complaining about her friend's promotion.
4.	The storms were unpredictable, so getting soaked was unpreventable.
5.	Their ignorance of the effects of pollution on health was due to their complete lack of information.
6.	His prediction regarding the reduction in pay discouraged the workers.
7.	The observant walker moved down the slippery stairs with great caution.
8.	Amazingly, the refreshments were prepared on time.
9.	The furnishings were so exact that the room had a look of great distinction.
10.	The suddenness with which he received the promotion surprised numerous other workers.

Activity Procedure: Have students read a sentence to themselves. Then, choose from several options of having students read the sentence together, to partners, or individually to the class.

1. Find Sentence 1 in Activity I. These sentences include words that we practiced today. Read the first sentence to yourself. When you can read all of the words in the sentence, put your thumb up. __

2. (When students can read the sentence, use one of the following options:

    a. Ask the students to read the sentence together, i.e., choral reading.

    b. Have students read the sentence to their partners. Then, call on one student to read the sentence to the group.

    c. Ask one student to read the sentence to the group.)

3. (Repeat these procedures with the remaining sentences. Be sure that you give ample thinking time for each sentence.)

Materials Needed

- Lesson 18 from the *Student Book*
- Overhead Transparencies 20 and 21
- Washable overhead transparency pen
- Paper or cardboard to use when covering the overhead transparencies
- Paper or cardboard for each student to use during spelling dictation

ACTIVITY A: **Vowel Combinations Review** (See the *Student Book*, page 64.)

1.	ea	a - e	e - e	au	ee
2.	oi	o - e	oo	oa	ow
3.	er	ir	ar	ai	ou

Activity Procedure: Have students review saying the sounds for letter combinations. When the letter combination has a box around it, ask students to tell you both sounds.

Note:
- Whenever you come to letters in a box, ask "What sound would you try first? What sound would you try next?"

1. Find Activity A. Let's review vowel combinations.

2. Point to the boxed letters in Line 1. What sound would you try first? __ What sound would you try next? __ Next sound? __ Next sound? __ Next sound? __ Next sound? __

3. (Continue Step 2 for letters in Lines 2 and 3.)

ACTIVITY B: **Vowel Conversions Review** (See the *Student Book*, page 64.)

e	i	a	o	u

Activity Procedure: Have students review saying the sound, then the name for each letter.

1. Find Activity B. When you are reading words and see these letters, what should you try first, the sound or the name? __ If it doesn't make a real word, what should you try? __

2. Point to the first letter. What sound? __ What name? __

3. Next letter. What sound? __ What name? __

4. Next letter. What sound? __ What name? __

5. Next letter. What sound? __ What name? __

6. Next letter. What sound? __ What name? __

ACTIVITY C: **Prefixes and Suffixes Review** (See the *Student Book*, page 64.)

Prefixes				
1. ab	in	con	pro	en
2. re	com	ad	per	ex

Suffixes				
3. ism	ary	ize	able	ous
4. ance	ent	ture	le	age
5. tive	er	ence	sive	ment

Activity Procedure: Have students review saying prefixes and suffixes aloud.

1. Find Activity C.

2. Point to the first prefix in Line 1. What prefix? __ Next? __ Next? __ Next? __ Next? __

3. (Repeat Step 2 for prefixes in Line 2.)

4. Point to the first suffix in Line 3. What suffix? __ Next? __ Next? __ Next? __ Next? __

5. (Repeat Step 4 for suffixes in Lines 4 and 5.)

ACTIVITY D: **Strategy Instruction** (See the *Student Book*, page 65.)

1.	exceptionally	independence
2.	uncomfortable	surrender
3.	invention	expectation
4.	disposable	development

Activity Procedure: First, use two words to show students how to use the strategy for figuring out longer words. Then, work with students to apply the strategy to the remaining words. For each word, ask students if the word has any prefixes or suffixes, then circle them. Underline the vowels and have students say the sounds. Finally, have students say the word, first part by part, and then as a whole word.

 Use Overhead 20: Activity D

1. Find Activity D.

2. Today we are going to practice the *REWARDS* strategy for figuring out longer words.

3. Look up here. Watch me use the strategy. (Point to the word **exceptionally**.)

4. First, I circle prefixes and suffixes. (First circle **ex**. Then, work backward and circle **ly** and **al** and **tion**. Point to each affix and ask...) What prefix? __ What suffix? __ What suffix? __ What suffix? __

5. Next, I underline the vowels in the rest of the word. (Underline **e** in **cep**. Point to the vowel and ask...) What sound? __

6. Next, I say the parts in the word. (Loop under each part and say the parts.)
ex cep tion al ly

7. Next, we say the whole word. It must be a real word. What word? __

8. (Repeat Steps 4–7 with **independence**.)

9. Let's read some more words.

10. (Point to the first word in Line 2.) Does the word have a prefix? __ (If the answer is yes, circle the prefix and ask...) What prefix? __

11. Does the word have a suffix? __ (If the answer is yes, circle the suffix and ask...) What suffix? __

12. (Underline the vowels in the rest of the word and ask...) What sound? __

13. Say the word by parts. (Loop under each part and ask...) What part? __ What part? __ What part? __ What part? __

14. (Run your finger under the whole word.) What word? __

15. (Repeat Steps 10–14 with each remaining word in Activity D.)

Note:
- You may wish to provide additional practice by having students read a line to the group or to a partner.

ACTIVITY E: **Strategy Practice** (See the *Student Book,* page 65.)

1.	permanently	amusement
2.	utterance	suddenly
3.	impersonal	existence
4.	importantly	indifferent
5.	deformity	containers

Activity Procedure: Have students circle prefixes and suffixes and underline the vowels. Assist students in checking their work, then reading each word, first part by part, and then as a whole word.

 Use Overhead 20: Activity E

1. Find Activity E.

2. Now it's your turn. For each word, circle prefixes and suffixes and underline the vowels in the rest of the word. Look up when you are done. __

3. (Show the overhead transparency.) Now check and fix any mistakes. __

4. (When students are done checking, assist them in reading each word on the overhead transparency, beginning with the first word in Line 1.) Look up here. __

   (Loop under each word part in **per man ent ly**.) What part? __ What part? __ What part? __ What part? __

   (Run your finger under the whole word.) What word? __

5. (Repeat Step 4 with all words in Activity E.)

Note:
- You may wish to provide additional practice by having students read a line to the group or to a partner.

ACTIVITY F: **Word Families** (See the *Student Book,* page 66.)

A	B
invent—to make something that has never been made before	develop—to take something that has been invented and make it better
invents	developed
inventor	developer
invention	developing
inventive	development
reinvent	developmental
reinvention	developmentally

Activity Procedure: Tell students the meaning of the first word in Column A. Have students read words in the first column to themselves, and then twice with the teacher. Then, have students read Column A to their partners. Repeat these procedures for the words in Column B, with opposite partners reading.

 Use Overhead 21: Activity F

1. Find Activity F.

2. Find the Column A word family. The first word is <u>invent</u>. Invent means "to make something that has never been made before." The words in Column A have similar meanings to the word <u>invent</u>. Say each word in Column A to yourself until I say "Stop." __

3. Now let's read the words together. Touch under the first word and read each word with me. (Read the list of words with students.)

4. Let's read those words together again. Touch under the first word and read with me. (Read the list of words with students.)

5. Touch under the first word in Column A again. Partner 1, read the list to your partner. Look up when you are done. __ (Monitor partner reading.)

6. Find the Column B word family. The first word is <u>develop</u>. Develop means "to take something that has been invented and make it better." The words in Column B have similar meanings to the word <u>develop</u>. Say each word in Column B to yourself until I say "Stop." __

7. (Repeat Steps 3–5 with words in Column B. In Step 5, have Partner 2 read.)

ACTIVITY G: **Spelling Dictation** (See the *Student Book,* page 66.)

1. independence	2. expectation
3. impersonal	4. importantly

Activity Procedure: For each word, tell students the word, then have students say the parts of the word with you. Have them say the parts to themselves as they write the word. Then, have students compare their words with your word and cross out and rewrite any misspelled words.

Note:
- Distribute a piece of light cardboard to each of the students.

1. Find Activity G.

2. The first word is **independence**. What word? __ Fist in the air. Say the parts of **independence** with me. First part? __ Next part? __ Next part? __ Next part? __ Say the parts in **independence** to yourself as you write the word. (Pause and monitor.)

3. (Write **independence** on the board or overhead transparency.) Check **independence**. If you misspelled it, cross it out and write it correctly.

4. The second word is **expectation**. What word? __ Fist in the air. Say the parts of **expectation** with me. First part? __ Next part? __ Next part? __ Next part? __ Say the parts in **expectation** to yourself as you write the word. (Pause and monitor.)

5. (Write **expectation** on the board or overhead transparency.) Check **expectation**. If you misspelled it, cross it out and write it correctly.

6. (Repeat the procedures for the words **impersonal** and **importantly**.)

ACTIVITY H: **Vocabulary** (See the *Student Book*, page 66.)

a.	the act of developing or making something (Activity D)	development
b.	not personal (Activity E)	impersonal
c.	the condition of being deformed (Activity E)	deformity

Special Vocabulary

1. expectation—When you think that something might happen, you have an <u>expectation</u>.

2. utterance—When you say something, the spoken words are called an <u>utterance</u>.

1. Find Activity H.

2. Listen to the first definition, "the act of developing or making something." Look back at the words in Activity D. Find the word and write it. (Pause and monitor.) What word means "the act of developing or making something"? (*development*)

3. Listen to the next definition, "not personal." Look back at the words in Activity E. Find the word and write it. (Pause and monitor.) What word means "not personal"? (*impersonal*)

4. Next definition. "The condition of being deformed." Look back at the words in Activity E. Find the word and write it. (Pause and monitor.) What word means "the condition of being deformed"? (*deformity*)

5. Find the *Special Vocabulary*. Find Line 1. (Pause.) Read the word to yourself. (Pause.) What word? (*expectation*)

6. Read the explanation with me. "When you think that something might happen, you have an expectation."

7. Marcus is absolutely certain that his parents will give him a bike for his birthday. Getting a bike for his birthday is Marcus's _____. (*expectation*)

8. On Thanksgiving Day, Anita's family and friends think they will eat turkey. Eating turkey on Thanksgiving Day is an _____. (*expectation*)

9. Partner 1, tell your partner some expectations that you have before you come into class each day. __

10. Partner 2, tell your partner some expectations that you have when you get home from school. __

11. Find Line 2. (Pause.) Read the word to yourself. (Pause.) What word? (*utterance*)

12. Read the explanation with me. "When you say something, the spoken words are called an <u>utterance</u>."

13. If you said, "This is a wonderful day," those words would be an _____. (*utterance*)

14. If the teacher said, "Get out your book," that would be an _____. (*utterance*)

15. Partner 2, tell your partner a short utterance. __

16. Partner 1, tell your partner a short utterance. __

ACTIVITY I: **Sentence Reading** (See the *Student Book*, page 67.)

---

1.   Reproduction allows the ongoing existence of plants and animals.

2.   Mario was so famished, he suddenly grabbed the disposable containers full of leftovers.

3.   The army was unwilling to surrender and, more importantly, to lose its country's independence.

4.   After the development of her invention, Mrs. Lopez got a promotion.

5.   The woman's utterances were so indifferent and impersonal that further discussion was impossible.

6.   Even though he was a beginner at basketball, Jason was persistent and had an expectation of perfection.

7.   Scientists have no explanation for why so many frogs and toads have a deformity.

8.   The development of the invention will reduce pollution in the community.

9.   The children seemed as if they wanted to stay at the amusement park permanently, but it was time to go home.

10.   Because of the newspaper's description of Kate, Mrs. Wood made a prediction that she would be exceptionally independent.

Activity Procedure: Have students read a sentence to themselves. Then, choose from several options of having students read the sentence together, to partners, or individually to the class.

1. Find Sentence 1 in Activity I. These sentences include words that we practiced today. Read the first sentence to yourself. When you can read all of the words in the sentence, put your thumb up. __

2. (When students can read the sentence, use one of the following options:
   a. Ask the students to read the sentence together, i.e., choral reading.
   b. Have students read the sentence to their partners. Then, call on one student to read the sentence to the group.
   c. Ask one student to read the sentence to the group.)

3. (Repeat these procedures with the remaining sentences. Be sure that you give ample thinking time for each sentence.)

Materials Needed

- Lesson 19 from the *Student Book*
- Overhead Transparencies 22 and 23
- Washable overhead transparency pen
- Paper or cardboard to use when covering the overhead transparencies
- Paper or cardboard for each student to use during spelling dictation

ACTIVITY A: **Vowel Combinations Review** (See the *Student Book*, page 68.)

1.	u - e	oy	or	oo	ee
2.	au	ar	e - e	er	i - e
3.	ow	oi	ea	ur	ay

> **Activity Procedure:** Have students review saying the sounds for letter combinations. When the letter combination has a box around it, ask students to tell you both sounds.

Note:

- Whenever you come to letters in a box, ask "What sound would you try first? What sound would you try next?"

1.   Find Activity A. Let's review vowel combinations.

2.   Point to the first letters in Line 1. What sound? __ Next sound? __ Next sound? __ Boxed letters. What sound would you try first? __ What sound would you try next? __ Next sound? __

3.   (Continue Step 2 for letters in Lines 2 and 3.)

ACTIVITY B: **Vowel Conversions Review** (See the *Student Book,* page 68.)

i	a	o	u	e

> **Activity Procedure:** Have students review saying the sound, then the name for each letter.

1. Find Activity B. When you are reading words and see these letters, what should you try first, the sound or the name? __ If it doesn't make a real word, what should you try? __

2. Point to the first letter. What sound? __ What name? __

3. Next letter. What sound? __ What name? __

4. Next letter. What sound? __ What name? __

5. Next letter. What sound? __ What name? __

6. Next letter. What sound? __ What name? __

ACTIVITY C: **Prefixes and Suffixes Review** (See the *Student Book,* page 68.)

Prefixes				
1.	im	mis	un	pre	be
2.	dis	de	con	a	en

Suffixes				
3.	ist	ate	ic	al	sion
4.	y	ity	ant	tive	ible
5.	er	tion	ly	ness	est

> **Activity Procedure:** Have students review saying prefixes and suffixes aloud.

1. Find Activity C.

2. Point to the first prefix in Line 1. What prefix? __ Next? __ Next? __ Next? __ Next? __

3. (Repeat Step 2 for prefixes in Line 2.)

4. Point to the first suffix in Line 3. What suffix? __ Next? __ Next? __ Next? __ Next? __

5. (Repeat Step 4 for suffixes in Lines 4 and 5.)

ACTIVITY D: **Strategy Instruction** (See the *Student Book*, page 69.)

1.	intolerable	combination
2.	amendment	instructional
3.	organization	understandable
4.	political	oxidize

> **Activity Procedure:** First, use two words to show students how to use the strategy for figuring out longer words. Then, work with students to apply the strategy to the remaining words. For each word, ask students if the word has any prefixes or suffixes, then circle them. Underline the vowels and have students say the sounds. Finally, have students say the word, first part by part, and then as a whole word.

 Use Overhead 22: Activity D

1. Find Activity D.

2. Today we are going to practice the *REWARDS* strategy for figuring out longer words.

3. Look up here. Watch me use the strategy. (Point to the word **intolerable**.)

4. First, I circle prefixes and suffixes. (First circle **in**. Then, work backward and circle **able** and **er**. Point to each affix and ask...) What prefix? __   What suffix? __   What suffix? __

5. Next, I underline the vowels in the rest of the word. (Underline **o** in **tol**. Point to the vowel and ask...) What sound? __

6. Next, I say the parts in the word. (Loop under each part and say the parts.) **in tol er able**

7. Next, we say the whole word. It must be a real word. What word? __

8. (Repeat Steps 4–7 with **combination**.)

9. Let's read some more words.

10. (Point to the first word in Line 2.) Does the word have a prefix? __   (If the answer is yes, circle the prefix and ask...) What prefix? __

11. Does the word have a suffix? __   (If the answer is yes, circle the suffix and ask...) What suffix? __

12. (Underline the vowels in the rest of the word and ask...) What sound? __

13. Say the word by parts. (Loop under each part and ask...) What part? __   What part? __   What part? __

14. (Run your finger under the whole word.) What word? __

15. (Repeat Steps 10–14 with each remaining word in Activity D.)

Note:
- You may wish to provide additional practice by having students read a line to the group or to a partner.

ACTIVITY E: **Strategy Practice** (See the *Student Book*, page 69.)

1.	reinvestigate	confident
2.	unsuspecting	government
3.	contribution	example
4.	medically	honesty
5.	executive	unspeakable

Activity Procedure: Have students circle prefixes and suffixes and underline the vowels. Assist students in checking their work, then reading each word, first part by part, and then as a whole word.

 Use Overhead 22: Activity E

1. Find Activity E.

2. Now it's your turn. For each word, circle prefixes and suffixes and underline the vowels in the rest of the word. Look up when you are done. __

3. (Show the overhead transparency.) Now check and fix any mistakes. __

4. (When students are done checking, assist them in reading each word on the overhead transparency, beginning with the first word in Line 1.) Look up here. __

   (Loop under each word part in **re in ves tig ate**.) What part? __ What part? __ What part? __ What part? __ What part? __

   (Run your finger under the whole word.) What word? __

5. (Repeat Step 4 with all words in Activity E.)

Note:
- You may wish to provide additional practice by having students read a line to the group or to a partner.

ACTIVITY F: **Word Families** (See the *Student Book,* page 70.)

A	B
instruct—to teach	contribute—to give money to a charity
instructed	contributes
instructing	contributed
instructor	contributing
instruction	contributor
instructional	contributory
instructive	contribution

Activity Procedure: Tell students the meaning of the first word in Column A. Have students read words in the first column to themselves, and then twice with the teacher. Then, have students read Column A to their partners. Repeat these procedures for the words in Column B, with opposite partners reading.

 Use Overhead 23: Activity F

1. Find Activity F.

2. Find the Column A word family. The first word is <u>instruct</u>. Instruct means "to teach." The words in Column A have similar meanings to the word <u>instruct</u>. Say each word in Column A to yourself until I say "Stop." __

3. Now let's read the words together. Touch under the first word and read each word with me. (Read the list of words with students.)

4. Let's read those words together again. Touch under the first word and read with me. (Read the list of words with students.)

5. Touch under the first word in Column A again. Partner 2, read the list to your partner. Look up when you are done. __ (Monitor partner reading.)

6. Find the Column B word family. The first word is <u>contribute</u>. Contribute can mean "to give money to a charity." The words in Column B have similar meanings to the word <u>contribute</u>. Say each word in Column B to yourself until I say "Stop." __

7. (Repeat Steps 3–5 with words in Column B. In Step 5, have Partner 1 read.)

ACTIVITY G: **Spelling Dictation** (See the *Student Book,* page 70.)

1.	instructional	2.	example
3.	understandable	4.	combination

Activity Procedure: For each word, tell students the word, then have students say the parts of the word with you. Have them say the parts to themselves as they write the word. Then, have students compare their words with your word and cross out and rewrite any misspelled words.

Note:
- Distribute a piece of light cardboard to each of the students.

1.   Find Activity G.

2.   The first word is **instructional**. What word? __ Fist in the air. Say the parts of **instructional** with me. First part? __ Next part? __ Next part? __ Next part? __ Say the parts in **instructional** to yourself as you write the word. (Pause and monitor.)

3.   (Write **instructional** on the board or overhead transparency.) Check **instructional**. If you misspelled it, cross it out and write it correctly.

4.   The second word is **example**. What word? __ Fist in the air. Say the parts of **example** with me. First part? __ Next part? __ Next part? __ Say the parts in **example** to yourself as you write the word. (Pause and monitor.)

5.   (Write **example** on the board or overhead transparency.) Check **example**. If you misspelled it, cross it out and write it correctly.

6.   (Repeat the procedures for the words **understandable** and **combination**.)

ACTIVITY H: **Vocabulary** (See the *Student Book,* page 70.)

a.	not able to be tolerated (Activity D)	_intolerable_
b.	able to be understood (Activity D)	_understandable_
c.	the money given to a charity (Activity E)	_contribution_

Special Vocabulary

1. amendment—When something is added to a document such as a constitution or a legal contract, the thing that is added is called an <u>amendment</u>.

2. combination—When you put or mix several things together, the result is a <u>combination</u>.

1. Find Activity H.

2. Listen to the first definition, "not able to be tolerated." Look back at the words in Activity D. Find the word and write it. (*Pause and monitor.*) What word means "not able to be tolerated"? (*intolerable*)

3. Listen to the next definition, "able to be understood." Look back at the words in Activity D. Find the word and write it. (*Pause and monitor.*) What word means "able to be understood"? (*understandable*)

4. Next definition. "The money given to a charity." Look back at the words in Activity E. Find the word and write it. (*Pause and monitor.*) What word means "the money given to a charity"? (*contribution*)

5. Find the *Special Vocabulary.* Find Line 1. (*Pause.*) Read the word to yourself. (*Pause.*) What word? (*amendment*)

6. Read the explanation with me. "When something is added to a document such as a constitution or a legal contract, the thing that is added is called an <u>amendment</u>."

7. When people add a new part to their constitution, it is called an _____. (*amendment*)

8. When a person adds a new part to his or her will, it is called an _____. (*amendment*)

9. Tell me if this example is an amendment. You wrote a letter to your friend. Is the letter an amendment? __ (*No*) If you later added something to the letter, could that be called an amendment? __ (*Yes*)

10. Find Line 2. (*Pause.*) Read the word to yourself. (*Pause.*) What word? (*combination*)

11. Read the explanation with me. "When you put or mix several things together, the result is a <u>combination</u>."

12. If you put fourth and fifth graders together into one room, you would have a class that was a _____. (*combination*)

13. If you put nails and bolts into the same drawer, you would have a _____. (*combination*)

14. Tell me if this is a combination. If you had boys and girls on the soccer team, would you have a combination of children on the team? __ (*Yes*) If you had boys and girls

from two different schools going to the same after-school program, would you have a combination of children? __ (*Yes*)

15. Tell me if this is a combination. If you poured milk into a glass, would you have a combination? __ (*No*) If you poured coffee, chocolate syrup, and milk into a glass and stirred, would you have a combination? __ (*Yes*)

ACTIVITY I: **Sentence Reading** (See the *Student Book*, page 71.)

1.	The enormity of the problem was both unpredictable and intolerable.
2.	The complicated math example was challenging and very instructive.
3.	Last week, the government passed a radical amendment to the historical law.
4.	If you see your doctor regularly, many problems are medically preventable.
5.	The consultant made numerous redundant suggestions to the executives.
6.	By listening carefully to their utterances, you can often determine someone's honesty.
7.	Because of his excellence, the employee had the distinction of getting the only promotion last year.
8.	The government is going to reinvestigate the unsuspecting political organization.
9.	By constantly complaining, Janet had an expectation of getting what she wanted.
10.	The combination of excellence and honesty made the president of the organization an exceptional example.

Activity Procedure: Have students read a sentence to themselves. Then, choose from several options of having students read the sentence together, to partners, or individually to the class.

1. Find Sentence 1 in Activity I. These sentences include words that we practiced today. Read the first sentence to yourself. When you can read all of the words in the sentence, put your thumb up. __

2. (When students can read the sentence, use one of the following options:

   a. Ask the students to read the sentence together, i.e., choral reading.

   b. Have students read the sentence to their partners. Then, call on one student to read the sentence to the group.

   c. Ask one student to read the sentence to the group.)

3. (Repeat these procedures with the remaining sentences. Be sure that you give ample thinking time.)

Materials Needed

- Lesson 20 from the *Student Book*
- Overhead Transparencies 24, 25, and 26
- Washable overhead transparency pen
- Paper or cardboard to use when covering the overhead transparencies
- Paper or cardboard for each student to use during spelling dictation

ACTIVITY A: **Vowel Combinations Review** (See the *Student Book*, page 72.)

1.	ir	o - e	ay	oo	a - e
2.	ow	ea	oi	ou	oa

Activity Procedure: Have students review saying the sounds for letter combinations. When the letter combination has a box around it, ask students to tell you both sounds.

Note:

- Whenever you come to letters in a box, ask "What sound would you try first? What sound would you try next?"

1. Find Activity A. Let's review vowel combinations.

2. Point to the first letters in Line 1. What sound? __ Next sound? __ Next sound? __ Boxed letters. What sound would you try first? __ What sound would you try next? __ Next sound? __

3. (Continue Step 2 for letters in Line 2.)

ACTIVITY B: **Vowel Conversions Review** (See the *Student Book,* page 72.)

u	e	a	i	o

> **Activity Procedure:** Have students review saying the sound, then the name for each letter.

1.   Find Activity B. When you are reading words and see these letters, what would you try first, the name or the sound? __

2.   Point to the first letter. What sound? __ What name? __

3.   Next letter. What sound? __ What name? __

4.   Next letter. What sound? __ What name? __

5.   Next letter. What sound? __ What name? __

6.   Next letter. What sound? __ What name? __

ACTIVITY C: **Prefixes and Suffixes Review** (See the *Student Book,* page 72.)

			Prefixes		
1.	ad	in	com	re	pro
2.	per	a	ab	con	im

			Suffixes		
3.	less	ish	sive	ary	ent
4.	ance	ous	ture	able	ize
5.	or	ful	ant	age	ment

> **Activity Procedure:** Have students review saying prefixes and suffixes aloud.

1.   Find Activity C.

2.   Point to the first prefix in Line 1. What prefix? __ Next? __ Next? __ Next? __ Next? __

3.   (Repeat Step 2 for prefixes in Line 2.)

4.   Point to the first suffix in Line 3. What suffix? __ Next? __ Next? __ Next? __ Next? __

5.   (Repeat Step 4 for suffixes in Lines 4 and 5.)

ACTIVITY D: **Strategy Instruction** (See the *Student Book,* page 73.)

1.	persistently	governmental
2.	famously	legendary
3.	attractiveness	economize
4.	disappointment	occurrence

Activity Procedure: Work with students to apply the strategy for figuring out longer words to all words in this activity. For each word, ask students if the word has any prefixes or suffixes, then circle them. Underline the vowels and have students say the sounds. Finally, have students say the word, first part by part, and then as a whole word.

 Use Overhead 24: Activity D

1. Find Activity D.
2. Look up here. Let's use the *REWARDS* strategy to figure out these words.
3. (Point to the first word in Line 1.) Does the word have a prefix? __ (If the answer is yes, circle the prefix and ask...) What prefix? __
4. Does the word have a suffix? __ (If the answer is yes, circle the suffix and ask...) What suffix? __
5. (Underline the vowels in the rest of the word and ask...) What sound? __
6. Say the word by parts. (Loop under each part and ask...) What part? __ What part? __ What part? __ What part? __
7. (Run your finger under the whole word.) What word? __
8. (Repeat Steps 3–7 with each remaining word in Activity D.)

Note:
- You may wish to provide additional practice by having students read a line to the group or to a partner.

ACTIVITY E: **Strategy Practice** (See the *Student Book,* page 73.)

1.	resistance	fascination
2.	unmentionable	intermission
3.	exterminate	undependable
4.	unimportance	contradiction
5.	inexpensive	invitation

Activity Procedure: Have students circle prefixes and suffixes and underline the vowels. Assist students in checking their work, then reading each word, first part by part, and then as a whole word.

 Use Overhead 24: Activity E

1. Find Activity E.

2. Now it's your turn. For each word, circle prefixes and suffixes and underline the vowels in the rest of the word. Look up when you are done. __

3. (Show the overhead transparency.) Now check and fix any mistakes. __

4. (When students are done checking, assist them in reading each word on the overhead transparency, beginning with the first word in Line 1.) Look up here. __

   (Loop under each word part in **re sist ance**.) What part? __ What part? __ What part? __

   (Run your finger under the whole word.) What word? __

5. (Repeat Step 4 with all words in Activity E.)

Note:
- You may wish to provide additional practice by having students read a line to the group or to a partner.

ACTIVITY F: **Word Families** (See the *Student Book*, page 74.)

A	B
resist—to not want to do something	attract—to bring attention to something
resisting	attracts
resister	attracted
resistive	attracting
resistible	attraction
resistibility	attractive
resistance	attractiveness

Activity Procedure: Tell students the meaning of the first word in Column A. Have students read words in the first column to themselves, and then twice with the teacher. Then, have students read Column A to their partners. Repeat these procedures for the words in Column B, with opposite partners reading.

 Use Overhead 25: Activity F

1. Find Activity F.

2. Find the Column A word family. The first word is <u>resist</u>. Resist means "to not want to do something." The words in Column A have similar meanings to the word <u>resist</u>. Say each word in Column A to yourself until I say "Stop." __

3. Now let's read the words together. Touch under the first word and read each word with me. (Read the list of words with students.)

4. Let's read those words together again. Touch under the first word and read with me. (Read the list of words with students.)

5. Touch under the first word in Column A again. Partner 1, read the list to your partner. Look up when you are done. __ (Monitor partner reading.)

6. Find Column B. These words belong to the same word family. The first word is <u>attract</u>. Attract means "to bring attention to something." The words in Column B have similar meanings to the word <u>attract</u>. Say each word in Column B to yourself until I say "Stop." __

7. (Repeat Steps 3–5 with words in Column B. In Step 5, have Partner 2 read.)

ACTIVITY G: **Spelling Dictation** (See the *Student Book*, page 74.)

1.	intermission	2.	inexpensive
3.	disappointment	4.	undependable

Activity Procedure: For each word, tell students the word, then have students say the parts of the word with you. Have them say the parts to themselves as they write the word. Then, have students compare their words with your word and cross out and rewrite any misspelled words.

Note:
- Distribute a piece of light cardboard to each of the students.

1. Find Activity G.

2. The first word is **intermission**. What word? __ Fist in the air. Say the parts of **intermission** with me. First part? __ Next part? __ Next part? __ Next part? __ Say the parts in **intermission** to yourself as you write the word. (Pause and monitor.)

3. (Write **intermission** on the board or overhead transparency.) Check **intermission**. If you misspelled it, cross it out and write it correctly.

4. The second word is **inexpensive**. What word? __ Fist in the air. Say the parts of **inexpensive** with me. First part? __ Next part? __ Next part? __ Next part? __ Say the parts in **inexpensive** to yourself as you write the word. (Pause and monitor.)

5. (Write **inexpensive** on the board or overhead transparency.) Check **inexpensive**. If you misspelled it, cross it out and write it correctly.

6. (Repeat the procedures for the words **disappointment** and **undependable**.)

ACTIVITY H: **Vocabulary** (See the *Student Book,* page 74.)

a.	relating to the government (Activity D)	_governmental_
b.	something that has occurred (Activity D)	_occurrence_
c.	not able to be mentioned or talked about (Activity E)	_unmentionable_

1. Find Activity H.

2. Listen to the first definition, "relating to the government." Look back at the words in Activity D. Find the word and write it. (Pause and monitor.) What word means "relating to the government"? __ (*governmental*)

3. Listen to the next definition, "something that has occurred." Look back at the words in Activity D. Find the word and write it. (Pause and monitor.) What word means "something that has occurred"? __ (*occurrence*)

4. Next definition. "Not able to be mentioned or talked about." Look back at the words in Activity E. Find the word and write it. (Pause and monitor.) What word means "not able to be mentioned or talked about"? __ (*unmentionable*)

ACTIVITY I: **Passage Preparation** (See the *Student Book*, page 75.)

Part 1—Tell

1.	nutrients	*n.*	what a plant or animal needs to stay alive
2.	nitrogen-poor	*adj.*	not having much nitrogen
*3.	dissolve	*v.*	to change a solid into a liquid
*4.	various	*adj.*	many different kinds
5.	electricity	*n.*	the power that makes appliances run
6.	electrical	*adj.*	having to do with electricity
7.	wriggles	*v.*	twists
8.	miniature	*adj.*	very small

Part 2—Strategy Practice

9.	carnivorous plants	*n.*	meat-eating plants
10.	capture	*v.*	to catch
*11.	digesting	*v.*	breaking down food so a plant or animal can use it
12.	digestive	*adj.*	related to digesting
13.	supplemental	*adj.*	extra
*14.	desperate	*adj.*	having no hope
15.	curious	*adj.*	eager to know or learn
16.	portray	*v.*	to tell about
17.	glistening	*adj.*	shining or sparkling
18.	environments	*n.*	surroundings

Activity Procedure: In this activity, students read words from the upcoming passage that are difficult to pronounce. Because the first set of words is difficult to read using the part-by-part strategy, tell students each word and have them read its definition. Then, have students practice reading the words themselves. The second set of words can be read using the part-by-part strategy. Have students circle prefixes and suffixes, then underline the vowels. Using the overhead transparency, assist students in checking their work. Next, have students read each word aloud, first part by part, and then as a whole word. Have them read the part of speech and definition aloud. Finally, use the scripted wording to introduce the four starred vocabulary words that provide a preview of the passage.

 Use Overhead 26: Activity I

Part 1—Tell

1. Beginning today, you will be applying your word reading strategy to interesting passages that contain many longer words. The longer words often hold the key to understanding the passage.

2. (Show the top half of Overhead 26.) Before we read the first passage, let's read the difficult words. (Point to **nutrients**.) The first word is **nutrients**. What word? __ Now read the definition with me. "What a plant or animal needs to stay alive."

3. (Point to **nitrogen-poor**.) The next words are **nitrogen-poor**. What words? __ Read the definition with me. "Not having much nitrogen."

4. (Pronounce each word in Part 1, and then have students repeat each word and read the definition with you.)

5. Find Activity I, Part 1, in your book. __ Let's read the words again. First word. __ Next word. __ (Continue for all words in Part 1.)

Part 2—Strategy Practice

1. Find Part 2. For each word, circle the prefixes and suffixes and underline the vowels. Look up when you are done. __

2. (Show the bottom half of Overhead 26.) Now check and fix any mistakes. __

3. (When students are done checking, assist them in reading each word on the overhead transparency, beginning with the first words in Part 2.) Look up here. __

   (Loop under each word part in **carnivorous plants**.) What part? __ What part? __ What part? __ What part? __ What part? __

   (Run your finger under each word.) What word? __ What word? __ Now, read the definition for "carnivorous plants." __

4. (Repeat Step 3 with all remaining words in Part 2.)

Note:
- You may wish to provide additional practice by having students read words to a partner.

Part 3—Starred Vocabulary

1. Let's study some of the words in Activity I. Find word #11. __ What word? (*digesting*) When a plant or animal breaks down food to use, it is digesting the food. After a meal, your body digests food. In this passage, we are going to learn that some plants catch insects and digest them.

2. Find #3. __ What word? (*dissolve*) If a solid changes into a liquid, the solid would _____. (*dissolve*) If you put sugar into hot water, the sugar would _____. (*dissolve*) If you dumped a package of Jell-O™ into boiling water, the Jell-O would _____. (*dissolve*) In this passage, we learn that the digestive juices of some plants actually will dissolve insects so that the plant can use the nutrients.

3. Find #4. __ What word? (*various*) If we have many different kinds, we have various kinds. In this passage, there are many different kinds of carnivorous plants. Thus, there are various kinds of carnivorous plants.

4. Find #14. __ What word? (*desperate*) If someone has no hope at all, they feel _____. (*desperate*) If an insect was caught by a carnivorous plant and couldn't escape, the insect would be _____. (*desperate*) If a fly was trapped by a Venus flytrap, the fly would be _____. (*desperate*)

ACTIVITY J: **Passage Reading and Comprehension** (See the *Student Book,* pages 76 and 77.)

	Meat-Eating Plants
	All plants need nutrients to stay alive, grow, and
9	reproduce. (#1) Most plants get these nutrients from the soil
18	and from the air. (#2) Some soil, however, is so nitrogen-
28	poor that plants cannot get enough nutrients. Plants that
37	live in nitrogen-poor areas sometimes get supplemental
45	nutrients from eating insects and small animals instead. We
54	call these plants **carnivorous**, or meat-eating, **plants**. (#3)
62	Carnivorous plants use various ways to attract and
70	capture the insects for food. Certain smells, bright colors
79	or patterns, or leaves covered with sparkling droplets draw
88	the insects toward them. (#4)
92	The sundew plant is a fascinating example of a
101	carnivorous plant. Tiny hairs cover the leaves of a sundew
111	plant. The hairs produce a sticky substance that clings
120	to the tips of the hairs. The sticky drops on the ends of
133	the hairs sparkle like dew in the sunlight. The glistening
143	droplets usually attract insects, such as flies. In some
152	environments, however, a sundew plant is large enough to
161	attract small animals, such as frogs. The insects or small
171	creatures approach the plant, hoping for water or food. (#5)
180	A curious fly gets too close to a sundew plant and
191	sticks to the hairs on the leaves. In a few seconds, the
203	plant traps the unsuspecting fly. When the fly wriggles and
213	tries to get away, its movement signals the sticky leaves to
224	curl tightly around it. As the leaf strangles the desperate
234	fly, the leaf pours digestive juices onto it. The juices
244	dissolve the prey, and the plant absorbs the nutrients it
254	needs. After the plant has finished digesting the fly, the leaf

265	uncurls and fills up with more sticky drops and waits for
276	its next meal. Some sundews are so sticky that people used
287	to hang them in their houses to catch flies. (#6)
296	The Venus flytrap is a legendary example of a
305	carnivorous plant. Its leaves attract insects with a sweet
314	smell, red coloring, and a broad shape that looks like a
325	good resting spot. (#7) Miniature hairs cover each leaf of
334	the plant. The moment the insect touches two or more
344	hairs, it triggers an electrical signal that tells the leaf to
355	slam shut and trap the insect. The two halves of the leaf
367	clamp together like jaws. Guard hairs along the edges of
377	the leaf prevent the insect from escaping its prison. The
387	leaf crushes the insect's body and dissolves it in order to
398	get the nutrients. (#8)
401	Although moviemakers portray carnivorous plants,
406	like the one in *Little Shop of Horrors*, as also eating
417	humans, man-eating plants don't exist in real life.
426	Fortunately for us, carnivorous plants eat only insects and
435	small animals. (#9)
437	

A. ☐ **Total number of words read**

B. ☐ **Total number of underlined words (mistakes)**

C. ☐ **Total number of words read correctly**

Activity Procedure: In this activity, students read a passage containing words they practiced in the previous activity. Reading this passage gives students the opportunity to practice using their strategy for figuring out longer words. In addition, it gives students an opportunity to work on rate development, that is, building fluency while reading difficult passages. Have students work on accuracy by having them read the passage silently to each embedded number, and then rereading the same section orally to a partner, together as a group, or individually. When students finish reading a section orally, ask the corresponding comprehension question. When the passage has been read, have students work on fluency by having them read the passage first to themselves twice, and then to a partner. Have students count the total number of words read and the number of words missed and subtract to find the number of words read correctly. You may also wish to have students graph their daily fluency.

Passage Reading—Accuracy

1. Find Activity J. You are going to read a passage and answer questions about what you've read. Today's passage is about carnivorous plants and how they capture insects so they can get the nutrients they need in order to live. Read the title with me. "Meat-Eating Plants."

2. Find #1 in the passage. (Pause.) Read to #1 silently. Look up when you are done. __

3. (Wait for students to complete the reading. Then have students reread the section by having them read orally to a partner, read together orally as a group, or read aloud individually.)

4. (Ask the question associated with the number. Provide feedback to students regarding their answers.)

5. (Repeat Steps 2, 3, and 4 for all sections of the passage.)

Comprehension Questions

(Numbers corresponding to these questions are placed throughout the passage at points at which they should be asked during oral reading.)

1. What do all plants need in order to stay alive? (*All plants need nutrients.*)

2. Where do most plants get these nutrients? (*Most plants get their nutrients from the soil and from the air.*)

3. What do we call plants that get supplemental nutrients by eating insects and small animals? (*These plants are called carnivorous or meat-eating plants.*)

4. How do carnivorous plants attract insects so they can eat them? (*They attract insects through smells, colors, or patterns, or with sparkling droplets on their leaves.*)

5. Why do insects or small animals approach the sundew plant? (*When they are looking for food or water, they are attracted to sticky drops that sparkle.*)

6. What happens to a fly that gets too close to the sundew plant? (*It sticks to the hairs on the leaves and then starts to wriggle to get away. The leaves curl around the fly and pour digestive juices onto it. The juices dissolve the fly's body, and the plant gets its nutrients.*)

7. How does the Venus flytrap attract insects? (*Its leaves have a sweet smell, red coloring, and a broad shape that looks like a good resting spot.*)

8. What happens when the insect lands on the leaf? (*The leaf slams shut and traps the fly. It crushes the fly's body and dissolves it to get the nutrients.*)

9. Why is it fortunate for us that carnivorous plants eat only insects and small animals? (*If they were man-eating, they would be dangerous to people.*)

Summative Question

10. Pretend your partner has not read this selection. Tell your partner how carnivorous plants get some of their nutrients. First Partner 1 and then Partner 2.

Passage Reading—Fluency

1. It is important that you read passages accurately. However, it is also important that you can read the material quickly. What are some benefits of reading quickly? __ (Call on individual students.)

2. In each of the remaining lessons, we will work to increase your reading fluency. First, you will practice reading the passage. Then, your partner will listen to you read.

3. Find the beginning of the passage. (Pause.) Get ready for your first practice. I want you to whisper-read so that I can hear you when I am close, but you will not disturb your neighbors. See how many words you can read in a minute. Begin. __ (Time students for one minute.) Stop. Circle the last word that you read. __

4. Let's practice again. Return to the beginning of the passage. __ Remember to whisper-read. See if you can read more words. Begin. __ (Time students for one minute.) Stop. Put a box around the last word that you read. __

5. Please exchange books with your partner. __ Partner 1, you are going to read first. Partner 2, you are going to listen carefully to your partner. If your partner makes a mistake or leaves out a word, underline the word. Ones, get ready to read quietly to your partner. Begin. __ (Time students for one minute.) Stop. Twos, cross out the last word that your partner read. __

6. Partner 2, you are going to read next. Partner 1, listen carefully to your partner. If your partner makes a mistake or leaves out a word, underline the word. Twos, get ready to read quietly to your partner. Begin. __ (Time students for one minute.) Stop. Ones, cross out the last word that your partner read. __

7. Please return your partner's book. __ Let's figure out the total number of words you read. Find the line containing the last word that you read. __ Now, find the number at the beginning of that line. __ Start with that number and count on until you get to your last word. __ Write that number in Box A at the end of the passage. __

8. Now, go back and count the number of words you missed. These words are underlined. __ Write that number in Box B. __

9. Please subtract to determine the number of words that you read correctly in one minute. __ Write that number in Box C. __

Note:
- Optional—You may select to have the students graph their daily fluency. For directions, see Appendix E, "Fluency Graph: Correct Words Per Minute" at the end of the *Teacher's Guide*. Each student's copy of the graph is on the last page of the *Student Book*.

Lesson 21

Materials Needed

- Lesson 21 from the *Student Book*
- Overhead Transparencies 27, 28, and 29
- Washable overhead transparency pen
- Paper or cardboard to use when covering the overhead transparencies
- Paper or cardboard for each student to use during spelling dictation

ACTIVITY A: **Vowel Combinations Review** (See the *Student Book*, page 78.)

1.	oo	oy	i - e	ai	ee
2.	e - e	or	u - e	er	ar

Activity Procedure: Have students review saying the sounds for letter combinations. When the letter combination has a box around it, ask students to tell you both sounds.

Note:
- Whenever you come to letters in a box, ask "What sound would you try first? What sound would you try next?"

1. Find Activity A. Let's review vowel combinations.

2. Point to the boxed letters in Line 1. What sound would you try first? __ What sound would you try next? __ Next sound? __ Next sound? __ Next sound? __ Next sound? __

3. (Continue Step 2 for letters in Line 2.)

ACTIVITY B: **Vowel Conversions Review** (See the *Student Book*, page 78.)

a	i	e	o	u

> **Activity Procedure:** Have students review saying the sound, then the name for each letter.

1. Find Activity B. When you are reading words and see these letters, what would you try first, the sound or the name? __

2. Point to the first letter. What sound? __ What name? __

3. Next letter. What sound? __ What name? __

4. Next letter. What sound? __ What name? __

5. Next letter. What sound? __ What name? __

6. Next letter. What sound? __ What name? __

ACTIVITY C: **Prefixes and Suffixes Review** (See the *Student Book*, page 78.)

		Prefixes			
1.	dis	be	un	ex	mis
2.	pre	de	en	ad	com

		Suffixes			
3.	ness	ate	ing	ist	ism
4.	ence	ous	ible	tive	y
5.	ity	est	er	le	sion

> **Activity Procedure:** Have students review saying prefixes and suffixes aloud.

1. Find Activity C.

2. Point to the first prefix in Line 1. What prefix? __ Next? __ Next? __ Next? __ Next? __

3. (Repeat Step 2 for prefixes in Line 2.)

4. Point to the first suffix in Line 3. What suffix? __ Next? __ Next? __ Next? __ Next? __

5. (Repeat Step 4 for suffixes in Lines 4 and 5.)

ACTIVITY D: **Strategy Instruction** (See the *Student Book,* page 79.)

1.	unforgettable	population
2.	experimental	probably
3.	vigilant	difficulty
4.	adventurous	pilgrimage

Activity Procedure: Work with students to apply the strategy for figuring out longer words to all words in this activity. For each word, ask students if the word has any prefixes or suffixes, then circle them. Underline the vowels and have students say the sounds. Finally, have students say the word, first part by part, and then as a whole word.

 Use Overhead 27: Activity D

1.   Find Activity D.

2.   Look up here. Let's use the *REWARDS* strategy to figure out these words.

3.   (Point to the first word in Line 1.) Does the word have a prefix? __ (If the answer is yes, circle the prefix and ask...) What prefix? __

4.   Does the word have a suffix? __ (If the answer is yes, circle the suffix and ask...) What suffix? __

5.   (Underline the vowels in the rest of the word and ask...) What sound? __ What sound? __

6.   Say the word by parts. (Loop under each part and ask...) What part? __ What part? __ What part? __ What part? __

7.   (Run your finger under the whole word.) What word? __

8.   (Repeat Steps 3–7 with each remaining word in Activity D.)

Note:
• You may wish to provide additional practice by having students read a line to the group or to a partner.

ACTIVITY E: **Strategy Practice** (See the *Student Book,* page 79.)

1.	dependability	incompetent
2.	disorganization	unexpectedness
3.	depression	defective
4.	unlikely	incorrectly
5.	inadmissible	prematurely

Activity Procedure: In this activity, have students apply the strategy for figuring out longer words by themselves. Have students circle prefixes and suffixes and underline the vowels. Have students say the word part by part to themselves and then as a whole word aloud.

 Use Overhead 27: Activity E

1. Find Activity E.

2. It's your turn to use the *REWARDS* strategy. For each word, circle prefixes and suffixes and underline the vowels in the rest of the word. Look up when you are done. __

3. (Show the overhead transparency.) Now check and fix any mistakes. __

4. Go back to the first word. __ Sound out the word to yourself. Put your thumb up when you can read the word. Be sure that it is a real word. __ What word? __

5. Next word. (Pause.) What word? __

6. (Repeat Step 5 with all words in Activity E.)

Note:
• You may wish to provide additional practice by having students read a line to the group or to a partner.

ACTIVITY F: **Word Families** (See the *Student Book,* page 79.)

A	**B**
organize—to put things in order	expect—to look forward to something happening
organized	expected
organizer	expecting
organization	expectance
organizational	expectation
disorganization	unexpected
reorganize	unexpectedness

Activity Procedure: Tell students the meaning of the first word in Column A. Have students read words in the first column to themselves, and then twice with the teacher. Then, have students read Column A to their partners. Repeat these procedures for the words in Column B, with opposite partners reading.

 Use Overhead 28: Activity F

1. Find Activity F.

2. Find the Column A word family. The first word is <u>organize</u>. Organize means "to put things in order." The words in Column A have similar meanings to the word <u>organize</u>. Say each word in Column A to yourself until I say "Stop." __

3. Now let's read the words together. Touch under the first word and read each word with me. (Read the list of words with students.)

4. Let's read those words together again. Touch under the first word and read with me. (Read the list of words with students.)

5. Touch under the first word in Column A again. Partner 2, read the list to your partner. Look up when you are done. __ (Monitor partner reading.)

6. Find the Column B word family. The first word is <u>expect</u>. Expect means "to look forward to something happening." The words in Column B have similar meanings to the word <u>expect</u>. Say each word in Column B to yourself until I say "Stop." __

7. (Repeat Steps 3–5 with words in Column B. In Step 5, have Partner 1 read.)

ACTIVITY G: **Spelling Dictation** (See the *Student Book,* page 80.)

1. population	2. disorganization
3. defective	4. difficulty

Activity Procedure: For each word, tell students the word, then have students say the parts of the word with you. Have them say the parts to themselves as they write the word. Then, have students compare their words with your word and cross out and rewrite any misspelled words.

Note:
- Distribute a piece of light cardboard to each of the students.

1. Find Activity G.

2. The first word is **population**. What word? __ Fist in the air. Say the parts of **population** with me. First part? __ Next part? __ Next part? __ Next part? __ Say the parts in **population** to yourself as you write the word. (Pause and monitor.)

3. (Write **population** on the board or overhead transparency.) Check **population**. If you misspelled it, cross it out and write it correctly.

4. The second word is **disorganization**. What word? __ Fist in the air. Say the parts of **disorganization** with me. First part? __ Next part? __ Next part? __ Next part? __ Next part? __ Next part? __ Say the parts in **disorganization** to yourself as you write the word. (Pause and monitor.)

5. (Write **disorganization** on the board or overhead transparency.) Check **disorganization**. If you misspelled it, cross it out and write it correctly.

6. (Repeat the procedures for the words **defective** and **difficulty**.)

ACTIVITY H: **Vocabulary** (See the *Student Book,* page 80.)

a.	not able to be forgotten (Activity D)	_unforgettable_
b.	in a manner that is not correct (Activity E)	_incorrectly_
c.	in a manner that is premature or before the best time (Activity E)	
	prematurely	

1. Find Activity H.

2. Listen to the first definition, "not able to be forgotten." Look back at the words in Activity D. Find the word and write it. (Pause and monitor.) What word means "not able to be forgotten"? __ (*unforgettable*)

3. Listen to the next definition, "in a manner that is not correct." Look back at the words in Activity E. Find the word and write it. (Pause and monitor.) What word means "in a manner that is not correct"? __ (*incorrectly*)

4. Next definition. "In a manner that is premature or before the best time." Look back at the words in Activity E. Find the word and write it. (Pause and monitor.) What word means "in a manner that is premature or before the best time"? __ (*prematurely*)

ACTIVITY I: **Passage Preparation** (See the *Student Book,* page 81.)

Part 1—Tell

1.	Wilma Rudolph	*n.*	a woman who was a fast runner
2.	pneumonia	*n.*	an illness
3.	polio	*n.*	an illness that causes weakness in muscles
4.	physical therapy	*n.*	treatment for problems in your body
5.	Olympic Games	*n.*	sports contest among nations
6.	tournament	*n.*	a contest involving many teams in a sport or game
*7.	triumph	*n.*	an outstanding success
*8.	obstacles	*n.*	things that stand in your way

Part 2—Strategy Practice

9.	Tennessee	*n.*	a state in the United States
10.	corrective	*adj.*	intended to correct (corrective braces)
*11.	encourage	*v.*	to give hope and support to others
*12.	persevered	*v.*	kept on trying to do something even if it was hard
13.	determination	*n.*	the act of not letting anything stop you
14.	decision	*n.*	the act of deciding or choosing something
15.	American	*adj.*	related to the United States of America
16.	international	*adj.*	involving more than one nation
17.	foundation	*n.*	an organization that has money to do special things
18.	inducted	*v.*	accepted as a member of a group or club

Activity Procedure: For the first set of words, tell students each word and have them read its definition. Then, have students practice reading the words themselves. The second set of words can be read using the part-by-part strategy. Have students circle prefixes and suffixes, then underline the vowels. Using the overhead transparency, assist students in checking their work. Next, have students read each word aloud, first part by part, and then as a whole word. Have them read the part of speech and definition aloud. Finally, use the scripted wording to introduce the four starred vocabulary words that provide a preview of the passage.

Use Overhead 29: Activity I

Part 1—Tell

1. (Show the top half of Overhead 29.) Before we read today's passage, let's read the difficult words. (Point to **Wilma Rudolph**.) The first words are **Wilma Rudolph**. What words? __ Now read the definition with me. "A woman who was a fast runner."

2. (Point to **pneumonia**.) The next word is **pneumonia**. What word? __ Read the definition with me. "An illness."

3. (Pronounce each word in Part 1, and then have students repeat each word and read the definition with you.)

4. Find Activity I, Part 1, in your book. __ Let's read the words again. First word. __ Next word. __ (Continue for all words in Part 1.)

Part 2—Strategy Practice

1. Find Part 2. For each word, circle the prefixes and suffixes and underline the vowels. Look up when you are done. __

2. (Show the bottom half of Overhead 29.) Now check and fix any mistakes. __

3. (When students are done checking, assist them in reading each word on the overhead transparency, beginning with the first word in Part 2.) Look up here. __

   (Loop under each word part in **Tennessee**.) What part? __ What part? __ What part? __

   (Run your finger under the whole word.) What word? __ Now, read the definition for "Tennessee." __

4. (Repeat Step 3 with all remaining words in Part 2.)

Note:
- You may wish to provide additional practice by having students read words to a partner.

Part 3—Starred Vocabulary

1. Let's study some of the words in Activity I. Find word #7. __ What word? (*triumph*) When we have a wonderful success at anything, it can be called a _____. (*triumph*) If you finally won a basketball game after losing many, that would be a _____. (*triumph*) If you read an entire book in a day, that would be a _____. (*triumph*) Even though Wilma Rudolph was very ill as a child, in sports she experienced a _____. (*triumph*)

2. Find #8. __ What word? (*obstacles*) If things stand in your way, they are _____. (*obstacles*) If you were writing a report and couldn't find your notes or any more information on your topic, these would be _____. (*obstacles*) Wilma Rudolph was very ill as a child and wore a metal brace on her leg. If you wanted to be a runner, these would be _____. (*obstacles*)

3. Find #11. __ What word? (*encourage*) If we encourage someone, we give them hope and support. Ones, tell your partner one person who might have encouraged Wilma in sports and what makes you think so. Twos, tell your partner another person who might have encouraged Wilma and what makes you think so.

4. Find #12. __ What word? (*persevered*) If you kept on trying to do something even if it was hard, you would have _____. (*persevered*) Wilma Rudolph kept trying and trying to be good at sports. She _____. (*persevered*)

ACTIVITY J: **Passage Reading and Comprehension** (See the *Student Book*, pages 82 and 83.)

	Wilma Rudolph, a True Hero
9	Wilma Rudolph's life story is one of hope and determination, adversity and triumph. She became one of
17	the most highly regarded athletes in history. (#1) The way
26	the story begins, however, does not sound like it could turn
37	out that way.
40	In 1940, Wilma was born at home, the 20th of 22
51	children. She was born prematurely and weighed only
59	4.5 pounds. Wilma soon experienced one illness after
67	another. Because of the Great Depression, Wilma's parents
75	were quite poor and could not afford medical care for her.
86	Instead, her mother took care of her. (#2)
93	She survived measles, mumps, scarlet fever, chicken
100	pox, and double pneumonia. When she was four years old,
110	her left leg was shrinking and getting weak, and Wilma's
120	mother had to take her 50 miles to visit a doctor. The doctor
133	said Wilma had polio and probably would not walk. (#3)
142	Most people would be discouraged and give up at that
152	point. Not Wilma and not Wilma's determined family! They
161	did not give up hope. After several years of hard work,
172	Wilma could walk with the aid of a metal brace.
182	Doctors also showed Wilma's mother how to do
190	physical therapy, and she showed all of Wilma's brothers
199	and sisters how to help. (#4) What happened next was
208	close to a miracle. By age 12, Wilma was walking without
219	crutches, braces, or corrective shoes. (#5)
224	Believing that sports would strengthen her leg further,
232	Wilma made a decision to become an athlete. (#6) In
241	junior high, she joined a basketball team. For three years,
251	the coach did not put her into a game. Wilma persevered,

262	however. She became a starting guard when she was in
272	tenth grade and led her team to the state championship.
282	During the tournament, the Tennessee State track coach
290	spotted her and invited her to a summer sports camp.
300	Wilma was on her way to becoming a track star. (#7)
310	When she was 16, Wilma Rudolph helped her team
319	win an Olympic medal in a relay race. Four years later,
330	Wilma became the first American woman to win three
339	gold medals in one Olympic Games. Everyone called her
348	the fastest woman in the world. She received numerous
357	awards and medals. In addition, she was inducted into the
367	Black Sports Hall of Fame, the International Sports Hall
376	of Fame, and the U.S. Olympic Hall of Fame. (#8) In 1982,
387	she started the Wilma Rudolph Foundation to encourage
395	children to overcome obstacles and follow their dreams,
403	just as her mother had taught her to do. (#9)
412	

A. ☐ **Total number of words read**

B. ☐ **Total number of underlined words (mistakes)**

C. ☐ **Total number of words read correctly**

Activity Procedure: Have students work on accuracy by having them read the passage silently to each embedded number and then rereading the same section orally to a partner, together as a group, or individually. When students finish reading a section orally, ask the corresponding comprehension question. When the passage has been read, have students work on fluency by having them read the passage first to themselves twice, and then to a partner. Have students count the total number of words read and the number of words missed and subtract to find the number of words read correctly. You may also wish to have students graph their daily fluency.

Passage Reading—Accuracy

1. Find Activity J. You are going to read a passage and answer questions about what you've read. Today's passage is about a remarkable woman who overcame obstacles to become an Olympic track star. The passage describes what the obstacles were and how Wilma Rudolph overcame them with her perseverance. Read the title with me. "Wilma Rudolph, a True Hero."

2. Find #1 in the passage. (Pause.) Read down to #1 silently. Look up when you are done. __

3. (Wait for students to complete the reading. Then have students reread the section by having them read orally to a partner, read together orally as a group, or read aloud individually.)

4. (Ask the question associated with the number. Provide feedback to students regarding their answers.)

5. (Repeat Steps 2, 3, and 4 for all sections of the passage.)

Comprehension Questions
(Numbers corresponding to these questions are placed throughout the passage at points at which they should be asked during oral reading.)

1. Who was Wilma Rudolph? (*She was one of the most highly regarded athletes in history.*)

2. When Wilma became very ill, why did her mother need to take care of her? (*Her parents were poor and could not afford medical care.*)

3. What disease affected Wilma's walking? (Polio.)

4. How did Wilma's family help her? (*They did not give up hope; Wilma's mother and brothers and sisters did physical therapy with her.*)

5. What happened when Wilma was 12 that was "close to a miracle"? (*Wilma walked without crutches, braces, or corrective shoes.*)

6. Why did Wilma decide to become an athlete? (*She believed it would help to strengthen her leg further.*)

7. How did Wilma's perseverance help her? (*She kept trying to play basketball until she became a championship player.*)

8. What honors did Wilma receive over her career? (*At the age of 16, she helped her team win an Olympic medal; four years later, she won three gold medals; she received other awards and medals; she was inducted into the Black Sports Hall of Fame, the International Sports Hall of Fame, and the U.S. Olympic Hall of Fame.*)

9. Why did she start the Wilma Rudolph Foundation? (*She wanted to encourage kids to overcome obstacles and follow their dreams.*)

Summative Question

10. Pretend that you interviewed Wilma Rudolph. She talked about the three most important highlights in her life. What do you think she told you? First Partner 1 and then Partner 2.

Passage Reading—Fluency

1. Now it's time for fluency building.

2. Find the beginning of the passage. (Pause.) Get ready for your first practice. I want you to whisper-read so that I can hear you when I am close, but you will not disturb your neighbors. See how many words you can read in a minute. Begin. __ (Time students for one minute.) Stop. Circle the last word that you read. __

3. Let's practice again. Return to the beginning of the passage. __ Remember to whisper-read. See if you can read more words. Begin. __ (Time students for one minute.) Stop. Put a box around the last word that you read. __

4. Please exchange books with your partner. __ Partner 2, you are going to read first. Partner 1, you are going to listen carefully to your partner. If your partner makes a mistake or leaves out a word, underline the word. Twos, get ready to read quietly to your partner. Begin. __ (Time students for one minute.) Stop. Ones, cross out the last word that your partner read. __

5. Partner 1, you are going to read next. Partner 2, listen carefully to your partner. If your partner makes a mistake or leaves out a word, underline the word. Ones, get ready to read quietly to your partner. Begin. __ (Time students for one minute.) Stop. Twos, cross out the last word that your partner read. __

6. Please return your partner's book. __ Let's figure out the total number of words you read. Find the line containing the last word that you read. __ Now, find the number at the beginning of that line. __ Start with that number and count on until you get to your last word. __ Write that number in Box A at the end of the passage. __

7. Now, go back and count the number of words you missed. These words are underlined. __ Write that number in Box B. __

8. Please subtract to determine the number of words that you read correctly in one minute. __ Write that number in Box C. __

Note:
- Optional—You may select to have the students graph their daily fluency. For directions, see Appendix E, "Fluency Graph: Correct Words Per Minute" at the end of the *Teacher's Guide*. Each student's copy of the graph is on the last page of the *Student Book*.

Materials Needed

- Lesson 22 from the *Student Book*
- Overhead Transparencies 30, 31, and 32
- Washable overhead transparency pen
- Paper or cardboard to use when covering the overhead transparencies
- Paper or cardboard for each student to use during spelling dictation

ACTIVITY A: **Vowel Combinations Review** (See the *Student Book*, page 84.)

1.	ow	au	ay	o - e	ir
2.	ou	ea	a - e	ur	oo

Activity Procedure: Have students review saying the sounds for letter combinations. When the letter combination has a box around it, ask students to tell you both sounds.

Note:
- Whenever you come to letters in a box, ask "What sound would you try first? What sound would you try next?"

1. Find Activity A. Let's review vowel combinations.

2. Point to the boxed letters in Line 1. What sound would you try first? __ What sound would you try next? __ Next sound? __ Next sound? __ Next sound? __ Next sound? __

3. (Continue Step 2 for letters in Line 2.)

ACTIVITY B: **Vowel Conversions Review** (See the *Student Book,* page 84.)

e	o	a	u	i

> **Activity Procedure:** Have students review saying the sound, then the name for each letter.

1. Find Activity B. When you are reading words and see these letters, what would you try first, the sound or the name? __

2. Point to the first letter. What sound? __ What name? __

3. Next letter. What sound? __ What name? __

4. Next letter. What sound? __ What name? __

5. Next letter. What sound? __ What name? __

6. Next letter. What sound? __ What name? __

ACTIVITY C: **Prefixes and Suffixes Review** (See the *Student Book,* page 84.)

	Prefixes				
1.	ab	in	con	re	pro
2.	per	a	im	mis	pre

	Suffixes				
3.	less	ic	al	or	tion
4.	ly	ant	ance	ible	ize
5.	ture	ent	ish	age	sive

> **Activity Procedure:** Have students review saying prefixes and suffixes aloud.

1. Find Activity C.

2. Point to the first prefix in Line 1. What prefix? __ Next? __ Next? __ Next? __ Next? __

3. (Repeat Step 2 for prefixes in Line 2.)

4. Point to the first suffix in Line 3. What suffix? __ Next? __ Next? __ Next? __ Next? __

5. (Repeat Step 4 for suffixes in Lines 4 and 5.)

ACTIVITY D: **Strategy Practice** (See the *Student Book*, page 85.)

1.	professionally	unfortunately
2.	exterminator	comparison
3.	instructionally	nonviolence
4.	immigration	eventually

Activity Procedure: In this activity, have students apply the strategy for figuring out longer words by themselves. Have students circle prefixes and suffixes and underline the vowels. Have students say the word part by part to themselves and then as a whole word aloud.

 Use Overhead 30: Activity D

1. Find Activity D.

2. It's your turn to use the *REWARDS* strategy. Circle prefixes and suffixes and underline the vowels. Look up when you are done. __

3. (Show the overhead transparency.) Now check and fix any mistakes. __

4. Go back to the first word. __ Sound out the word to yourself. Put your thumb up when you can read the word. Be sure that it is a real word. __ What word? __

5. Next word. (Pause.) What word? __

6. (Repeat Step 5 with all words in Activity D.)

Note:
• You may wish to provide additional practice by having students read a line to the group or to a partner.

ACTIVITY E: **Independent Strategy Practice** (See the *Student Book,* page 85.)

1.	misinformation	enlargement
2.	communicate	conversational
3.	conditionally	accomplishment
4.	destructive	organism
5.	returnable	governmentally

Activity Procedure: In this activity, students independently apply the strategy for figuring out longer words without circling and underlining. Have students look carefully at each word; locate prefixes, suffixes, and vowels; and figure out the word to themselves. Then, have students say the word aloud.

 Use Overhead 30: Activity E

1. Find Activity E.

2. Find the first word in Line 1. Without circling and underlining, look carefully for prefixes and suffixes. Look for vowels in the rest of the word. If you have difficulty figuring out the word, use your pencil. Put your thumb up when you can say the word. __ (Give ample thinking time.)

3. (When students have decoded the word, ask…) What word? __

4. Next word. Put your thumb up when you can say the word. __ (Give ample thinking time.) What word? __

5. (Repeat Step 4 for the remaining words.)

Note:
• You may wish to provide additional practice by having students read a line to the group or to a partner.

ACTIVITY F: **Word Families** (See the *Student Book,* page 86.)

A	B
inform—to tell someone something	destroy—to ruin something
informer	destruction
informant	destructive
information	destructiveness
informational	destructible
informative	indestructible
misinformation	indestructibility

Activity Procedure: Tell students the meaning of the first word in Column A. Have students read words in the first column to themselves, and then twice with the teacher. Then, have students read Column A to their partners. Repeat these procedures for the words in Column B, with opposite partners reading.

 Use Overhead 31: Activity F

1. Find Activity F.

2. Find the Column A word family. The first word is <u>inform</u>. Inform means "to tell someone something." The words in Column A have similar meanings to the word <u>inform</u>. Say each word in Column A to yourself until I say "Stop." __

3. Now let's read the words together. Touch under the first word and read each word with me. (Read the list of words with students.)

4. Let's read those words together again. Touch under the first word and read with me. (Read the list of words with students.)

5. Touch under the first word in Column A again. Partner 1, read the list to your partner. Look up when you are done. __ (Monitor partner reading.)

6. Find the Column B word family. The first word is <u>destroy</u>. Destroy means "to ruin something." The words in Column B have similar meanings to the word <u>destroy</u>. Say each word in Column B to yourself until I say "Stop." __

7. (Repeat Steps 3–5 with words in Column B. In Step 5, have Partner 2 read.)

ACTIVITY G: **Spelling Dictation** (See the *Student Book,* page 86.)

1.	professionally	2.	communicate
3.	exterminator	4.	conversational

> **Activity Procedure:** For each word, tell students the word, then have students say the parts of the word with you. Have them say the parts to themselves as they write the word. Then, have students compare their words with your word and cross out and rewrite any misspelled words.

Note:
 • Distribute a piece of light cardboard to each of the students.

1. Find Activity G.

2. The first word is **professionally**. What word? __ Fist in the air. Say the parts of **professionally** with me. First part? __ Next part? __ Next part? __ Next part? __ Next part? __ Say the parts in **professionally** to yourself as you write the word. (Pause and monitor.)

3. (Write **professionally** on the board or overhead transparency.) Check **professionally**. If you misspelled it, cross it out and write it correctly.

4. The second word is **communicate**. What word? __ Fist in the air. Say the parts of **communicate** with me. First part? __ Next part? __ Next part? __ Next part? __ Say the parts in **communicate** to yourself as you write the word. (Pause and monitor.)

5. (Write **communicate** on the board or overhead transparency.) Check **communicate**. If you misspelled it, cross it out and write it correctly.

6. (Repeat the procedures for the words **exterminator** and **conversational**.)

ACTIVITY H: **Vocabulary** (See the *Student Book,* page 86.)

a.	not having fortune or good luck; regretfully (Activity D)	_unfortunately_
b.	the result of accomplishing or completing something (Activity E)	
	accomplishment	
c.	able to be returned (Activity E)	_returnable_

1. Find Activity H.

2. Listen to the first definition, "not having fortune or good luck; regretfully." Look back at the words in Activity D. Find the word and write it. (Pause and monitor.) What word means "not having fortune or good luck; regretfully"? __ (*unfortunately*)

3. Listen to the next definition, "the result of accomplishing or completing something." Look back at the words in Activity E. Find the word and write it. (Pause and monitor.) What word means "the result of accomplishing or completing something"? __ (*accomplishment*)

4. Next definition. "Able to be returned." Look back at the words in Activity E. Find the word and write it. (Pause and monitor.) What word means "able to be returned"? __ (*returnable*)

ACTIVITY I: **Passage Preparation** (See the *Student Book,* page 87.)

Part 1—Tell

1.	Cesar Chavez	*n.*	a man who worked for migrant workers' rights
2.	Mexico	*n.*	a country in North America
3.	United States	*n.*	a country in North America
4.	Arizona	*n.*	a state in the United States
5.	California	*n.*	a state in the United States
6.	English	*n.*	a language
7.	believed	*v.*	accepted as true
8.	noticed	*v.*	saw something or somebody

Part 2—Strategy Practice

9.	ancestors	*n.*	people who came before us, such as our grandparents
10.	immigrate	*v.*	come into a country and settle there
*11.	migrant workers	*n.*	people who move from place to place to find work in farming
12.	vegetables	*n.*	foods such as carrots, lettuce, and beets
*13.	boycott	*n.*	a group's refusal to deal with an organization in protest
14.	supermarkets	*n.*	big grocery stores
*15.	sacrifice	*n.*	a thing given up for something of more value
*16.	nonviolent	*adj.*	not using violence or force
17.	elementary	*adj.*	referring to grades one to six
18.	attention	*n.*	the act of thinking carefully about something

Activity Procedure: For the first set of words, tell students each word and have them read its definition. Then, have students practice reading the words themselves. The second set of words can be read using the part-by-part strategy. Have students circle prefixes and suffixes, then underline the vowels. Using the overhead transparency, assist students in checking their work. Next, have students read each word aloud, first part by part, and then as a whole word. Have them read the part of speech and definition aloud. Finally, use the scripted wording to introduce the four starred vocabulary words that provide a preview of the passage.

Use Overhead 32: Activity I

Part 1—Tell

1. (Show the top half of Overhead 32.) Before we read today's passage, let's read the difficult words. (Point to **Cesar Chavez**.) The first words are **Cesar Chavez**. What words? __ Now read the definition with me. "A man who worked for migrant workers' rights."

2. (Point to **Mexico**.) The next word is **Mexico**. What word? __ Read the definition with me. "A country in North America."

3. (Pronounce each word in Part 1, and then have students repeat each word and read the definition with you.)

4. Find Activity I, Part 1, in your book. __ Let's read the words again. First word. __ Next word. __ (Continue for all words in Part 1.)

Part 2—Strategy Practice

1. Find Part 2. For each word, circle the prefixes and suffixes and underline the vowels. Look up when you are done. __

2. (Show the bottom half of Overhead 32.) Now check and fix any mistakes. __

3. (When students are done checking, assist them in reading each word on the overhead transparency, beginning with the first word in Part 2.) Look up here. __

   (Loop under each word part in **ancestors**.) What part? __ What part? __ What part? __

   (Run your finger under the whole word.) What word? __ Now, read the definition for "ancestors." __

4. (Repeat Step 3 with all remaining words in Part 2.)

Note:
- You may wish to provide additional practice by having students read words to a partner.

Part 3—Starred Vocabulary

1. Let's study some of the words in Activity I. Find word #11. __ What words? (*migrant workers*) People who move from place to place to locate farm work are called _____. (*migrant workers*) If Manuel Lopez worked in apple orchards in Washington state and then in the lettuce fields of California, he would be a _____. (*migrant worker*) In this passage, we are going to learn about Cesar Chavez, a man who tried to make the lives of migrant workers better.

2. Find #13. __ What word? (*boycott*) If your family refused to shop at a grocery store because you did not like the store's policies, you would be involved in a _____. (*boycott*) To get grape farmers to provide better conditions for migrant workers, Cesar Chavez asked people to refuse to buy grapes. These people participated in a grape _____. (*boycott*)

3. Find #15. __ What word? (*sacrifice*) If you give a thing up because something else is more important to you, you make a _____. (*sacrifice*) Because Cesar Chavez thought that making the lives of migrant workers better was important, he made many _____. (*sacrifices*) For example, he starved himself to bring attention to the difficult lives of migrant workers.

4. Find #16. __ What word? (*nonviolent*) If you protested the bad treatment of migrant workers, but you didn't use force or hurt people, your actions would be _____. (*nonviolent*) Chavez asked people to take actions that were _____. (*nonviolent*)

ACTIVITY J: **Passage Reading and Comprehension** (See the *Student Book*, pages 88 and 89.)

Cesar Chavez, Fighter for Human Dignity

	Cesar Chavez (1927–1993) devoted his life to human
9	dignity and fairness. Throughout his life, he made
17	sacrifices so that migrant workers' lives could be better. (#1)
26	Cesar's ancestors immigrated to the United States from
34	Mexico. They left their homeland to find a better life. (#2)
44	Cesar's grandparents established a large ranch in the
52	Arizona desert and worked as farmers. Cesar was born on
62	the family ranch.
65	In 1937, when Cesar was 10 years old, the Chavez
75	family moved to California and became migrant workers.
83	"Migrant" means moving from one place to another. As
92	migrant workers, they moved from one farm to another
101	and worked for the farm owners. (#3)
107	The farm owners paid them very little to pick fruits
117	and vegetables. The migrant workers worked long hours in
126	the hot sun. Because they did not own houses, they slept
137	in small shacks that had no bathrooms, no electricity, and
147	no running water. Sometimes the shacks were so crowded,
156	they even slept in their pickup trucks. (#4)
163	Cesar said that school was very difficult for him. As
173	the families moved around, the children kept changing
181	schools. Cesar attended school sometimes for only a
189	day or two and sometimes for a few weeks or months.
200	He estimated that he went to 65 elementary schools
209	altogether! In addition, his family spoke only Spanish at
218	home, so learning to read and write English was hard for
229	him. The other students taunted (made fun of) him. (#5) In
239	spite of difficulties, Cesar was able to graduate from eighth

249	grade. Graduating was an unusual accomplishment for
256	migrant workers in those days.
261	As Cesar grew up, he noticed how difficult the migrant
271	workers' lives were. He wanted to do something about it.
281	Cesar took part in his first nonviolent protest of low wages
272	and poor working conditions by going on strike. (#6) For
301	several years, he was part of an organization called the
311	Community Service Organization. Eventually, he left to
318	form his own organization, now known as the United Farm
328	Workers (UFW).
330	Cesar Chavez and the UFW led many strikes and
339	boycotts against farm owners who refused to change the
348	working conditions. In addition, Cesar Chavez fasted, or
356	starved himself, to draw more attention to the issues. (#7)
365	People did pay attention. For example, many Americans
373	joined the boycott against table grapes. They refused to
382	buy them at their local supermarkets. The grape boycott
391	lasted for five years, but the farm owners finally made
401	some changes. (#8)
403	When Cesar Chavez died, he was 66 years old. His
413	tireless work for other people and all the fasting he did
424	were hard on his body. Nevertheless, he believed strongly
433	in making sacrifices so that other people could have better
443	lives. Today his children still work for migrant workers'
452	rights. (#9)
452	

A.	☐	**Total number of words read**
B.	☐	**Total number of underlined words (mistakes)**
C.	☐	**Total number of words read correctly**

Activity Procedure: Have students work on accuracy by having them read the passage silently to each embedded number and then reread the same section orally to a partner, together as a group, or individually. When students finish reading a section orally, ask the corresponding comprehension question. When the passage has been read, have students work on fluency by having them read the passage first to themselves twice, and then to a partner. Have students count the total number of words read and the number of words missed, and subtract to find the number of words read correctly. You may also wish to have students graph their daily fluency.

Passage Reading—Accuracy

1. Find Activity J. You are going to read a passage and answer questions about what you've read. Today's passage is about an admirable man who fought tirelessly for the rights of migrant workers. You will find out why the migrant workers needed more rights and what Cesar Chavez did to fight for them. Read the title with me. "Cesar Chavez, Fighter for Human Dignity."

2. Find #1 in the passage. (Pause.) Read down to #1 silently. Look up when you are done. __

3. (Wait for students to complete the reading. Then have students reread the section by having them read orally to a partner, read together orally as a group, or read aloud individually.)

4. (Ask the question associated with the number. Provide feedback to students regarding their answers.)

5. (Repeat Steps 2, 3, and 4 for all sections of the passage.)

Comprehension Questions

(Numbers corresponding to these questions are placed throughout the passage at points at which they should be asked during oral reading.)

1. Why did Cesar Chavez make sacrifices? (*So that migrant workers' lives could be better.*)

2. Why did Cesar's ancestors immigrate to the United States? (*In order to find a better life.*)

3. What happened when Cesar was 10 years old? (*His family became migrant workers, moving from one farm to another to work.*)

4. What were the lives of migrant workers like? (*They were paid very little, worked long hours, and did not own houses. They slept in small shacks with no bathrooms, electricity, or running water. Some slept in their trucks.*)

5. Why was school difficult for Cesar? (*He moved a lot, attended school sometimes only a day or two or for a few weeks or months; he attended 65 elementary schools; his family spoke only Spanish at home so learning English was hard; other students made fun of him.*)

6. Why did Cesar take part in nonviolent protests? (*He wanted to do something for the migrant workers.*)

7. What did Cesar and the United Farm Workers (UFW) do to help migrant workers? (*They led strikes and boycotts. Cesar fasted to draw attention to issues.*)

8. What happened during the grape boycott? (*People refused to buy grapes for five years. The farmers started to make some changes.*)

9. Why might we think of Cesar Chavez as a hero? (*He made sacrifices for others; he formed organizations that worked on behalf of migrant workers and made things better for them.*)

Summative Question

10. Many groups of humans have major problems that need to be solved. Partner 1, tell your partner a group of humans that need assistance and why. Partner 2, tell your partner a different group that needs assistance and why.

Passage Reading—Fluency

1. Now it's time for fluency building.

2. Find the beginning of the passage. (Pause.) Remember to whisper-read. See how many words you can read in a minute. Begin. ___ (Time students for one minute.) Stop. Circle the last word that you read. ___

3. Let's practice again. Return to the beginning of the passage. ___ Remember to whisper-read. See if you can read more words. Begin. ___ (Time students for one minute.) Stop. Put a box around the last word that you read. ___

4. Please exchange books with your partner. ___ Partner 1, you are going to read first. Partner 2, you are going to listen carefully to your partner. If your partner makes a mistake or leaves out a word, underline the word. Ones, get ready to read quietly to your partner. Begin. ___ (Time students for one minute.) Stop. Twos, cross out the last word that your partner read. ___

5. Partner 2, you are going to read next. Partner 1, listen carefully to your partner. If your partner makes a mistake or leaves out a word, underline the word. Twos, get ready to read quietly to your partner. Begin. ___ (Time students for one minute.) Stop. Ones, cross out the last word that your partner read. ___

6. Please return your partner's book. ___ Let's figure out the total number of words you read. Find the line containing the last word that you read. ___ Now, find the number at the beginning of that line. ___ Start with that number and count on until you get to your last word. ___ Write the number. ___

7. Now, go back and count the number of words you missed. These words are underlined. ___ Write the number. ___

8. Please subtract to determine the number of words that you read correctly in one minute. ___ Write the number. ___

Note:
- Optional—You may select to have the students graph their daily fluency. For directions, see Appendix E, "Fluency Graph: Correct Words Per Minute" at the end of the *Teacher's Guide*. Each student's copy of the graph is on the last page of the *Student Book*.

Lesson 23

Materials Needed

- Lesson 23 from the *Student Book*
- Overhead Transparencies 33, 34, and 35
- Washable overhead transparency pen

- Paper or cardboard to use when covering the overhead transparencies
- Paper or cardboard for each student to use during spelling dictation

---

ACTIVITY A: **Vowel Combinations Review** (See the *Student Book*, page 90.)

1.	or	oo	i - e	oy	ar
2.	ee	e - e	oi	ai	er

> **Activity Procedure:** Have students review saying the sounds for letter combinations. When the letter combination has a box around it, ask students to tell you both sounds.

Note:
- Whenever you come to letters in a box, ask "What sound would you try first? What sound would you try next?"

1. Find Activity A. Let's review vowel combinations.

2. Point to the first letters in Line 1. What sound? __ Boxed letters. What sound would you try first? __ What sound would you try next? __ Next sound? __ Next sound? __ Next sound? __

3. (Continue Step 2 for letters in Line 2.)

ACTIVITY B: Vowel Conversions Review (See the *Student Book*, page 90.)

u	a	i	e	o

Activity Procedure: Have students review saying the sound, then the name for each letter.

1. Find Activity B. When you are reading words and see these letters, what would you try first, the name or the sound? __
2. Point to the first letter. What sound? __ What name? __
3. Next letter. What sound? __ What name? __
4. Next letter. What sound? __ What name? __
5. Next letter. What sound? __ What name? __
6. Next letter. What sound? __ What name? __

ACTIVITY C: Prefixes and Suffixes Review (See the *Student Book*, page 90.)

Prefixes				
1. dis	de	un	ex	ad
2. en	com	be	per	ab

Suffixes				
3. sive	able	ment	ful	ary
4. le	ate	ism	ous	ence
5. tive	ity	sion	y	er

Activity Procedure: Have students review saying prefixes and suffixes aloud.

1. Find Activity C.
2. Point to the first prefix in Line 1. What prefix? __ Next? __ Next? __ Next? __ Next? __
3. (Repeat Step 2 for prefixes in Line 2.)
4. Point to the first suffix in Line 3. What suffix? __ Next? __ Next? __ Next? __ Next? __
5. (Repeat Step 4 for suffixes in Lines 4 and 5.)

ACTIVITY D: **Strategy Practice** (See the *Student Book*, page 91.)

1.	reorganization	comparatively
2.	jealousy	immediately
3.	investigator	communication
4.	dissatisfaction	disadvantage

Activity Procedure: Have students circle prefixes and suffixes and underline the vowels. Have students say the word part by part to themselves and then as a whole word aloud.

 Use Overhead 33: Activity D

1. Find Activity D.

2. Circle prefixes and suffixes and underline the vowels. Look up when you are done. __

3. (Show the overhead transparency.) Now check and fix any mistakes. __

4. Go back to the first word. __ Sound out the word to yourself. Put your thumb up when you can read the word. Be sure that it is a real word. __ What word? __

5. Next word. (Pause.) What word? __

6. (Repeat Step 5 with all words in Activity D.)

Note:
• You may wish to provide additional practice by having students read a line to the group or to a partner.

ACTIVITY E: **Independent Strategy Practice** (See the *Student Book,* page 91.)

1.	administrative	vertically
2.	educationally	departmentally
3.	impossibility	operator
4.	completely	intentionally
5.	noisiest	discouragement

Activity Procedure: Have students look carefully at each word; locate prefixes, suffixes, and vowels; and figure out the word to themselves. Then, have students say the word aloud.

Use Overhead 33: Activity E

1. Find Activity E.

2. Find the first word in Line 1. Without circling and underlining, look carefully for prefixes and suffixes. Look for vowels in the rest of the word. If you have difficulty figuring out the word, use your pencil. Put your thumb up when you can say the word. __ (Give ample thinking time.)

3. (When students have decoded the word, ask...) What word? __

4. Next word. Put your thumb up when you can say the word. __ (Give ample thinking time.) What word? __

5. (Repeat Step 4 for the remaining words.)

Note:
• You may wish to provide additional practice by having students read a line to the group or to a partner.

ACTIVITY F: **Word Families** (See the *Student Book*, page 92.)

A	B
compare—to see how two things are alike	educate—to teach
comparison	education
comparable	educational
comparability	educationally
comparative	reeducate
comparatively	reeducating
incomparable	reeducation

Activity Procedure: Tell students the meaning of the first word in Column A. Have students read words in the first column to themselves, and then twice with the teacher. Then, have students read Column A to their partners. Repeat these procedures for the words in Column B, with opposite partners reading.

 Use Overhead 34: Activity F

1. Find Activity F.

2. Find the Column A word family. The first word is <u>compare</u>. Compare means "to see how two things are alike." The words in Column A have similar meanings to the word <u>compare</u>. Say each word in Column A to yourself until I say "Stop." __

3. Now let's read the words together. Touch under the first word and read each word with me. (Read the list of words with students.)

4   Let's read those words together again. Touch under the first word and read with me. (Read the list of words with students.)

5. Touch under the first word in Column A again. Partner 2, read the list to your partner. Look up when you are done. __   (Monitor partner reading.)

6. Find the Column B word family. The first word is <u>educate</u>. Educate means "to teach." The words in Column B have similar meanings to the word <u>educate</u>. Say each word in Column B to yourself until I say "Stop." __

7. (Repeat Steps 3–5 with words in Column B. In Step 5, have Partner 1 read.)

ACTIVITY G: **Spelling Dictation** (See the *Student Book,* page 92.)

1.	disadvantage	2.	administrative
3.	impossibility	4.	investigator

Activity Procedure: For each word, tell students the word, then have students say the parts of the word with you. Have them say the parts to themselves as they write the word. Then, have students compare their words with your word and cross out and rewrite any misspelled words.

Note:
- Distribute a piece of light cardboard to each of the students.

1. Find Activity G.

2. The first word is **disadvantage**. What word? __ Fist in the air. Say the parts of **disadvantage** with me. First part? __ Next part? __ Next part? __ Next part? __ Say the parts in **disadvantage** to yourself as you write the word. (Pause and monitor.)

3. (Write **disadvantage** on the board or overhead transparency.) Check **disadvantage**. If you misspelled it, cross it out and write it correctly.

4. The second word is **administrative**. What word? __ Fist in the air. Say the parts of **administrative** with me. First part? __ Next part? __ Next part? __ Next part? __ Next part? __ Say the parts in **administrative** to yourself as you write the word. (Pause and monitor.)

5. (Write **administrative** on the board or overhead transparency.) Check **administrative**. If you misspelled it, cross it out and write it correctly.

6. (Repeat the procedures for the words **impossibility** and **investigator**.)

ACTIVITY H: **Vocabulary** (See the *Student Book,* page 92.)

a.	the result of organizing again (Activity D)	reorganization
b.	a person who investigates or studies (Activity D)	investigator
c.	in a manner that is educational (Activity E)	educationally

1. Find Activity H.

2. Listen to the first definition, "the result of organizing again." Look back at the words in Activity D. Find the word and write it. (Pause and monitor.) What word means "the result of organizing again"? __ (*reorganization*)

3. Listen to the next definition, "a person who investigates or studies." Look back at the words in Activity D. Find the word and write it. (Pause and monitor.) What word means "a person who investigates or studies"? __ (*investigator*)

4. Next definition. "In a manner that is educational." Look back at the words in Activity E. Find the word and write it. (Pause and monitor.) What word means "in a manner that is educational"? __ (*educationally*)

ACTIVITY I: **Passage Preparation** (See the *Student Book,* page 93.)

Part 1—Tell

1.	*Scientific American*	*n.*	a magazine
2.	Missouri	*n.*	a state in the United States
3.	Minnesota	*n.*	a state in the United States
4.	Australia	*n.*	a country
5.	scientists	*n.*	people having knowledge of science
6.	weird	*adj.*	very odd or strange
7.	bizarre	*adj.*	freaky
*8.	unfamiliar	*adj.*	not well known

Part 2—Strategy Practice

9.	century	*n.*	100 years
10.	multiple	*adj.*	many
*11.	witness	*n.*	a person who saw something happen
12.	incidents	*n.*	events
*13.	phenomenon	*n.*	an unusual event
*14.	explanation	*n.*	that which is said or written that makes something clear
15.	logical	*adj.*	having to do with logic or with making sense
16.	precipitation	*n.*	rain, snow, or hail
17.	manufacture	*v.*	to make things with machines, usually in a factory
18.	thudded	*v.*	made a heavy, dull sound

Activity Procedure: For the first set of words, tell students each word and have them read its definition. Then, have students practice reading the words themselves. The second set of words can be read using the part-by-part strategy. Have students circle prefixes and suffixes, then underline the vowels. Using the overhead transparency, assist students in checking their work. Next, have students figure out each word to themselves, then say it aloud. Have them read the part of speech and definition aloud. Finally, use the scripted wording to introduce the four starred vocabulary words that provide a preview of the passage.

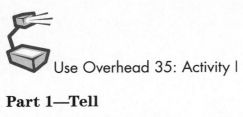

Use Overhead 35: Activity I

Part 1—Tell

1. (Show the top half of Overhead 35.) Before we read today's passage, let's read the difficult words. (Point to **Scientific American**.) The first words are **Scientific American**. What words? __ Now read the definition with me. "A magazine."

2. (Point to **Missouri**.) The next word is **Missouri**. What word? __ Read the definition with me. "A state in the United States."

3. (Pronounce each word in Part 1, and then have students repeat each word and read the definition with you.)

4. Find Activity I, Part 1, in your book. __ Let's read the words again. First word. __ Next word. __ (Continue for all words in Part 1.)

Part 2—Strategy Practice

1. Find Part 2. For each word, circle the prefixes and suffixes and underline the vowels. Look up when you are done. __

2. (Show the bottom half of Overhead 35.) Now check and fix any mistakes. __

3. Go back to the first word. __ Sound out the word to yourself. Put your thumb up when you can read the word. Be sure that it is a real word. __ What word? __ Now, read the definition. __

4. (Continue Step 3 with all remaining words in Part 2.)

Note:
- You may wish to provide additional practice by having students read words to a partner.

Part 3—Starred Vocabulary

1. Let's study some of the words in Activity I. Find word #8. __ What word? (*unfamiliar*) When something is not well known, we say it is _____. (*unfamiliar*) If you had never seen a lunar eclipse, it would be _____. (*unfamiliar*) If you had never seen snow, it would be __ (*unfamiliar*) In this passage, you will learn about a weather event that is _____. (*unfamiliar*)

2. Find #11. __ What word? (*witness*) When a person sees an event happen, that person is a _____. (*witness*). If people saw a crime being committed, they would be _____. (*witnesses*) In this passage, unfamiliar weather events are seen by _____. (*witnesses*)

3. Find #13. __ What word? (*phenomenon*) A very unusual event is called a _____. (*phenomenon*) Having animals fall from the sky would be a strange _____. (*phenomenon*)

4. Find #14. __ What word? (*explanation*) When you write or say something that makes something clear, you are giving an _____. (*explanation*) When scientists write about the phenomenon of animals falling from the sky and try to explain it, the scientists are giving an _____. (*explanation*)

ACTIVITY J: **Passage Reading and Comprehension** (See the *Student Book,* pages 94 and 95.)

Weird Rain

9	When someone says, "It's raining cats and dogs," we don't expect to look out the window and see animals. We
20	know the person is talking about a downpour, or heavy
30	rainfall. (#1) As far as we know, no cats or dogs have
41	actually fallen from the sky. But, what if someone said it
52	was raining frogs and toads? Is that another way of saying
63	the same thing as "raining cats and dogs"? Not according
73	to multiple news accounts of unusual occurrences. (#2)
80	For more than a century, people have reported bizarre
89	incidents in which rain has included frogs, fish, or frozen
99	turtles. Try to picture in your mind what this might look
110	like. In 1873, *Scientific American* described a shower of
119	frogs that darkened the air and fell to the ground during a
131	rainstorm in Missouri. (#3) In 1901, witnesses in Minnesota
139	told a rare story. They said that they heard an unfamiliar
150	plopping outside. It sounded like falling lumps of mud,
159	not like rain or hail. Outside, they saw a huge green mass
171	coming down from the sky. When the storm was over, they
182	saw hundreds of frogs and toads piled three inches deep
192	and covering more than four blocks! (#4)
198	Many other animals have thudded to the ground
206	as well. Different kinds of fish have fallen on priests in
217	Australia, golfers in England, and families in Singapore.
225	Sometimes birds frozen like hailstones have dropped to
233	the earth. In 1930, *Nature* magazine told a story about a
244	turtle wrapped in ice that fell during a hailstorm. (#5)
253	How does this strange precipitation happen? Some
260	scientists believe they have a logical explanation for the
269	weird rain or hail. They tell us that a violent thunderstorm
280	picks up animals from shallow ponds or creeks and pulls
290	the animals high into the air. Then these whirlwinds carry
300	the animals for hundreds of miles before throwing them
309	to the ground. They compare this phenomenon to what
318	happens in dry areas where huge, whirling dust storms are
328	constantly dropping rubbish out of the sky. (#6)
335	Other scientists say that we don't really know how
344	weird rain happens. In another odd event, however, a
353	tornado dropped unopened soft drink cans. The cans were

362	marked with the name of the manufacturing plant. The
371	plant was 150 miles away from where the full cans landed.
382	Whether the logical explanations are proved or not, let's
391	hope the weatherperson doesn't start predicting soft drink
399	showers for tomorrow's weather. (#7)
403	

A.	☐	**Total number of words read**
B.	☐	**Total number of underlined words (mistakes)**
C.	☐	**Total number of words read correctly**

Activity Procedure: Have students work on accuracy by having them read the passage silently to each embedded number, and then reread the same section orally to a partner, together as a group, or individually. When students finish reading a section orally, ask the corresponding comprehension question. When the passage has been read, have students work on fluency by having them read the passage first to themselves twice, and then to a partner. Have students determine the number of words read correctly and graph it (if you have chosen this option).

Passage Reading—Accuracy

1. Find Activity J. You are going to read a passage and answer questions about what you've read. Today's passage is about a weird and unfamiliar weather phenomenon. You will learn about things that witnesses claimed to have seen all the way back to 1873. Read the title with me. "Weird Rain."

2. Find #1 in the passage. (Pause.) Read down to #1 silently. Look up when you are done. __

3. (Wait for students to complete the reading. Then have students reread the section by having them read orally to a partner, read together orally as a group, or read aloud individually.)

4. (Ask the question associated with the number. Provide feedback to students regarding their answers.)

5. (Repeat Steps 2, 3, and 4 for all sections of the passage.)

Comprehension Questions
(Numbers corresponding to these questions are placed throughout the passage at points at which they should be asked during oral reading.)

1. What do people usually mean when they say "it's raining cats and dogs"? (*There is a downpour, or heavy rainfall.*)

2. Does "raining frogs and toads" mean the same thing as "raining cats and dogs"? (*No.*)

3. According to an article in *Scientific American*, what happened in Missouri in 1873? (*During a rainstorm, frogs fell to the ground.*)

4. According to witnesses, what happened in Minnesota in 1901? (*Hundreds of frogs and toads fell from the sky and piled up to three inches deep.*)

5. What other animals have people reported as falling from the sky? (*Different kinds of fish and birds, and a turtle.*)

6. What do some scientists believe is a logical explanation? (*Violent thunderstorms pick up animals from shallow ponds, and whirlwinds carry them for hundreds of miles and then drop them.*)

7. How did full soda cans travel 150 miles from the manufacturer and drop from the sky? (*They were sucked up in a tornado, carried 150 miles away, and then dropped.*)

Summative Question

8. What response would you have if you were a witness to this phenomenon? Talk it over with your partner.

Passage Reading—Fluency

1. Now it's time for fluency building.

2. Find the beginning of the passage. (Pause.) Whisper-read. See how many words you can read in a minute. Begin. __ (Time students for one minute.) Stop. Circle the last word that you read. __

3. Let's practice again. Return to the beginning of the passage. __ See if you can read more words. Begin. __ (Time students for one minute.) Stop. Put a box around the last word that you read. __

4. Please exchange books with your partner. __ Partner 2, you are going to read first. Partner 1, listen and underline any mistakes or words left out. Twos, begin. __ (Time students for one minute.) Stop. Ones, cross out the last word that your partner read. __

5. Partner 1, you are going to read next. Partner 2, listen and underline any mistakes or words left out. Ones, begin. __ (Time students for one minute.) Stop. Twos, cross out the last word that your partner read. __

6. Please return your partner's book. __ Figure out the total number of words you read correctly and write it in Box C. __

Note:
- Optional—You may select to have the students graph their daily fluency. For directions, see Appendix E, "Fluency Graph: Correct Words Per Minute" at the end of the *Teacher's Guide*. Each student's copy of the graph is on the last page of the *Student Book*.

Lesson 24

Materials Needed

- Lesson 24 from the *Student Book*
- Overhead Transparencies 36, 37, and 38
- Washable overhead transparency pen
- Paper or cardboard to use when covering the overhead transparencies
- Paper or cardboard for each student to use during spelling dictation

ACTIVITY A: **Vowel Combinations Review** (See the *Student Book*, page 96.)

1.	u - e	ea	au	oa	o - e
2.	ay	ou	oo	ow	ur

Activity Procedure: Have students review saying the sounds for letter combinations. When the letter combination has a box around it, ask students to tell you both sounds.

Note:
- Whenever you come to letters in a box, ask "What sound would you try first? What sound would you try next?"

1. Find Activity A. Let's review vowel combinations.

2. Point to the first letters in Line 1. What sound? __ Boxed letters. What sound would you try first? __ What sound would you try next? __ Next sound? __ Next sound? __ Next sound? __

3. (Continue Step 2 for letters in Line 2.)

ACTIVITY B: **Vowel Conversions Review** (See the *Student Book,* page 96.)

o	i	e	u	a

> **Activity Procedure:** Have students review saying the sound, then the name for each letter.

1. Find Activity B. When you are reading words and see these letters, what would you try first, the sound or the name? __

2. Point to the first letter. What sound? __ What name? __

3. Next letter. What sound? __ What name? __

4. Next letter. What sound? __ What name? __

5. Next letter. What sound? __ What name? __

6. Next letter. What sound? __ What name? __

ACTIVITY C: **Prefixes and Suffixes Review** (See the *Student Book,* page 96.)

Prefixes				
1.	mis	in	con	pre	pro
2.	a	im	re	com	ad

Suffixes				
3.	ness	ing	ist	est	ant
4.	ance	ture	ible	ize	ent
5.	sive	ish	al	or	tion

> **Activity Procedure:** Have students review saying prefixes and suffixes aloud.

1. Find Activity C.

2. Point to the first prefix in Line 1. What prefix? __ Next? __ Next? __ Next? __ Next? __

3. (Repeat Step 2 for prefixes in Line 2.)

4. Point to the first suffix in Line 3. What suffix? __ Next? __ Next? __ Next? __ Next? __

5. (Repeat Step 4 for suffixes in Lines 4 and 5.)

ACTIVITY D: **Strategy Practice** (See the *Student Book,* page 97.)

1.	productivity	escalator
2.	unmistakable	imperfectly
3.	tantalize	redundantly
4.	unavoidable	unmanageable

Activity Procedure: Have students circle prefixes and suffixes and underline the vowels. Have students say the word part by part to themselves and then as a whole word aloud.

 Use Overhead 36: Activity D

1.   Find Activity D.

2.   Circle prefixes and suffixes and underline the vowels. Look up when you are done. __

3.   (Show the overhead transparency.) Now check and fix any mistakes. __

4.   Go back to the first word. __ Sound out the word to yourself. Put your thumb up when you can read the word. Be sure that it is a real word. __What word? __

5.   Next word. (Pause.) What word? __

6.   (Repeat Step 5 with all words in Activity D.)

Note:
• You may wish to provide additional practice by having students read a line to the group or to a partner.

ACTIVITY E: **Independent Strategy Practice** (See the *Student Book,* page 97.)

1.	unattractiveness	exceptionality
2.	preparation	disagreements
3.	meaningfulness	publicize
4.	dramatically	radiant
5.	inconsistence	reactionary

Activity Procedure: Have students look carefully at each word; locate prefixes, suffixes, and vowels; and figure out the word to themselves. Then, have students say the word aloud.

 Use Overhead 36: Activity E

1. Find Activity E.

2. Find the first word in Line 1. Without circling and underlining, look carefully for prefixes and suffixes. Look for vowels in the rest of the word. If you have difficulty figuring out the word, use your pencil. Put your thumb up when you can say the word. __ (Give ample thinking time.)

3. (When students have decoded the word, ask...) What word? __

4. Next word. Put your thumb up when you can say the word. __ (Give ample thinking time.) What word? __

5. (Repeat Step 4 for the remaining words.)

Note:
  • You may wish to provide additional practice by having students read a line to the group or to a partner.

ACTIVITY F: **Word Families** (See the *Student Book,* page 98.)

A	B
continue—to keep doing something	consist—to be made up of
continued	consistent
continuing	consistently
continuation	consistence
continual	consistency
continually	inconsistent
continuous	inconsistence

Activity Procedure: Tell students the meaning of the first word in Column A. Have students read words in the first column to themselves, and then twice with the teacher. Then, have students read Column A to their partners. Repeat these procedures for the words in Column B, with opposite partners reading.

 Use Overhead 37: Activity F

1. Find Activity F.

2. Find the Column A word family. The first word is <u>continue</u>. Continue means "to keep doing something." The words in Column A have similar meanings to the word <u>continue</u>. Say each word in Column A to yourself until I say "Stop." __

3. Now let's read the words together. Touch under the first word and read each word with me. (Read the list of words with students.)

4. Let's read those words together again. Touch under the first word and read with me. (Read the list of words with students.)

5. Touch under the first word in Column A again. Partner 1, read the list to your partner. Look up when you are done. __ (Monitor partner reading.)

6. Find the Column B word family. The first word is <u>consist</u>. Consist means "to be made up of." The words in Column B have similar meanings to the word <u>consist</u>. Say each word in Column B to yourself until I say "Stop." __

7. (Repeat Steps 3–5 with words in Column B. In Step 5, have Partner 2 read.)

ACTIVITY G: **Spelling Dictation** (See the *Student Book,* page 98.)

1. imperfectly	2. unavoidable
3. publicize	4. disagreements

Activity Procedure: For each word, tell students the word, then have students say the parts of the word with you. Have them say the parts to themselves as they write the word. Then, have students compare their words with your word and cross out and rewrite any misspelled words.

Note:
- Distribute a piece of light cardboard to each of the students.

1. Find Activity G.

2. The first word is **imperfectly**. What word? __ Fist in the air. Say the parts of **imperfectly** with me. First part? __ Next part? __ Next part? __ Next part? __ Say the parts in **imperfectly** to yourself as you write the word. (Pause and monitor.)

3. (Write **imperfectly** on the board or overhead transparency.) Check **imperfectly**. If you misspelled it, cross it out and write it correctly.

4. The second word is **unavoidable**. What word? __ Fist in the air. Say the parts of **unavoidable** with me. First part? __ Next part? __ Next part? __ Next part? __ Say the parts in **unavoidable** to yourself as you write the word. (Pause and monitor.)

5. (Write **unavoidable** on the board or overhead transparency.) Check **unavoidable**. If you misspelled it, cross it out and write it correctly.

6. (Repeat the procedures for the words **publicize** and **disagreements**.)

ACTIVITY H: **Vocabulary** (See the *Student Book*, page 98.)

a.	the state of being productive or making a lot (Activity D) <u>productivity</u>
b.	not able to be managed or controlled (Activity D) <u>unmanageable</u>
c.	the act of preparing something or making something ready for use (Activity E) <u>preparation</u>

1. Find Activity H.

2. Listen to the first definition, "the state of being productive or making a lot." Look back at the words in Activity D. Find the word and write it. (Pause and monitor.) What word means "the state of being productive or making a lot"? __ (*productivity*)

3. Listen to the next definition, "not able to be managed or controlled." Look back at the words in Activity D. Find the word and write it. (Pause and monitor.) What word means "not able to be managed or controlled"? __ (*unmanageable*)

4. Next definition. "The act of preparing something or making something ready for use." Look back at the words in Activity E. Find the word and write it. (Pause and monitor.) What word means "the act of preparing something or making something ready for use"? __ (*preparation*)

ACTIVITY I: **Passage Preparation** (See the *Student Book,* page 99.)

Part 1—Tell

*1.	record breaker	*n.*	someone or something that beats a previous record
2.	measured	*v.*	figured out the amount in inches, meters, miles, etc.
3.	koala bear	*n.*	an animal of Australia
4.	eucalyptus	*n.*	a tree of Australia
5.	Galapagos Islands	*n.*	islands of South America
6.	tortoise	*n.*	a turtle
7.	endangered species	*n.*	a species of animal or plant that may die out
8.	Thailand	*n.*	a country

Part 2—Strategy Practice

9.	explorers	*n.*	people who travel to new places to learn about them
*10.	category	*n.*	a group of ideas or things
*11.	feature	*n.*	a distinct part of something, such as a part of your face
12.	imaginable	*adj.*	able to be imagined
13.	contrast	*n.*	a difference
*14.	amazing	*adj.*	surprising
15.	hibernate	*v.*	to sleep through the winter
16.	caterpillar	*n.*	wormlike animal that becomes a butterfly or moth
17.	multitude	*n.*	a very large number of people or things
18.	host	*n.*	a very large number of people or things

Activity Procedure: For the first set of words, tell students each word and have them read its definition. Then, have students practice reading the words themselves. The second set of words can be read using the part-by-part strategy. Have students circle prefixes and suffixes, then underline the vowels. Using the overhead transparency, assist students in checking their work. Next, have students figure out each word to themselves, then say it aloud. Have them read the part of speech and definition aloud. Finally, use the scripted wording to introduce the four starred vocabulary words that provide a preview of the passage.

Use Overhead 38: Activity I

Part 1—Tell

1. (Show the top half of Overhead 38.) Before we read today's passage, let's read the difficult words. (Point to **record breaker**.) The first words are **record breaker**. What words? __ Now read the definition with me. "Someone or something that beats a previous record."

2. (Point to **measured**.) The next word is **measured**. What word? __ Read the definition with me. "Figured out the amount in inches, meters, miles, etc."

3. (Pronounce each word in Part 1, and then have students repeat each word and read the definition with you.)

4. Find Activity I, Part 1, in your book. __ Let's read the words again. First word. __ Next word. __ (Continue for all words in Part 1.)

Part 2—Strategy Practice

1. Find Part 2. For each word, circle the prefixes and suffixes and underline the vowels. Look up when you are done. __

2. (Show the bottom half of Overhead 38.) Now check and fix any mistakes. __

3. Go back to the first word. __ Sound out the word to yourself. Put your thumb up when you can read the word. Be sure that it is a real word. __ What word? __ Now, read the definition. __

4. (Continue Step 3 with all remaining words in Part 2.)

Note:
- You may wish to provide additional practice by having students read words to a partner.

Part 3—Starred Vocabulary

1. Let's study some of the words in Activity I. Find word #1. __ What words? (*record breaker*) When someone or something beats a previous record, they would be called a _____. (*record breaker*) If you ran faster than anyone else, you would be a _____. (*record breaker*) If an animal was larger than any other animal, it would be a _____. (*record breaker*) This fascinating passage is about animals that are _____. (*record breakers*)

2. Find #10. __ What word? (*category*) A group of ideas or things can be called a _____. (*category*) When you think of humans, women form one group or _____. (*category*) Men form another group or _____. (*category*) Ones, tell your partner some categories of animals. __

3. Find #11. __ What word? (*feature*) A distinct part of something such as your face is called a _____. (*feature*) A nice smile, dark brown eyes, dimples, and large ears are all _____. (*features*) For a dog, soft fur, a long snout, a pink nose, and a fuzzy tail would be called _____. (*features*) Twos, tell your partner some features of a turtle.

4. Find #14. __ What word? (*amazing*) When something is very surprising, it is
    sometimes called _____. (*amazing*) For example, the huge size of the tortoise
    on the Galapagos Islands is so surprising, we would say it is _____. (*amazing*)
    The amount that some caterpillars eat is so surprising, we would say it is _____.
    (*amazing*) In this passage, you will learn about some amazing animals.

ACTIVITY J: **Passage Reading and Comprehension** (See the *Student Book,* pages 100
and 101.)

Record Breakers in the Animal World

9	In the animal world, record breakers exist in every category imaginable. People could tell you which animal
17	is the biggest, the tallest, the smallest, and the heaviest of
28	all animals. People could tell you which animal is fussiest,
38	hungriest, thirstiest, and quietest. Animals hold records
45	for shouting the loudest, diving the deepest, hibernating
53	the longest, and digging the biggest burrows. (#1)
60	Record breakers in the animal world live on every
69	continent on earth. Some live on only one continent, and
79	some live on every continent. The fussiest eater, the koala
89	bear, lives only in Australia. (#2) Even though more than
98	100 types of eucalyptus trees grow in Australia, the koala
108	bear eats leaves from only 12 types. In fact, the koala
119	bear is so fussy, it cannot eat anything except eucalyptus
129	leaves. (#3)
130	The hungriest animal on earth lives on all continents.
139	Perhaps you have heard of the hungry caterpillar. It eats
149	constantly. From the time it hatches until it turns into a
160	butterfly, it eats so much that its weight can increase as
171	much as 3,000 times. (#4)
175	The longest earthworm in the world lives in southern
184	Africa. Someone actually measured the biggest one he or
193	she found, and it was more than 6 meters (20 feet) long.
205	That is longer than three tall men lying on the ground head
217	to toe. (#5)
219	In contrast, the world's smallest mammal is no bigger
228	than a human's thumb. Thailand's bumblebee bat weighs
236	less than a penny. Bumblebee bats are one of the 12 most
248	endangered species. At last count, the Thai government
256	could find only 160. (#6)
260	A multitude of howler monkeys still exist, though, in
269	Central and South America. The male howlers have the

278	distinction of being the world's noisiest land animal.
286	A special box in their throat makes their shouts so loud,
297	they can be heard almost 10 miles away! (#7)
305	The tortoise that lives on the Galapagos Islands is the
315	largest tortoise found anywhere. (#8) The word *galápago*
322	is Spanish for "tortoise," which is why explorers gave the
332	islands that name. A mature Galapagos tortoise can weigh
341	as much as 700 pounds, measure 4 feet in length, and live
353	as long as 200 years. (#9)
358	Most humans never tire of finding out which animals
367	break records for speed, size, amount they eat or drink,
377	number of offspring they bring into the world at one time,
388	or a host of other animal features. Whether they are the
399	oldest, loudest, or most endangered, animals are quite
407	amazing. (#10)
408	

A.   ☐   **Total number of words read**

B.   ☐   **Total number of underlined words (mistakes)**

C.   ☐   **Total number of words read correctly**

Activity Procedure: Have students work on accuracy by having them read the passage silently to each embedded number, and then reread the same section orally to a partner, together as a group, or individually. When students finish reading a section orally, ask the corresponding comprehension question. When the passage has been read, have students work on fluency by having them read the passage first to themselves twice, and then to a partner. Have students determine the number of words read correctly and graph it (if you have chosen this option).

Passage Reading—Accuracy

1. Find Activity J. You are going to read a passage and answer questions about what you've read. Today's passage is about some amazing animals. You will learn about the fussiest, the hungriest, and the longest animals, as well as other record breakers. Read the title with me. "Record Breakers in the Animal World."

2. Read down to #1 silently. Look up when you are done. __

3. (When students finish reading, have them reread the section orally to a partner, together orally as a group, or aloud individually.)

4. (Ask the question associated with the number. Provide feedback for students' answers.)

5. (Repeat Steps 2, 3, and 4 for all sections of the passage.)

Comprehension Questions

(Numbers corresponding to these questions are placed throughout the passage at points at which they should be asked during oral reading.)

1. What are some records held by animals? (*Biggest, tallest, smallest, heaviest, fussiest, hungriest, thirstiest, quietest. Shouting the loudest, diving the deepest, hibernating the longest, digging the biggest burrows.*)

2. Where do the fussiest eaters of the animal kingdom live? (*In Australia.*)

3. Why are koalas called the fussiest eaters of the animal world? (*They eat only eucalyptus leaves; of those available, they eat leaves from only 12 types of eucalyptus trees.*)

4. Which animal is the hungriest on earth? (*The caterpillar.*)

5. How long is the longest earthworm on earth? (*More than 6 meters or 20 feet long; longer than three tall men lying head to toe.*)

6. Why are Thailand's bumblebee bats considered to be among the 12 most endangered species? (*The Thai government could find only 160 of them at last count.*)

7. What makes howler monkeys the noisiest land animal? (*They have a special box in their throats; they are so loud, they can be heard 10 miles away.*)

8. Where is the largest tortoise in the world found? (*On the Galapagos Islands.*)

9. Describe a mature Galapagos tortoise. (*It can weigh up to 700 pounds, measure 4 feet in length, and live up to 200 years.*)

Summative Question

10. Which record were you the most amazed by? Why? First Ones and then Twos.

Passage Reading—Fluency

1. Now it's time for fluency building.

2. Find the beginning of the passage. (Pause.) Whisper-read. See how many words you can read in a minute. Begin. __ (Time students for one minute.) Stop. Circle the last word that you read. __

3. Let's practice again. Return to the beginning of the passage. (Pause.) See if you can read more words. Begin. __ (Time students for one minute.) Stop. Put a box around the last word that you read. __

4. Please exchange books with your partner. __ Partner 1, you are going to read first. Partner 2, listen and underline any mistakes or words left out. Ones, begin. __ (Time students for one minute.) Stop. Twos, cross out the last word that your partner read. __

5. Partner 2, you are going to read next. Partner 1, listen and underline any mistakes or words left out. Twos, begin. __ (Time students for one minute.) Stop. Ones, cross out the last word that your partner read. __

6. Please return your partner's book. __ Figure out the total number of words you read correctly and write it in Box C. __ (Optional: Have students graph it.)

Lesson 25

Materials Needed

- Lesson 25 from the *Student Book*
- Overhead Transparencies 39, 40, and 41
- Washable overhead transparency pen
- Paper or cardboard to use when covering the overhead transparencies
- Paper or cardboard for each student to use during spelling dictation

ACTIVITY A: **Vowel Combinations Review** (See the *Student Book*, page 102.)

1.	a - e	oo	i - e	ir	oy
2.	ee	ai	ar	or	ow

Activity Procedure: Have students review saying the sounds for letter combinations. When the letter combination has a box around it, ask students to tell you both sounds.

Note:
- Whenever you come to letters in a box, ask "What sound would you try first? What sound would you try next?"

1. Find Activity A.

2. Point to the first letters in Line 1. What sound? __ Boxed letters. What sound would you try first? __ What sound would you try next? __ Next sound? __ Next sound? __ Next sound? __

3. (Continue Step 2 for letters in Line 2.)

ACTIVITY B: **Vowel Conversions Review** (See the *Student Book,* page 102.)

a	u	i	e	o

> **Activity Procedure:** Have students review saying the sound, then the name for each letter.

1. Find Activity B. When you are reading words and see these letters, what would you try first, the name or the sound? __
2. Point to the first letter. What sound? __ What name? __
3. Next letter. What sound? __ What name? __
4. Next letter. What sound? __ What name? __
5. Next letter. What sound? __ What name? __
6. Next letter. What sound? __ What name? __

ACTIVITY C: **Prefixes and Suffixes Review** (See the *Student Book,* page 102.)

Prefixes				
1. un	dis	per	en	ex
2. ab	com	de	con	be

Suffixes				
3. less	ic	ful	sion	tive
4. y	ment	ly	ous	able
5. ate	ism	age	ary	ence

> **Activity Procedure:** Have students review saying prefixes and suffixes aloud.

1. Find Activity C.
2. Point to the first prefix in Line 1. What prefix? __ Next? __ Next? __ Next? __ Next? __
3. (Repeat Step 2 for prefixes in Line 2.)
4. Point to the first suffix in Line 3. What suffix? __ Next? __ Next? __ Next? __ Next? __
5. (Repeat Step 4 for suffixes in Lines 4 and 5.)

ACTIVITY D: **Strategy Practice** (See the *Student Book*, page 103.)

1.	unrepairable	respectability
2.	individuality	occasionally
3.	mismanagement	generosity
4.	environmentally	disappearance

Activity Procedure: Have students circle prefixes and suffixes and underline the vowels. Have students say the word part by part to themselves and then as a whole word aloud.

 Use Overhead 39: Activity D

1.   Find Activity D.

2.   Circle prefixes and suffixes and underline the vowels. Look up when you are done. __

3.   (Show the overhead transparency.) Now check and fix any mistakes. __

4.   Go back to the first word. __ Sound out the word to yourself. Put your thumb up when you can read the word. Be sure that it is a real word. __ What word? __

5.   Next word. (Pause.) What word? __

6.   (Repeat Step 5 with all words in Activity D.)

Note:
• You may wish to provide additional practice by having students read a line to the group or to a partner.

ACTIVITY E: **Independent Strategy Practice** (See the *Student Book*, page 103.)

1.	competition	tremendously
2.	instrumentalist	superintendent
3.	additionally	dissimilarity
4.	impracticality	fundamentally
5.	indescribable	unconventionality

Activity Procedure: Have students figure out each word to themselves. Then, have students say the word aloud.

 Use Overhead 39: Activity E

1.   Find Activity E.

2.   Find the first word in Line 1. Put your thumb up when you can say the word. __ (Give ample thinking time.)

3.   (When students have decoded the word, ask...) What word? ___

4.   Next word. Put your thumb up when you can say the word. __ (Give ample thinking time.) What word? __

5.   (Repeat Step 4 for the remaining words.)

Note:
• You may wish to provide additional practice by having students read a line to the group or to a partner.

ACTIVITY F: **Word Families** (See the *Student Book,* page 104.)

A	B
manage—to tell a group what to do	appear—to come into sight
manager	appearance
management	disappear
manageable	disappears
mismanage	disappearing
mismanaged	disappearance
unmanageable	disappearances

Activity Procedure: Tell students the meaning of the first word in Column A. Have students read words in the first column to themselves, and then twice with the teacher. Then, have students read Column A to their partners. Repeat these procedures for the words in Column B, with opposite partners reading.

 Use Overhead 40: Activity F

1. Find Activity F.

2. Find the Column A word family. The first word is <u>manage</u>. Manage means "to tell a group what to do." The words in Column A have similar meanings to the word <u>manage</u>. Say each word in Column A to yourself until I say "Stop." __

3. Now let's read the words together. Touch under the first word and read each word with me. (Read the list of words with students.)

4. Let's read those words together again. Touch under the first word and read with me. (Read the list of words with students.)

5. Touch under the first word in Column A again. Partner 2, read the list to your partner. Look up when you are done. __ (Monitor partner reading.)

6. Find the Column B word family. The first word is <u>appear</u>. Appear means "to come into sight." The words in Column B have similar meanings to the word <u>appear</u>. Say each word in Column B to yourself until I say "Stop." __

7. (Repeat Steps 3–5 with words in Column B. In Step 5, have Partner 1 read.)

ACTIVITY G: **Spelling Dictation** (See the *Student Book,* page 104.)

1.	tremendously	2.	competition
3.	individuality	4.	generosity

Activity Procedure: For each word, tell students the word, then have students say the parts of the word with you. Have them say the parts to themselves as they write the word. Then, have students compare their words with your word and cross out and rewrite any misspelled words.

Note:
- Distribute a piece of light cardboard to each of the students.

1. Find Activity G.

2. The first word is **tremendously**. What word? ___ Fist in the air. Say the parts of **tremendously** with me. First part? ___ Next part? ___ Next part? ___ Next part? ___ Say the parts in **tremendously** to yourself as you write the word. (Pause and monitor.)

3. (Write **tremendously** on the board or overhead transparency.) Check **tremendously**. If you misspelled it, cross it out and write it correctly.

4. The second word is **competition**. What word? ___ Fist in the air. Say the parts of **competition** with me. First part? ___ Next part? ___ Next part? ___ Next part? ___ Say the parts in **competition** to yourself as you write the word. (Pause and monitor.)

5. (Write **competition** on the board or overhead transparency.) Check **competition**. If you misspelled it, cross it out and write it correctly.

6. (Repeat the procedures for the words **individuality** and **generosity**.)

ACTIVITY H: **Vocabulary** (See the *Student Book,* page 104.)

a.	not able to be repaired or fixed (Activity D)	_unrepairable_
b.	someone who makes music on an instrument (Activity E)	_instrumentalist_
c.	not able to be described (Activity E)	_indescribable_

1. Find Activity H.

2. Listen to the first definition, "not able to be repaired or fixed." Look back at the words in Activity D. Find the word and write it. (Pause and monitor.) What word means "not able to be repaired or fixed"? __ (*unrepairable*)

3. Listen to the next definition, "someone who makes music on an instrument." Look back at the words in Activity E. Find the word and write it. (Pause and monitor.) What word means "someone who makes music on an instrument"? __ (*instrumentalist*)

4. Next definition. "Not able to be described." Look back at the words in Activity E. Find the word and write it. (Pause and monitor.) What word means "not able to be described"? __ (*indescribable*)

ACTIVITY I: **Passage Preparation** (See the *Student Book*, page 105.)

Part 1—Tell

1.	Soviet Union	*n.*	the name of a former country
2.	Russian	*adj.*	related to the country of Russia
3.	cosmonaut	*n.*	a Russian astronaut
4.	Laika	*n.*	the name of a dog that went into space
*5.	knowledge	*n.*	facts that have been learned
6.	atmosphere	*n.*	the air above the earth
7.	species	*n.*	a specific kind of plant or animal
8.	medicines	*n.*	drugs used to treat diseases

Part 2—Strategy Practice

9.	vertical	*adj.*	standing or pointing straight up
10.	capsule	*n.*	a closed container
11.	researchers	*n.*	people who study something
12.	monument	*n.*	a building or statue built in memory of a person or event
13.	memorial	*n.*	something in memory of a person or event including a monument
*14.	monitor	*v.*	to keep a close watch on
*15.	respond	*v.*	to give an answer
*16.	resemble	*v.*	to look like
17.	good-natured	*adj.*	nice; easygoing
18.	weightlessness	*n.*	the state of having little or no weight—especially when out in space

---

Activity Procedure: For the first set of words, tell students each word and have them read its definition. Then, have students practice reading the words themselves. The second set of words can be read using the part-by-part strategy. Have students circle prefixes and suffixes, then underline the vowels. Using the overhead transparency, assist students in checking their work. Next, have students figure out each word to themselves, then say it aloud. Have them read the part of speech and definition aloud. Finally, use the scripted wording to introduce the four starred vocabulary words that provide a preview of the passage.

Use Overhead 41: Activity I

Part 1—Tell

1. (Show the top half of Overhead 41.) Before we read today's passage, let's read the difficult words. (Point to **Soviet Union**.) The first words are **Soviet Union**. What words? __ Now read the definition with me. "The name of a former country."

2. (Point to **Russian**.) The next word is **Russian**. What word? __ Read the definition with me. "Related to the country of Russia."

3. (Pronounce each word in Part 1, and then have students repeat each word and read the definition with you.)

4. Find Activity I, Part 1, in your book. __ Let's read the words again. First word. __ Next word. __ (Continue for all words in Part 1.)

Part 2—Strategy Practice

1. Find Part 2. For each word, circle the prefixes and suffixes and underline the vowels. Look up when you are done. __

2. (Show the bottom half of Overhead 41.) Now check and fix any mistakes. __

3. Go back to the first word. __ Sound out the word to yourself. Put your thumb up when you can read the word. Be sure that it is a real word. __ What word? __ Now, read the definition. __

4. (Continue Step 3 with all remaining words in Part 2.)

Note:
• You may wish to provide additional practice by having students read words to a partner.

Part 3—Starred Vocabulary

1. Let's study some of the words in Activity I. Find #5. __ What word? (*knowledge*) The facts that we learn about things can be called _____. (*knowledge*) One way that we have extended our knowledge is through space exploration. You have all heard of the astronauts who went into space, but you may not know about all the animals that have traveled into space so that we could gain more _____. (*knowledge*)

2. Find #14. __ What word? (*monitor*) If you keep a close watch on something, it would be _____. (*monitored*) If teachers closely watch children who have gone out to recess, the children would be _____. (*monitored*) If guards closely watch prisoners in the jail cafeteria, the prisoners would be _____. (*monitored*) When animals go into outer space, everything about them is carefully _____. (*monitored*)

3. Find #15. __ What word? (*respond*) If your parents ask you a question and you give an answer, you _____. (*respond*) If a teacher asks a boy a question and he answers, he _____. (*responds*)

4. Find #16. __ What word? (*resemble*) If James looks like Scott, we could say that James resembles _____. (*Scott*) If Mary looked like Val, we could say that Mary resembles _____. (*Val*) In the passage, we will learn that the home of one of the space animals resembled a familiar object.

ACTIVITY J: **Passage Reading and Comprehension** (See the *Student Book,* pages 106 and 107.)

	Animals in Space
	Before the first humans blasted into space, animals
8	became the first astronauts. Beginning in the 1940s,
16	humans sent many kinds of animals into space, including
25	monkeys, dogs, cats, fish, frogs, and many other species.
34	(#1) Scientists used the animals to study many aspects
42	of space travel to prepare for the first human flight. For
53	example, the animals tested what it was like to travel in
64	small space capsules. The animals helped identify possible
72	dangers to humans and taught humans important things
80	about how to live and work in space. (#2)
88	One of the most famous animal astronauts was
96	Laika, the dog. She was the first living creature to leave
107	the earth's atmosphere and orbit the earth. Laika was a
117	mongrel, or mutt, with no owner or home and lived on
128	the streets of Moscow. Suddenly, some Soviet researchers
136	captured her. They took her to a Soviet research center
146	and promoted her to the rank of cosmonaut, the name that
157	the Soviet Union uses for its astronauts. (#3)
164	Laika, a good-natured dog, responded well to her
173	spaceflight training. She learned to live and sleep while
182	wearing a special harness. She also learned to eat and drink
193	from special containers prepared just for her flight. (#4)
201	Laika's cabin resembled an egg-shaped nest. Soft
209	padded fabric covered the vertical walls of the cabin.
218	Measuring tools filled every nook and cranny of her
227	new home.
229	On November 5, 1957, Laika's spacecraft, *Sputnik 2,*
237	was launched into space. While Laika traveled around the
246	earth, scientists monitored her heartbeat, blood pressure,
253	and breathing rate. They hoped to learn how humans
262	might behave on future spaceflights. Laika helped humans

270	answer questions about the effects of escaping the earth's
279	atmosphere, living in such a small space, and how a body
290	would respond to weightlessness. (#5)
294	Today, more than 40 years after Laika's spaceflight,
302	her statue is part of a monument to Russian cosmonauts
312	that stands outside of Moscow. Laika is the only animal
322	that is part of the memorial. Some people consider her
332	contribution to science to be as important as that of any
343	human astronaut.
345	Animals are still going into orbit. All kinds of birds,
355	insects, and animals, even 2,000 jellyfish, have gone
363	into space. Animals in outer space contribute to new
372	understandings about the human body, disease prevention,
379	and the development of medicines. Animals in space help
388	humans understand life, growth, and development. This
395	research adds to our knowledge of humans, animals, and
404	every aspect of our planet. (#6)
409	

A. ☐ **Total number of words read**

B. ☐ **Total number of underlined words (mistakes)**

C. ☐ **Total number of words read correctly**

Activity Procedure: Have students work on accuracy by having them read the passage silently to each embedded number, and then reread the same section orally to a partner, together as a group, or individually. When students finish reading a section orally, ask the corresponding comprehension question. When the passage has been read, have students work on fluency by having them read the passage first to themselves twice, and then to a partner. Have students determine the number of words read correctly and graph it (if you have chosen this option).

Passage Reading—Accuracy

1. Find Activity J. You are going to read a passage and answer questions about what you've read. Today's passage is about astronauts and cosmonauts that are animals instead of humans. You will learn about one of the most famous animals in space, Laika, the dog. Read the title with me. "Animals in Space."

2. Read down to #1 silently. Look up when you are done. __

3. (When students finish reading, have them reread the section orally to a partner, together orally as a group, or aloud individually.)

4. (Ask the question associated with the number. Provide feedback for students' answers.)

5. (Repeat Steps 2, 3, and 4 for all sections of the passage.)

Comprehension Questions

(Numbers corresponding to these questions are placed throughout the passage at points at which they should be asked during oral reading.)

1. Who were the first astronauts? (*Animals—monkeys, dogs, cats, fish, frogs.*)

2. Why did scientists choose to first send animals into space and not humans? (*Animals helped identify possible dangers to humans and taught us important things about how to live and work in space.*)

3. How did Laika become a cosmonaut? (*Soviet researchers captured her and promoted her to cosmonaut.*)

4. What did Laika learn in her spaceflight training? (*She learned how to live and sleep in a special harness and to eat and drink from special containers.*)

5. How did scientists learn from Laika when she was in space? (*They monitored her heartbeat, blood pressure, and breathing rate; they learned how the body would respond to weightlessness.*)

6. Why are animals still being sent into space? (*To help us understand more about the human body and about disease prevention, and to help in the development of medicines. They help us understand life, growth, and development.*)

Summative Question

7. Do you think we should keep sending animals into space? Why? Why not? First Ones and then Twos.

Passage Reading—Fluency

1. Now it's time for fluency building.

2. Find the beginning of the passage. (Pause.) Whisper-read. See how many words you can read in a minute. Begin. __ (Time students for one minute.) Stop. Circle the last word that you read. __

3. Let's practice again. Return to the beginning of the passage. (Pause.) See if you can read more words. Begin. __ (Time students for one minute.) Stop. Put a box around the last word that you read. __

4. Please exchange books with your partner. __ Partner 2, you are going to read first. Partner 1, listen and underline any mistakes or words left out. Twos, begin. __ (Time students for one minute.) Stop. Ones, cross out the last word that your partner read. __

5. Partner 1, you are going to read next. Partner 2, listen and underline any mistakes or words left out. Ones, begin. __ (Time students for one minute.) Stop. Twos, cross out the last word that your partner read. __

6. Please return your partner's book. __ Figure out the total number of words you read correctly and write it in Box C. __ (Optional: Have students graph it.)

Blackline Masters for Overhead Transparencies

Description

The overhead transparencies contain stimuli that are essential to each lesson. They are used for modeling strategies and for providing students with feedback about their responses.

Use of overhead transparencies when teaching a group of four or more.

If you are teaching a group of four or more children, we recommend that you use an overhead projector. To prepare for the lessons you can:

- Use the overhead transparencies sold by Sopris West as supplemental material for *REWARDS Intermediate*

  OR

- Make your own overhead transparencies using the blackline masters found on the following pages.

Have a piece of paper handy that you can place under the transparency to frame the stimulus that you wish the students to attend to.

Use of photocopies of blackline masters when teaching a small group.

If you are teaching an individual or a small group of two or three, make a copy of the blackline master and place the copy on a clipboard. Use the copy in the same manner as the transparency in the lesson.

ACTIVITY E: Underlining Vowels in Words

1. pathway   waist   pigtail

2. maintain   midday   rapid

3. backspin   haystack   milkman

4. railway   panic   strain

5. midway   mailman   mainsail

ACTIVITY H: Circling Prefixes and Suffixes

1. misfit   dismiss   abstract

2. dash   misplay   addict

3. disband   misprint   disclaim

4. dismay   mint   distract

5. display   admit   mislaid

6. aim   district   disdain

7. abstain   mishap   miscast

ACTIVITY E: Underlining Vowels in Words

1. ransack	vault	raisin
2. v<u>i</u>ct<u>i</u>m	w<u>ai</u>stb<u>a</u>nd	fr<u>au</u>d
3. t<u>i</u>m<u>i</u>d	f<u>au</u>lt	v<u>a</u>l<u>i</u>d
4. j<u>au</u>nt	cl<u>ai</u>m	c<u>au</u>se
5. c<u>a</u>pt<u>ai</u>n	<u>au</u>d<u>i</u>t	c<u>a</u>nd<u>i</u>d

ACTIVITY H: Circling Prefixes and Suffixes

1. (in)sist	(com)mit	(im)print
2. camp	(in)laid	(con)sist
3. (dis)tinct	(in)habit	dim
4. (con)vict	(in)grain	(im)plant
5. (com)plain	(im)pact	cash
6. (in)flict	(com)mand	(mis)lay
7. (im)pair	(con)trast	(in)fant

ACTIVITY E: **Underlining Vowels in Words**

1.	curtail	birthday	turn
2.	auto*	astronaut*	random
3.	launch	verdict	vitamin*
4.	birdbath	turban	whirlwind
5.	auburn	server	taunt

ACTIVITY H: **Circling Prefixes and Suffixes**

1.	prefer	disturb	canvas
2.	proclaim	betray	defraud
3.	behind	complaint	decay
4.	confirm	detail	reclaim
5.	absurd	prepay	restrain
6.	prohibit	distant	behold
7.	restrict	invalid	prison

ACTIVITY E: **Underlining Vowels in Words**

1.   blizzard   holiday   haunt

2.   mermaid   shortstop   partner

3.   northern   cargo*   hardship

4.   border   vermin   overhaul*

5.   garland   backyard   barbershop

ACTIVITY H: **Circling Prefixes and Suffixes**

1.   constrict   deprogram   cannon

2.   across   misinform   repay

3.   deform   unfit   unafraid

4.   absorb   perform   preserve

5.   perturb   impart   prefix

6.   record   alert   discard

7.   unchain   persist   prolong

ACTIVITY E: **Underlining Vowels in Words**

1.   costume   timberline   turnstile

2.   stampede   autumn   backbone

3.   shipmate   maximum   sunstroke

4.   frustrate   marlin   murmur

5.   popcorn   tornado   obsolete
                         ＊ ＊   ＊

ACTIVITY H: **Circling Prefixes and Suffixes**

1.   explain   disgust   reconstruct

2.   promote   unalike   berate

3.   combine   alarm   exact

4.   entire   readjust   impose

5.   enthrone   unpaid   misbehave

6.   prescribe   exclude   entail

7.   conclude   advise   extreme

ACTIVITY E: Underlining Vowels in Words

1. turmoil   corduroy   boycott

2. corrode   void   spoilsport

3. barter   poison   joyride

4. pauper   oyster   hoist

5. loiter   launder   ordain

ACTIVITY H: Circling Prefixes and Suffixes

1. extrinsic   hardness   hopelessness

2. demanded   regardless   alarming

3. dominates   relaxing   carelessness

4. happiness   classic   captivates

5. discriminate   frantic   rejoin

6. graduate   destroy   fantastic

7. softness   departed   completeness

ACTIVITY E: Underlining Vowels in Words

1. streetcar   uniform   fifteenth

2. forget   textile   sweepstake

3. freedom   forest   canteen

4. female   leftover   forlorn

5. penmanship   homeland   benefit

ACTIVITY H: Circling Prefixes and Suffixes

1. alarmist   vanish   astonishing

2. punish   unselfish   interested

3. pessimism   comprehends   famish

4. respected   untrusting   heroism

5. intrude   conducted   optimism

6. humanist   advertise   smartest

7. disarm   florist   blemish

ACTIVITY E: **Underlining Vowels in Words**

1.   southwestern   cloudburst   seventeen

2.   carload   railroad   coach

3.   roadside   electrode   playground

4.   faucet   spellbound   northwestern

5.   coatrack   greenhouse   census

ACTIVITY H: **Circling Prefixes and Suffixes**

1.   loyalist   employer   percent

2.   consider   sailor   proposal

3.   author   consumers   respectful

4.   advertiser   personal   historical

5.   arrival   explode   cinder

6.   spectator   ungrateful   unfortunate

7.   untruthful   abnormal   successful

ACTIVITY E: **Underlining Vowels in Words**

1. pillow   chowder   roadway

2. succeed   elbow   cinch

3. flowerpot   willow   outgrow

4. snowplow   embrace   sundown

5. thirteenth   shallow   windowpane

ACTIVITY H: **Circling Prefixes and Suffixes**

1. manage   computers   struggle

2. reconsider   priceless   programmer

3. mishandle   absence   regretful

4. successor   bemoan   mileage

5. elevator   harvested   huddle

6. barbarism   unfaithful   shortage

7. resemble   sausage   entertainers

ACTIVITY E: **Underlining Vowels in Words**

1.	rainbow	margin	township
2.	shadow	lifeboat	oblige
3.	boatload	germfree	downtown
4.	snowflake	outgrowth	downhill
5.	sirloin	cowboy	marshmallow

ACTIVITY H: **Circling Prefixes and Suffixes**

1.	expansive	protection	permissive
2.	novelist	repulsive	civilization
3.	percussionist	gigantic	invasion
4.	postage	expression	caution
5.	refusal	completion	regenerate
6.	conditional	effective	demonstrations
7.	unintentional	panelist	professional

ACTIVITY E: **Underlining Vowels in Words**

1. cartoon	toothpick	igloo
2. footprint	monsoon	riverbank
3. cookbook	shampoo	showboat
4. sagebrush	fishhook	loophole
5. woodshed	macaroon	boomerang

ACTIVITY H: **Circling Prefixes and Suffixes**

1. precaution	dictionary	celery
2. injury	dismissal	belabor
3. disability	absurdity	complexity
4. grocery	energetic	voluntary
5. nationally	similarity	relatively
6. adhesive	disloyal	perfectionist
7. personality	intensive	contaminate

ACTIVITY E: Underlining Vowels in Words

1. raccoon   scapegoat   uproot

2. outlook   fluke   boyhood

3. rooftop   scrapbook   firstborn

4. balloon   classroom   girlhood

5. toothbrush   kangaroo   schoolyard

ACTIVITY H: Circling Prefixes and Suffixes

1. complimentary   continent   racism

2. different   documentary   challenging

3. servant   passage   suggestive

4. cartoonist   permanent   assistant

5. excitement   princely   examination

6. independently   enjoyment   entertainment

7. disinfectant   unemployment   construction

ACTIVITY E: **Underlining Vowels in Words**

1. steamboat   bedroom   streambed

2. meadow   peanut   widespread

3. showdown   streamline   meant

4. seashell   headstrong   meantime

5. oatmeal   daydream   gingerbread

ACTIVITY H: **Circling Prefixes and Suffixes**

1. explanation   difference   dependence

2. importance   fictional   refinance

3. gently   endurance   baggage

4. powerfully   confectionary   attendance

5. admittance   intolerant   magnetism

6. maintenance   misunderstand   confidence

7. significance   performance   consistent

ACTIVITY E: Underlining Vowels in Words

1. peacock	threadbare	steamship
2. breakfast	gemstone	moonbeam
3. footpath	soybean	letterhead
4. health	seamstress	sweatshirt
5. seaweed	proofread	southeastern

ACTIVITY H: Circling Prefixes and Suffixes

1. marvelous	continuous	healthy
2. inactive	literature	orphanage
3. enormous	tremendous	absorbent
4. departure	instructors	elementary
5. excessive	conformity	vulture
6. adventure	ineffective	confession
7. investigation	inconclusive	identification

ACTIVITY E: Underlining Vowels in Words

1.   teammate   h<u>ea</u>ddr<u>e</u>ss   m<u>a</u>rk<u>e</u>tpl<u>a</u>ce

2.   m<u>o</u>n<u>o</u>r<u>ai</u>l   t<u>i</u>nf<u>oi</u>l   r<u>ea</u>s<u>o</u>n

3.   s<u>ea</u>s<u>i</u>ck   s<u>u</u>rr<u>ou</u>nd   b<u>a</u>b<u>oo</u>n

4.   b<u>e</u>dspr<u>ea</u>d   t<u>o</u>rp<u>e</u>d<u>o</u>   d<u>ow</u>nstr<u>ea</u>m

5.   b<u>oo</u>kc<u>a</u>se   f<u>oo</u>tst<u>oo</u>l   s<u>u</u>nb<u>ea</u>m

ACTIVITY H: Circling Prefixes and Suffixes

1.   (in)cons<u>i</u>stent(ly)   (im)poss(ible)   (re)spons(ible)

2.   (pre)dict(able)   (a)vail(able)   civil(ize)

3.   drink(able)   norm(a)(lize)   (de)scrip(tive)

4.   lamin(ate)   (in)flex(ible)   (pre)vent(able)

5.   (in)cap(able)   (in)cred(ible)   leg(a)(lize)

6.   (mis)(un)derstand(ing) (en)joy(able) steril(ize)

7.   (de)part(ment)   (re)pro(duction)   (un)(con)ven(tion)(al)

ACTIVITY D: **Strategy Instruction**

1.   prevention   description

2.   estimate   unlucky

3.   excellence   redundant

4.   appearance   adversity

5.   community   enormity

6.   remainder   prediction

ACTIVITY E: **Strategy Practice**

1.   help(less)(ness)   (dis)(tinc)(tion)

2.   (pro)(ject)(or)   nu(mer)(ous)

3.   (con)(sult)(ant)   (con)(nec)(tion)

ACTIVITY F: **Word Families**

<table>
<tr><td align="center">**A**</td><td align="center">**B**</td></tr>
<tr><td>prevent—to keep from happening</td><td>connect—to join or fasten together</td></tr>
<tr><td>prevents</td><td>connected</td></tr>
<tr><td>prevented</td><td>connecting</td></tr>
<tr><td>preventing</td><td>connection</td></tr>
<tr><td>prevention</td><td>reconnect</td></tr>
<tr><td>preventable</td><td>reconnecting</td></tr>
<tr><td>unpreventable</td><td>reconnection</td></tr>
</table>

ACTIVITY D: **Strategy Instruction**

1. temporary   perfection

2. complaining   beginner

3. suddenness   reduction

4. pollution   productive

5. observant   propeller

6. extinction   mismanage

ACTIVITY E: **Strategy Practice**

1. convertible   ignorance

3. refreshments   amazingly

4. unpredictable   promotion

ACTIVITY F: **Word Families**

A	**B**
predict—to tell about something before it happens	produce—to make something
predicts	production
predicted	productive
predicting	productivity
predictor	productiveness
prediction	reproduce
unpredictable	reproduction

ACTIVITY D: **Strategy Instruction**

1.   exceptionally   independence

2.   uncomfortable   surrender

3.   invention   expectation

4.   disposable   development

ACTIVITY E: **Strategy Practice**

1.   permanently   amusement

2.   utterance   suddenly

3.   impersonal   existence

4.   importantly   indifferent

5.   deformity   containers

ACTIVITY F: **Word Families**

<table>
<tr><td align="center">A</td><td align="center">B</td></tr>
<tr><td>invent—to make something that has never been made before</td><td>develop—to take something that has been invented and make it better</td></tr>
<tr><td>invents</td><td>developed</td></tr>
<tr><td>inventor</td><td>developer</td></tr>
<tr><td>invention</td><td>developing</td></tr>
<tr><td>inventive</td><td>development</td></tr>
<tr><td>reinvent</td><td>developmental</td></tr>
<tr><td>reinvention</td><td>developmentally</td></tr>
</table>

ACTIVITY D: **Strategy Instruction**

1.   intolerable   combination

2.   amendment   instructional

3.   organization   understandable

4.   political   oxidize

ACTIVITY E: **Strategy Practice**

1.   reinvestigate   confident

2.   unsuspecting   government

3.   contribution   example

4.   medically   honesty

5.   executive   unspeakable

ACTIVITY F: **Word Families**

A	**B**
instruct—to teach	contribute—to give money to a charity
instructed	contributes
instructing	contributed
instructor	contributing
instruction	contributor
instructional	contributory
instructive	contribution

ACTIVITY D: **Strategy Instruction**

1. persistently   governmental

2. famously   legendary

3. attractiveness   economize

4. disappointment   occurrence

ACTIVITY E: **Strategy Practice**

1. resistance   fascination

2. unmentionable   intermission

3. exterminate   undependable

4. unimportance   contradiction

5. inexpensive   invitation

ACTIVITY F: **Word Families**

A	**B**
resist—to not want to do something	attract—to bring attention to something
resisting	attracts
resister	attracted
resistive	attracting
resistible	attraction
resistibility	attractive
resistance	attractiveness

ACTIVITY I: **Passage Preparation**

Part 1—Tell

1. nutrients	*n.*	what a plant or animal needs to stay alive
2. nitrogen-poor	*adj.*	not having much nitrogen
*3. dissolve	*v.*	to change a solid into a liquid
*4. various	*adj.*	many different kinds
5. electricity	*n.*	the power that makes appliances run
6. electrical	*adj.*	having to do with electricity
7. wriggles	*v.*	twists
8. miniature	*adj.*	very small

Part 2—Strategy Practice

9. carnivorous plants	*n.*	meat-eating plants
10. capture	*v.*	to catch
*11. digesting	*v.*	breaking down food so a plant or animal can use it
12. digestive	*adj.*	related to digesting
13. supplemental	*adj.*	extra
*14. desperate	*adj.*	having no hope
15. curious	*adj.*	eager to know or learn
16. portray	*v.*	to tell about
17. glistening	*adj.*	shining or sparkling
18. environments	*n.*	surroundings

ACTIVITY D: **Strategy Instruction**

1. unforgettable   population

2. experimental   probably

3. vigilant   difficulty

4. adventurous   pilgrimage

ACTIVITY E: **Strategy Practice**

1. dependability   incompetent

2. disorganization   unexpectedness

3. depression   defective

4. unlikely   incorrectly

5. inadmissible   prematurely

ACTIVITY F: **Word Families**

A	**B**
organize—to put things in order	expect—to look forward to something happening
organized	expected
organizer	expecting
organization	expectance
organizational	expectation
disorganization	unexpected
reorganize	unexpectedness

ACTIVITY I: **Passage Preparation**

Part 1—Tell

1.	Wilma Rudolph	*n.*	a woman who was a fast runner
2.	pneumonia	*n.*	an illness
3.	polio	*n.*	an illness that causes weakness in muscles
4.	physical therapy	*n.*	treatment for problems in your body
5.	Olympic Games	*n.*	sports contest among nations
6.	tournament	*n.*	a contest involving many teams in a sport or game
*7.	triumph	*n.*	an outstanding success
*8.	obstacles	*n.*	things that stand in your way

Part 2—Strategy Practice

9.	Tennessee	*n.*	a state in the United States
10.	corrective	*adj.*	intended to correct (corrective braces)
*11.	encourage	*v.*	to give hope and support to others
*12.	persevered	*v.*	kept on trying to do something even if it was hard
13.	determination	*n.*	the act of not letting anything stop you
14.	decision	*n.*	the act of deciding or choosing something
15.	American	*adj.*	related to the United States of America
16.	international	*adj.*	involving more than one nation
17.	foundation	*n.*	an organization that has money to do special things
18.	inducted	*v.*	accepted as a member of a group or club

ACTIVITY D: **Strategy Practice**

1.   professionally   unfortunately

2.   exterminator   comparison

3.   instructionally   nonviolence

4.   immigration   eventually

ACTIVITY E: **Independent Strategy Practice**

1.   misinformation   enlargement

2.   communicate   conversational

3.   conditionally   accomplishment

4.   destructive   organism

5.   returnable   governmentally

ACTIVITY F: **Word Families**

<table>
<tr><th>A</th><th>B</th></tr>
<tr><td>inform—to tell someone something</td><td>destroy—to ruin something</td></tr>
<tr><td>informer</td><td>destruction</td></tr>
<tr><td>informant</td><td>destructive</td></tr>
<tr><td>information</td><td>destructiveness</td></tr>
<tr><td>informational</td><td>destructible</td></tr>
<tr><td>informative</td><td>indestructible</td></tr>
<tr><td>misinformation</td><td>indestructibility</td></tr>
</table>

ACTIVITY I: **Passage Preparation**

Part 1—Tell

1.	Cesar Chavez	*n.*	a man who worked for migrant workers' rights
2.	Mexico	*n.*	a country in North America
3.	United States	*n.*	a country in North America
4.	Arizona	*n.*	a state in the United States
5.	California	*n.*	a state in the United States
6.	English	*n.*	a language
7.	believed	*v.*	accepted as true
8.	noticed	*v.*	saw something or somebody

Part 2—Strategy Practice

9.	ancestors	*n.*	people who came before us, such as our grandparents
10.	immigrate	*v.*	come into a country and settle there
*11.	migrant workers	*n.*	people who move from place to place to find work in farming
12.	vegetables	*n.*	foods such as carrots, lettuce, and beets
*13.	boycott	*n.*	a group's refusal to deal with an organization in protest
14.	supermarkets	*n.*	big grocery stores
*15.	sacrifice	*n.*	a thing given up for something of more value
*16.	nonviolent	*adj.*	not using violence or force
17.	elementary	*adj.*	referring to grades one to six
18.	attention	*n.*	the act of thinking carefully about something

ACTIVITY D: **Strategy Practice**

1. reorganization   comparatively

2. jealousy   immediately

3. investigator   communication

4. dissatisfaction   disadvantage

ACTIVITY E: **Independent Strategy Practice**

1. administrative   vertically

2. educationally   departmentally

3. impossibility   operator

4. completely   intentionally

5. noisiest   discouragement

ACTIVITY F: **Word Families**

A	**B**
compare—to see how two things are alike	educate—to teach
comparison	education
comparable	educational
comparability	educationally
comparative	reeducate
comparatively	reeducating
incomparable	reeducation

ACTIVITY I: **Passage Preparation**

Part 1—Tell

1. *Scientific American*	*n.*	a magazine
2. Missouri	*n.*	a state in the United States
3. Minnesota	*n.*	a state in the United States
4. Australia	*n.*	a country
5. scientists	*n.*	people having knowledge of science
6. weird	*adj.*	very odd or strange
7. bizarre	*adj.*	freaky
*8. unfamiliar	*adj.*	not well known

Part 2—Strategy Practice

9. century	*n.*	100 years
10. multiple	*adj.*	many
*11. witness	*n.*	a person who saw something happen
12. incidents	*n.*	events
*13. phenomenon	*n.*	an unusual event
*14. explanation	*n.*	that which is said or written that makes something clear
15. logical	*adj.*	having to do with logic or with making sense
16. precipitation	*n.*	rain, snow, or hail
17. manufacture	*v.*	to make things with machines, usually in a factory
18. thudded	*v.*	made a heavy, dull sound

ACTIVITY D: **Strategy Practice**

1. productivity   escalator

2. unmistakable   imperfectly

3. tantalize   redundantly

4. unavoidable   unmanageable

ACTIVITY E: **Independent Strategy Practice**

1. unattractiveness   exceptionality

2. preparation   disagreements

3. meaningfulness   publicize

4. dramatically   radiant

5. inconsistence   reactionary

ACTIVITY F: **Word Families**

A	**B**
continue—to keep doing something	consist—to be made up of
continued	consistent
continuing	consistently
continuation	consistence
continual	consistency
continually	inconsistent
continuous	inconsistence

ACTIVITY I: **Passage Preparation**

Part 1—Tell

*1. record breaker   *n.*   someone or something that beats a previous record

2. measured   *v.*   figured out the amount in inches, meters, miles, etc.

3. koala bear   *n.*   an animal of Australia

4. eucalyptus   *n.*   a tree of Australia

5. Galapagos Islands   *n.*   islands of South America

6. tortoise   *n.*   a turtle

7. endangered species   *n.*   a species of animal or plant that may die out

8. Thailand   *n.*   a country

Part 2—Strategy Practice

9. explorers   *n.*   people who travel to new places to learn about them

*10. category   *n.*   a group of ideas or things

*11. feature   *n.*   a distinct part of something, such as a part of your face

12. imaginable   *adj.*   able to be imagined

13. contrast   *n.*   a difference

*14. amazing   *adj.*   surprising

15. hibernate   *v.*   to sleep through the winter

16. caterpillar   *n.*   wormlike animal that becomes a butterfly or moth

17. multitude   *n.*   a very large number of people or things

18. host   *n.*   a very large number of people or things

ACTIVITY D: **Strategy Practice**

1.   (un)(re)p(ai)r(able)   (re)sp(e)ct(a)b(ili)ty

2.   (in)d(i)v(i)d(u)(ali)ty   (o)cc(a)s(ion)(al)ly

3.   (mis)m(a)n(age)(ment)   g(e)n(e)ro(si)ty

4.   (en)v(iron)(ment)(al)ly   (dis)(a)pp(ea)r(ance)

ACTIVITY E: **Independent Strategy Practice**

1.   competition   tremendously

2.   instrumentalist   superintendent

3.   additionally   dissimilarity

4.   impracticality   fundamentally

5.   indescribable   unconventionality

ACTIVITY F: **Word Families**

A	**B**
manage—to tell a group what to do	appear—to come into sight
manager	appearance
management	disappear
manageable	disappears
mismanage	disappearing
mismanaged	disappearance
unmanageable	disappearances

ACTIVITY I: **Passage Preparation**

Part 1—Tell

1. Soviet Union	*n.*	the name of a former country
2. Russian	*adj.*	related to the country of Russia
3. cosmonaut	*n.*	a Russian astronaut
4. Laika	*n.*	the name of a dog that went into space
*5. knowledge	*n.*	facts that have been learned
6. atmosphere	*n.*	the air above the earth
7. species	*n.*	a specific kind of plant or animal
8. medicines	*n.*	drugs used to treat diseases

Part 2—Strategy Practice

9. vertical	*adj.*	standing or pointing straight up
10. capsule	*n.*	a closed container
11. researchers	*n.*	people who study something
12. monument	*n.*	a building or statue built in memory of a person or event
13. memorial	*n.*	something in memory of a person or event including a monument
*14. monitor	*v.*	to keep a close watch on
*15. respond	*v.*	to give an answer
*16. resemble	*v.*	to look like
17. good-natured	*adj.*	nice; easygoing
18. weightlessness	*n.*	the state of having little or no weight—especially when out in space

Strategies for Reading Long Words

The following chart outlines the strategies that students are taught for attacking unknown long words. Initially, they are taught a strategy that involves the overt acts of circling prefixes and suffixes and underlining the letters that represent vowel sounds to assist the student in segmenting the word into decodable chunks. These overt steps are gradually faded until the students use only the covert (metacognitive) steps unless they have difficulty with a word.

This chart can be used in several ways:

1. **Overhead transparency**—After students have finished the program, periodically review the strategy by displaying an overhead transparency.

   (Note: This transparency is included in the set of transparencies sold by Sopris West.)

2. **Student Reference Chart**—When you begin Lesson 16, give each student a copy of the strategies or refer students to the back of their *Student Book*, where they will find a copy of the strategy.

3. **Poster**—When you purchased *REWARDS Intermediate*, you also received a **poster** of the strategies for display in your classroom. The poster will serve as a visual reminder for the students and teacher and can be used for review.

Strategies
for Reading Long Words

Overt Strategy

    1.   Circle the prefixes.

    2.   Circle the suffixes.

    3.   Underline the vowels.

    4.   Say the parts of the word.

    5.   Say the whole word.

    6.   Make it a real word.

EXAMPLE

Covert Strategy

    1.   Look for prefixes, suffixes, and vowels.

    2.   Say the parts of the word.

    3.   Say the whole word.

    4.   Make it a real word.

Student Reference Chart: Prefixes, Suffixes, and Vowel Combinations

Give this chart to students to assist them in circling prefixes and suffixes and underlining vowels. Because the chart includes all affixes and vowels taught in the first 15 lessons, to avoid confusion with untaught material, distribute the chart when you introduce Lesson 16, or refer students to the back of the *Student Book* where they will find a copy of this chart.

It will also be useful to maintain a cumulative chart in your room that students can refer to. Divide the chart into three parts and label the parts Prefixes, Suffixes, and Vowel Combinations. When a new affix or vowel combination is introduced, write it on an index card and add it to your chart. When the program is complete, additional affixes that you or your students find while reading can be added.

Prefixes, Suffixes, and Vowel Combinations

<table>
<tr><th>Decoding Element</th><th>Key Word</th><th>Decoding Element</th><th>Key Word</th><th>Decoding Element</th><th>Key Word</th></tr>
<tr><td colspan="6">Prefixes</td></tr>
<tr><td>a</td><td>above</td><td>de</td><td>depart</td><td>mis</td><td>mistake</td></tr>
<tr><td>ab</td><td>absent</td><td>dis</td><td>disagree</td><td>per</td><td>permit</td></tr>
<tr><td>ad</td><td>addition</td><td>en</td><td>enlist</td><td>pre</td><td>prevent</td></tr>
<tr><td>be</td><td>belong</td><td>ex</td><td>export</td><td>pro</td><td>protect</td></tr>
<tr><td>com</td><td>compare</td><td>im</td><td>immature</td><td>re</td><td>return</td></tr>
<tr><td>con</td><td>continue</td><td>in</td><td>incomplete</td><td>un</td><td>unfair</td></tr>
<tr><td colspan="6">Suffixes</td></tr>
<tr><td>able</td><td>comfortable</td><td>ful</td><td>careful</td><td>ment</td><td>argument</td></tr>
<tr><td>age</td><td>courage</td><td>ible</td><td>reversible</td><td>ness</td><td>kindness</td></tr>
<tr><td>al</td><td>final</td><td>ic</td><td>athletic</td><td>or</td><td>tailor</td></tr>
<tr><td>ance</td><td>disturbance</td><td>ing</td><td>running</td><td>ous</td><td>famous</td></tr>
<tr><td>ant</td><td>dormant</td><td>ish</td><td>selfish</td><td>s</td><td>birds</td></tr>
<tr><td>ary</td><td>missionary</td><td>ism</td><td>realism</td><td>sion</td><td>discussion</td></tr>
<tr><td>ate</td><td>regulate</td><td>ist</td><td>artist</td><td>sive</td><td>expensive</td></tr>
<tr><td>ed</td><td>landed</td><td>ity</td><td>oddity</td><td>tion</td><td>action</td></tr>
<tr><td>ence</td><td>influence</td><td>ize</td><td>memorize</td><td>tive</td><td>attentive</td></tr>
<tr><td>ent</td><td>persistent</td><td>le</td><td>cradle</td><td>ture</td><td>picture</td></tr>
<tr><td>er</td><td>farmer</td><td>less</td><td>useless</td><td>y</td><td>thirsty</td></tr>
<tr><td>est</td><td>biggest</td><td>ly</td><td>safely</td><td></td><td></td></tr>
<tr><td colspan="6">Vowel Combinations</td></tr>
<tr><td>ai</td><td>rain</td><td>oo</td><td>moon, book</td><td>or</td><td>torn</td></tr>
<tr><td>au</td><td>sauce</td><td>ou</td><td>loud</td><td>ur</td><td>turn</td></tr>
<tr><td>ay</td><td>say</td><td>ow</td><td>low, down</td><td>a - e</td><td>make</td></tr>
<tr><td>ea</td><td>meat, thread</td><td>oy</td><td>boy</td><td>e - e</td><td>Pete</td></tr>
<tr><td>ee</td><td>deep</td><td>ar</td><td>farm</td><td>i - e</td><td>side</td></tr>
<tr><td>oa</td><td>boat</td><td>er</td><td>her</td><td>o - e</td><td>hope</td></tr>
<tr><td>oi</td><td>boil</td><td>ir</td><td>bird</td><td>u - e</td><td>use</td></tr>
</table>

Pretest/Posttest and Generalization Test

Two curriculum-based assessment tools for measuring students' gains from *REWARDS Intermediate* are included in this section. The first assessment tool is a pretest/posttest that contains words taught in the program. The second measure, the generalization test, contains words that, although not taught in the program, contain elements that have been introduced. You may select to administer the pretest/posttest before beginning the program and readminister it on completion. The generalization test would be given only on completion of the program. All data can be recorded on the Class Summary Chart found at the end of Appendix C.

Preparation: Reproduce one copy of the Student Test Copy. Reproduce one Teacher Recording Form for each student.

Administration: **Pretest**—Hand the Student Test Copy to the student. Tell the student, "This is a list of long words. I don't expect you to know all of these words so just do your best. Please read down the list."

Posttest—Hand the Student Test Copy to the student. Tell the student, "These are words that you have read in *REWARDS*. Use what you have learned to figure out each word."

Generalization Test—Hand the Student Test Copy to the student. Tell the student, "These are words that you have not read in *REWARDS* . Use what you have learned to figure out each word."

Recording: As the student reads, cross out the word parts that are pronounced incorrectly in the Word Parts Correct column. Put a plus (+) in the final column if a word is pronounced correctly and a minus (–) for incorrectly pronounced words. If the student takes longer than four seconds to read a word, have him or her read the next word. If the student mispronounces four consecutive words, terminate the test.

Scoring: Determine the total number of correct words read by counting the pluses in the final column. Determine the total number of word parts read correctly by counting the parts that you crossed out and subtracting from 78. Notice that the parts do not always correspond to syllables; instead, they reflect word parts taught in the program. For example, *ity* is one word part, not two. The analysis of word parts is more sensitive than the word measure. Through the word part analysis you will be able to see if the student deletes whole parts of words, which is a common error of poor decoders. Finally, in each column, divide the top number by the total to calculate a percentage.

Pretest/Posttest
Student Test Copy

1. container	11. entertainment
2. advertise	12. unavoidable
3. promotion	13. unpredictable
4. abnormal	14. permanently
5. completeness	15. immigration
6. argument	16. investigation
7. disturbance	17. instrumentalist
8. combination	18. exceptionality
9. inexpensive	19. inconsistently
10. meaningfulness	20. communication

Pretest/Posttest
Teacher Recording Form

Word	Word Parts Correct (Cross out incorrect word parts)		Words Correct (+)/ Words Incorrect (−)
1. container	1. con tain er	3	
2. advertise	2. ad ver tise	3	
3. promotion	3. pro mo tion	3	
4. abnormal	4. ab norm al	3	
5. completeness	5. com plete ness	3	
6. argument	6. ar gu ment	3	
7. disturbance	7. dis turb ance	3	
8. combination	8. com bin a tion	4	
9. inexpensive	9. in ex pen sive	4	
10. meaningfulness	10. mean ing ful ness	4	
11. entertainment	11. en ter tain ment	4	
12. unavoidable	12. un a void able	4	
13. unpredictable	13. un pre dict able	4	
14. permanently	14. per man ent ly	4	
15. immigration	15. im mi gra tion	4	
16. investigation	16. in ves ti ga tion	5	
17. instrumentalist	17. in stru ment al ist	5	
18. exceptionality	18. ex cep tion al ity	5	
19. inconsistently	19. in con sist ent ly	5	
20. communication	20. com mun i ca tion	5	
Total number of correct word parts _____/78			Total correct words _____/20
Percentage correct _____%			_____%

Generalization Test
Student Test Copy

1. progression

2. communism

3. bedazzle

4. conference

5. reflective

6. miserable

7. donation

8. expenditure

9. deliberate

10. admiration

11. competitor

12. affectionate

13. continuous

14. explosively

15. hospitality

16. perpetually

17. proportionately

18. enthusiastic

19. international

20. irregularity

Generalization Test
Teacher Recording Form

Word	Word Parts Correct (Cross out incorrect word parts)		Words Correct (+)
1. progression	1. pro gres sion	3	
2. communism	2. com mun ism	3	
3. bedazzle	3. be dazz le	3	
4. conference	4. con fer ence	3	
5. reflective	5. re flec tive	3	
6. miserable	6. mis er able	3	
7. donation	7. do na tion	3	
8. expenditure	8. ex pen di ture	4	
9. deliberate	9. de lib er ate	4	
10. admiration	10. ad mir a tion	4	
11. competitor	11. com pet it or	4	
12. affectionate	12. af fec tion ate	4	
13. continuous	13. con tin u ous	4	
14. explosively	14. ex plo sive ly	4	
15. hospitality	15. hos pit al ity	4	
16. perpetually	16. per pet u al ly	5	
17. proportionately	17. pro por tion ate ly	5	
18. enthusiastic	18. en thu si ast ic	5	
19. international	19. in ter na tion al	5	
20. irregularity	20. ir reg u lar ity	5	
Total number of correct word parts _____/78			Total correct words _____/20
Percentage correct _____%			_____%

Class Summary Chart

Name of Student	Pretest Words /20	Posttest Words /20	Pretest Word Parts /78	Posttest Word Parts /78	Generalization Test Words /20	Fluency Pretest CWPM*	Fluency Posttest CWPM*	Days Absent

*CWPM = correct words per minute

Pretest/Posttest Reading Fluency

The goal of *REWARDS Intermediate* is not only to increase students' reading accuracy, but also to increase their reading fluency—the number of correct words that they can read in a minute. The ability to decode longer words should increase students' reading fluency and also their comprehension as they turn their attention from decoding to the meaning of text that they are reading.

The following procedures can be used to assess students' oral reading fluency.

Fluency Assessment Procedure

1. Administer the following fluency measure to each student before they begin *REWARDS Intermediate* and again after they complete the program.

2. Make copies of the passage on the next page (one copy per student for recording data and one copy for students to read).

3. Ask each student to read the passage as quickly and as carefully as possible.

4. Have the student read for one minute. Use a stopwatch or timer.

5. Record data as the student reads.
   - Underline all mispronunciations.
   - If the student immediately corrects a mispronunciation, give credit for the word.
   - If the student reverses the order of words, both words are errors.
   - Cross out words that are omitted. They will not be counted.
   - Write in all additions. However, these will not be counted.

6. When the minute is complete, ask the student to stop.

7. Determine the total number of words read by counting on from the number at the beginning of the last line read. Subtract any mispronunciations. Determine the number of words read correctly in one minute.

8. Keep a record of the pretest and posttest fluency scores on the Class Summary Chart found in Appendix C.

Taking Pictures

11	Have you ever taken a picture with a camera? How does what you see through the viewfinder get onto the film? How
22	
34	does that film become a picture you can show your friends? To understand how photography works, you need to know a little
44	bit about light and chemistry.
49	Light is not made up of waves (like sound is) or particles
61	(like objects), but instead it has properties of both of these. The
73	energy in light can be focused, like sound waves can. We see
85	different colors based on how tightly focused the wavelength of
95	light is. But the energy travels in small packets called photons.
106	Each photon contains a certain amount of energy. The shorter
116	the wavelength, the greater the energy.
122	When you focus your camera on a subject, and then push
133	the button, the shutter opens for a fraction of a second. During
145	this tiny amount of time, the light being reflected off your
156	subject enters the lens of the camera, where it meets the film.
168	The film in your camera is coated with several layers of
179	special chemicals. Some of these chemicals act as light filters.
189	Some of the chemicals will be part of the developing process.
200	But the chemical that enables your picture to become imprinted
210	on the film is called silver halide. These tiny silver halide
221	crystals are photosensitive—they react to light. Each photon
230	of light reacts differently with the crystals. The varying energy
240	levels in the photons are what create different colors on your
251	pictures if you are using color film, or different shades of grey if
264	you are using black and white.
270	

Appendix E

Fluency Graph:
Correct Words Per Minute

In Lessons 20–25, students engage in daily repeated reading activities to increase their reading fluency. First, students whisper-read the passage for one minute. Next, they whisper-read the same material for a minute trying to increase the number of words read in one minute. Then students read to their partners. The partners (coaches) underline any word errors that they detect. When both students have read for a minute, they determine the total number of words they have read correctly in one minute and graph their totals on a copy of the following page or on the graph at the back of their *Student Book.*

Many teachers have continued the fluency building activities after the completion of *REWARDS Intermediate,* using content area passages from their own textbooks or parts of stories from their core reading program.

Fluency Graph

Name _____

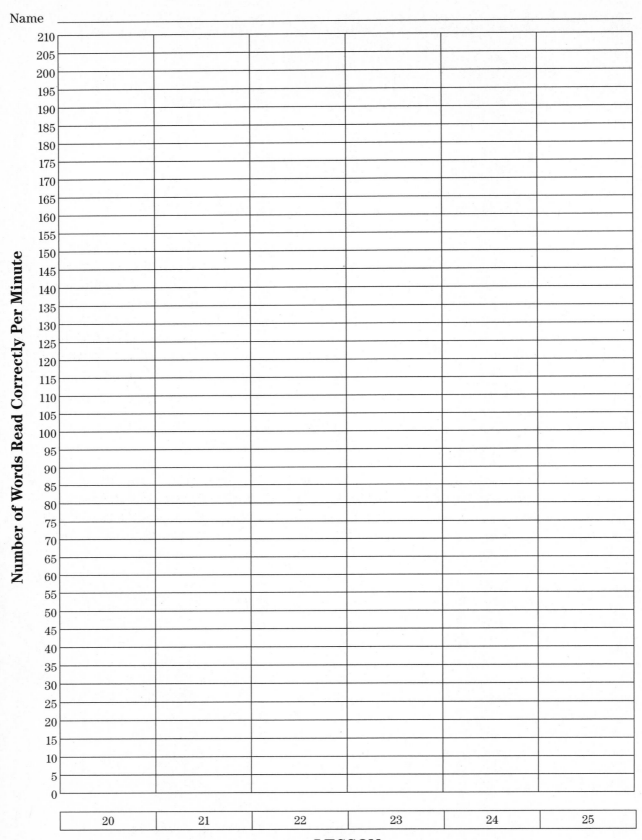

Number of Words Read Correctly Per Minute

| | 20 | 21 | 22 | 23 | 24 | 25 |

LESSON

Incentive Program

Make copies and distribute the *REWARDS* Chart to each student or refer students to the back of their *Student Book*. This will allow students to record their own points when you award them. During the lesson, award points for each segment of the lesson. These points can also be used to determine a lesson grade and an overall grade for the student. For some classes, you may decide to have your students earn points toward a special event (popcorn party, free reading period, or video viewing) or prizes (e.g., a book, school supplies, or treats). The following procedures can be used for awarding points.

Lessons 1–15

1. After each page in the *Student Book* is completed, award Participation Points. If students have followed your behavioral guidelines, paid attention, participated, and responded accurately, award three points. If students performed below your expectations, award zero, one, or two points.

2. For the **Reading Check**, ask each student to read one line of three words in Activity H. If the student makes no errors, award three points. Award two points if one error is made, one point if two errors are made.

3. Award Bonus Points for excellent reading and/or behavior.

4. At the end of the lesson, have students total their points.

Lessons 16–19

1. After each page in the *Student Book* is completed, award Participation Points as you did in Lessons 1–15.

2. For the **Reading Check**, ask each student to read one of the sentences in Activity I, Sentence Reading. If the student makes no

errors, award three points. Award two points if one error is made, one point if two errors are made.

3. Award Bonus Points for excellent reading and/or behavior.

4. At the end of the lesson, have students total their points.

Lessons 20–25

1. After each page in the *Student Book* is completed, award Participation Points as you did in Lessons 1–19.

2. For the **Fluency Check**, use students' correct words per minute (CWPM) on their last reading of the passage in Activity J. If the student reads between 100 and 150 CWPM, award three points. Award two points for 80–99 CWPM and one point for 60–79 CWPM.

3. Award Bonus Points for excellent reading and/or behavior.

4. At the end of the lesson, have students total their points.

Lesson Grade

You may wish to award students a lesson grade. If you choose to do this, determine the number of points needed for each grade. The following may be used as a guide.

Total possible points	= 12
11 or 12 points	= A
9 or 10 points	= B
7 or 8 points	= C
5 or 6 points	= D
Fewer than 6 points	= F

Other Incentives

Group Incentives

You may select to have special events to encourage participation and accurate reading. Often it is easier to offer group incentives rather than individual incentives, thus encouraging the students to support the academic and behavioral efforts of their peers. Group incentives could be one of the following: a popcorn party, 10 minutes to visit, a word game, or a special edible treat.

While you may determine your own way of awarding the group incentives, the following may be used as a guide.

1. Set a goal of all As or Bs for five lessons.

2. At the end of each lesson, examine the students' point sheets to determine if everyone received an A or B. If so, record a group point in a prominent place (e.g., a bulletin board).

3. When students have earned all As or Bs for five lessons, celebrate with the selected event.

Individual Incentives

If you are teaching a small group that includes students with learning challenges, you may wish to award individual prizes when a certain number of A or B lessons are earned. For example, individual students could earn a special treat for achieving all As or Bs for five lessons.

REWARDS Chart

Name _____

Lesson	First Page Activities A, B, C, D	Second Page Activities E, F, and G	Third Page Activities H, I, and J	Reading Check Line in H	Bonus Points	Total Points	Lesson Grade
Lesson 1							
Lesson 2							
Lesson 3							
Lesson 4							
Lesson 5							
Lesson 6							
Lesson 7							
Lesson 8							
Lesson 9							
Lesson 10							
Lesson 11							
Lesson 12							
Lesson 13							
Lesson 14							
Lesson 15							

Lesson	First Page Activities A, B, and C	Second Page Activities D, E, and F	Third Page Activities G and H	Reading Check Sentence in I	Bonus Points	Total Points	Lesson Grade
Lesson 16							
Lesson 17							
Lesson 18							
Lesson 19							

Lesson	First Page Activities A, B, and C	Second Page Activities D, E, and F	Third Page Activities G and H	Fluency Check Passage in J	Bonus Points	Total Points	Lesson Grade
Lesson 20							
Lesson 21							
Lesson 22							
Lesson 23							
Lesson 24							
Lesson 25							

	Total Points	Overall Grade

Participation Points (3 possible points)
- Following behavioral guidelines
- Paying attention and participating
- Responding accurately

Fluency Check
100–150 CWPM* = 3 points
80–99 CWPM = 2 points
60–79 CWPM = 1 point

* CWPM = correct words per minute

Reading Check (line or sentence)
No errors = 3 points
1 error = 2 points
2 errors = 1 point

Lesson Grade (12 possible points)
11 or 12 points = A
9 or 10 points = B
7 or 8 points = C
5 or 6 points = D
Fewer than 6 = F

Appendix G

Research on *REWARDS*

What is the research base for this program?

In the past, research on the acquisition of decoding skills has concentrated largely on monosyllabic (single-syllable) word reading. However, a need exists for research about multisyllabic (two or more syllables) word reading and how students accomplish the learning necessary to read these longer words. Beginning with fourth grade material, multisyllabic words account for anywhere from 10% to 80% of the words students read in a passage. Yet few curriculum materials exist to teach students to read longer words. The development of the *REWARDS* program and conducting research regarding its effectiveness was initiated to meet these needs.

Various versions of the *REWARDS* program have been field tested and used widely with poor readers and students with reading disabilities. Before any formal studies were conducted, data were collected in several field tests and in at least four pilot studies. Using the grade equivalent (GE) scores of two subtests from the *Woodcock Reading Mastery Tests* (Word Attack and Word Identification) (Woodcock, 1973), substantial gains in short periods of time were documented. In approximately five weeks, some students gained as little as one year's worth of reading, while other students showed a gain that was equivalent to eight years on the Word Attack subtest. Anita Archer (1981) found in the pilot studies that flexible syllabication procedures focusing on vowel sounds (e.g., **ai**, **ea**, **ou**), word parts, vowel conversions, and approximate pronunciations—in conjunction with a word building strategy that taught students to break longer words down into smaller recognizable word parts, read part by part, then read the whole word—were effective in teaching low-performing fourth and fifth grade students to read multisyllabic words.

To validate the strong field-test and pilot-test results and confirm that the intervention was responsible for the results, two studies were completed using previous versions of the *REWARDS* program as the intervention. In the first study, the experimenter tried three versions of *REWARDS* and compared them with a program not specifically designed to teach multisyllabic words. In the second study, different versions of the *REWARDS* program were implemented requiring different success levels for different groups (80% versus 90%) and providing different practice modes (sentences versus whole paragraphs). Each study will be described briefly.

1. **Archer, A. L., Gleason, M. M., Vachon, V., & Hollenbeck, K. (2006).** *Instructional strategies for teaching struggling fourth and fifth grade students to read long words.* **Manuscript submitted for review.**

   In the first experimental study, fourth and fifth graders were nominated by their teachers as reading-deficient and randomly assigned to one of three treatment groups or one control group. Participants' reading scores on the Word Identification and Word Attack subtests of the *Woodcock Reading Mastery Tests* (Woodcock, 1973) ranged from 2.7 to 3.5 grade equivalent on the first subtest and 2.5 to 3.8 grade equivalent on the second subtest. In addition, participants were decidedly deficient in decoding multisyllabic words. On a multisyllabic word reading pretest, students ranged from 2 correct responses to 13 correct responses out of 48 words.

   Each of the three treatment groups engaged in the same instruction during the first half of the intervention. The three groups received 30 minutes of preskill instruction for nine days. The preskills taught were:

   a. blending of word parts from an orally segmented model presented by the teacher;

   b. saying isolated vowel sounds for vowel letter combinations;

   c. vowel conversions;

   d. circling vowel graphemes in words and saying the phonemes for the graphemes;

   e. silently sounding out and orally reading word parts;

   f. correcting close approximations using context;

   g. pronunciation of affixes in isolation; and

   h. locating and reading affixes by circling and pronouncing word parts found at the beginning and end of words.

   After preskills training, a criterion test (Preskill Posttest) was administered to measure the level of mastery that occurred across the three treatment groups and to ensure that similar levels of attainment occurred for the groups but not for the control group (which did not receive preskill training). The groups then received an additional nine days of instruction followed by administration of the posttest measures, similar to those included in the *Teacher's Guide* for

REWARDS Intermediate. The posttest measures required students to read three- and four-syllable words in isolation and in sentences.

During the additional nine days of instruction, the three groups and the control group received different kinds of instruction. The Preskill Training Only group continued to work 30 minutes a day with the teacher. They received five minutes of review on three preskills taught during the initial training: pronouncing vowel combinations, saying the letter sound or name for single-letter graphemes (vowel conversions), and pronouncing prefixes and suffixes. This was followed by instruction in lessons from a commercial program, in which students practiced reading word lists and passages that consisted primarily of monosyllabic words.

The second group, the Strategy Training group, received 30 minutes of instruction a day on how to apply the *REWARDS* strategy while decoding individual multisyllabic words as well as these words in sentences. The strategy required students to put together the separate skills taught during the initial nine days of the study (preskill training). The strategy involved the following steps:

a. segmenting the word into decodable parts by locating and circling word parts at the beginning and end of the word (prefixes and suffixes);

b. orally reading these affixes;

c. locating and underlining vowel graphemes in the middle parts of the word;

d. reading the vowel sounds;

e. segmenting by reading all words part by part;

f. blending by saying the whole word; and

g. correcting the pronunciation of the word if necessary.

Student participation in this condition included watching the teacher model word reading, engaging in guided practice of reading similar words, and independently applying the strategy to more and more difficult review words, novel words, and words embedded in sentences. Over the course of the nine days, overt use of the strategy was reduced and covert strategy use was increased by both teachers and students.

The last group, the Word Build-Up group, did not use all eight preskills introduced during the nine days of strategy training. Unlike the Strategy Training group, students did not independently segment a word into decodable parts; that is, they did not locate and circle affixes or locate and underline vowel graphemes or pronounce vowel sounds. Instead, the instructor indicated decodable parts in the word by putting a dot between the word parts. This visual partitioning was done by the teacher during both teacher modeling and guided practice. Affixes and vowel sounds were not pronounced orally by teachers or students, but students did read each of the words part by part, blend the parts by saying the whole word, and correct their pronunciation to match oral/aural language or the sentence context. As in the Strategy Training group, students watched the teacher model word reading, engaged in guided practice, and independently applied the strategy to review words, novel words, and words embedded in sentences. Again, as in the Strategy Training group, the gradual fading of prompts occurred. Thus, the Strategy Training and Word Build-Up strategies were two variations of a strategy for reading longer words.

Subjects in the monosyllabic training condition served as the control group. They received 30 minutes of instruction from a commercial program for each of the 18 days. The program being used did not focus on teaching students to read multisyllabic words; instead, it was designed to bring students to mastery on phonetic and structural analysis skills, which are prerequisite skills for reading multisyllabic words.

Statistically significant differences in reading skills were observed on criterion measures of multisyllabic word reading (three- and four-syllable words) and multisyllabic word reading in sentences for students who were directly taught the two variations of the strategy that is now embedded in the *REWARDS* program. Students in the two strategy groups (Strategy Training and Word Build-Up), who read an average of approximately 8 out of 48 multisyllabic words on the pretest, were able to read an average of 31 out of 48 words after learning the strategy. In contrast, students who were not taught the strategy, but worked instead on preskills, read an average of approximately 14 out of the 48 words by the end of the study. In addition, performance on the Word Identification and Word Attack subtests of the *Woodcock Reading Mastery Tests* (Woodcock, 1973) indicated that specific instruction related to multisyllabic word reading increased students' general word recognition skills.

Comparing the scores before and after the study shows that, on average, students who were reading at second and third grade levels before they learned the strategy could read at the fourth grade level afterward. Though standardized measures are not expected to be as sensitive to the effects of short-term treatments, they do provide information on students' abilities to read real and nonsense words of graduated difficulty. And, because of the controlled research design, the results of the study can be attributed to the intervention. This attribution was also confirmed by the fact that students in the control group, who received a structured monosyllabic approach to reading, did not make significant gains. These results suggest that students significantly benefit when taught the necessary decoding preskills as well as the strategies for recognizing word parts in a flexible manner (versus following strict syllabication rules) and using the word parts to put together a whole word.

2. **Vachon, V., & Gleason, M. M. (2006).** *The effects of mastery teaching and varying practice contexts on middle school students' acquisition of multisyllabic word reading strategies.* **Manuscript in preparation.**

The purpose of this study was to examine the effects of mastery learning on multisyllabic word reading component skills and the effects of practice context on word and text reading skills of middle school students (sixth, seventh, and eighth grade) with reading deficiencies, including students with learning disabilities (LD). A factorial design was used to examine the effects of mastery and context. Sixty-five subjects, including 25 students with LD, were matched according to oral reading fluency and then randomly assigned to one of four treatment conditions (groups): high mastery/passage, high mastery/sentence, low mastery/passage, and low mastery/sentence. Participants' reading scores on the Word Identification and Word Attack subtests of the *Woodcock Reading Mastery Tests* (Woodcock, 1973) ranged from 3.0 to 5.0 grade equivalent on the two subtests. In addition, on a multisyllabic word reading pretest, students averaged 20 correct responses out of 36 words, slightly higher than the fourth and fifth grade students in the first study. In social studies passages, these students read an average of 73 correct words per minute with an average of seven errors.

Over the course of seven weeks, groups learned and practiced multisyllabic word reading strategies for 40 minutes a day using an earlier version of the *REWARDS* program. Some groups completed 18 lessons while others completed fewer. Each lesson took from one to three days to complete. After another eight weeks, students were given maintenance tests, bringing the research study to a duration of 15 weeks.

For the first nine lessons, high-mastery groups *required* scores of 90% or higher on daily probes of component skills in order to progress to the next lesson. The high-mastery groups *achieved* a 95% level on daily probes. Low-mastery groups progressed regardless of probe performance. But, in spite of being called low-mastery, their mastery level, according to probe data, was calculated as 85%.

On the last nine lessons, groups progressed at a lesson per day and practiced reading either social studies passages or those same passages arranged as randomly numbered sentences. The passages were drawn from grade-appropriate social studies textbooks. It was hypothesized that a high component skill mastery would result in stronger word identification skills, and that passage practice would result in higher gains in oral reading fluency and in stronger transfer to science text reading skills. Word identification skills were measured by standardized and criterion measures. Oral reading fluency was measured as correct words per minute in the social studies text and later in the science text.

Students from both high- and low-mastery groups made statistically significant gains in word and text reading skills, accompanied by a significant decrease in errors. Over the course of 15 weeks, regardless of the assigned intervention condition (group), students made statistically significant gains in their ability to decode multisyllabic words and in their ability to apply the strategy of identifying word parts when encountering unfamiliar words. However, no significant differences were observed between the high- and low-mastery groups on any index of word reading ability during post or maintenance testing. In other words, it didn't matter whether the mastery level they demonstrated while learning the strategy was 85% or 95%, as long as students kept practicing and reviewing the skills (demonstrating at least 80% mastery level before moving on to new lessons). Similarly, oral reading fluency was comparable for passage and sentence groups on posttest and maintenance measures, indicating that it didn't matter if students practiced reading multisyllabic words in sentences or in passages. Either way, their oral reading fluency improved significantly from pretest to maintenance test. On average, students gained 14 correct words read per minute. Students who were reading within a range of 40 to 95 words per minute before the study were now reading between 45 and 122 words per minute after the study. Overall errors decreased by 2.4 words or 36%, and multisyllabic word reading errors decreased by 1.8 words or 38% from pretest to maintenance test.

On criterion measures that required students to read lists of three-, four-, and five-syllable words, students read substantially better at the end of the study than at the beginning. By the end of the study, they read more total multisyllabic words and more word parts within multisyllabic words, even if they couldn't read the total word. They also read more fluently, as denoted by a substantial gain in correct word parts read per minute. Students read a mean of 26 out of 36 multisyllabic words correctly. They read 126 out of 144 word parts correctly, and they read 75 word parts per minute (compared with 59 word parts per minute at the beginning of the study).

In addition, by the second half of the intervention, students began making only an average of 2.3 errors per 100 words of connected text. This was due largely to learning the preskills in the first nine lessons and beginning to use the entire *REWARDS* strategy each time they came to a multisyllabic word within a social studies passage. However, students still needed help when they couldn't apply the strategy. Each time they made an error, the teacher briefly prompted students by reminding them to use what they had learned from the first nine lessons. In response to the brief strategy prompt, students on average successfully corrected 50% of their multisyllabic word reading errors, which brought them, by the end of the study, to a 98% to 99% level of reading success in grade-level social studies material. When they couldn't apply the strategy, the teacher gave more structured prompts similar to those given in the first nine lessons. In addition to reading well in social studies text, students demonstrated transfer of this oral reading accuracy to grade-level science text.

Gains for special education and low-ability students were statistically comparable to the group as a whole, thus demonstrating that the *REWARDS* program would benefit a range of diverse learners with reading problems. Only a few individual students needed more work on basic phonetic skills before participating in the program. A stronger phonetic foundation would have assisted them in benefiting from the program more than they did.

The *REWARDS* program provides students with the necessary decoding preskills, a highly generalizable strategy for reading longer words, and the practice necessary to read words, sentences, and passages in various subject areas successfully and independently. The two research studies cited describe successful use of this program with low-performing fourth and fifth grade students and with sixth, seventh, and eighth grade students with reading deficiencies (as defined by rate and accuracy measures). The second study also demonstrated that learning to read with the *REWARDS* program transfers to successful reading of the kinds of passages encountered in general education textbooks.

Word List for *REWARDS Intermediate*

The following alphabetized list contains all of the words that were presented in the practice activities of *REWARDS Intermediate*. Additional long words found in the sentences and passages are not included in this list.

Word List for *REWARDS Intermediate*

Word	Lessons	Activity
abnormal	8	H
above	4	G
absence	9	H
absent	1	G
absorb	4	H
absorbent	14	H
abstain	1	H
abstract	1	H
absurd	3	H
absurdity	11	H
accomplishment	22	E
across	4	H
action	10	G
addict	1	H
addition	1	G
additionally	25	E
adhesive	11	H
administrative	23	E
admit	1	H
admittance	13	H
adventure	14	H
adventurous	21	D
adversity	16	D
advertise	7	H
advertiser	8	H
advise	5	H
aim	1	H
alarm	5	H

Word	Lessons	Activity
alarming	6	H
alarmist	7	H
alert	4	H
amazing	24	I
amazingly	17	E
amendment	19	D
American	21	I
amusement	18	E
ancestors	22	I
appear	25	F
appearance	16	D
appearance	25	F
argument	12	G
Arizona	22	I
arrival	8	H
artist	7	G
assistant	12	H
astonishing	7	H
astronaut	3	E
athletic	6	G
atmosphere	25	I
attendance	13	H
attention	22	I
attentive	10	G
attract	20	F
attracted	20	F
attracting	20	F
attraction	20	F

Word	Lessons	Activity
attractive	20	F
attractiveness	20	D
attractiveness	20	F
attracts	20	F
auburn	3	E
audit	2	E
Australia	23	I
author	8	H
auto	3	E
autumn	5	E
available	15	H
baboon	15	E
backbone	5	E
backspin	1	E
backyard	4	E
baggage	13	H
balloon	12	E
barbarism	9	H
barbershop	4	E
barter	6	E
bedroom	13	E
bedspread	15	E
beginner	17	D
behind	3	H
behold	3	H
belabor	11	H
believed	22	I
belong	3	G
bemoan	9	H
benefit	7	E
berate	5	H

Word	Lessons	Activity
betray	3	H
biggest	7	G
birdbath	3	E
birds	6	G
birthday	3	E
bizarre	23	I
blemish	7	H
blizzard	4	E
boatload	10	E
bookcase	15	E
boomerang	11	E
border	4	E
boycott	6	E
boycott	22	I
boyhood	12	E
breakfast	14	E
California	22	I
camp	2	H
candid	2	E
cannon	4	H
canteen	7	E
canvas	3	H
capsule	25	I
captain	2	E
captivates	6	H
capture	20	I
careful	8	G
carelessness	6	H
cargo	4	E
carload	8	E
carnivorous plants	20	I

Word	Lessons	Activity
cartoon	11	E
cartoonist	12	H
cash	2	H
category	24	I
caterpillar	24	I
cause	2	E
caution	10	H
celery	11	H
cellar	8	B
census	8	E
cent	8	B
cent	9	B
center	9	B
century	23	I
Cesar Chavez	22	I
challenging	12	H
change	10	B
chowder	9	E
cinch	9	E
cinder	8	H
citrus	9	B
city	8	B
city	9	B
civil	8	B
civilization	10	H
civilize	15	H
claim	2	E
classic	6	H
classroom	12	E
cloudburst	8	E
coach	8	E

Word	Lessons	Activity
coatrack	8	E
combination	19	D
combine	5	H
comfortable	15	G
command	2	H
commit	2	H
communicate	22	E
communication	23	D
community	16	D
comparability	23	F
comparable	23	F
comparative	23	F
comparatively	23	D
comparatively	23	F
compare	2	G
compare	23	F
comparison	22	D
comparison	23	F
competition	25	E
complain	2	H
complaining	17	D
complaint	3	H
completely	23	E
completeness	6	H
completion	10	H
complexity	11	H
complimentary	12	H
comprehends	7	H
computers	9	H
conclude	5	H
conditional	10	H

Word	Lessons	Activity
conditionally	22	E
conducted	7	H
confectionary	13	H
confession	14	H
confidence	13	H
confident	19	E
confirm	3	H
conformity	14	H
connect	16	F
connected	16	F
connecting	16	F
connection	16	E
connection	16	F
consider	8	H
consist	2	H
consist	24	F
consistence	24	F
consistency	24	F
consistent	13	H
consistent	24	F
consistently	24	F
constrict	4	H
construction	12	H
consultant	16	E
consumers	8	H
containers	18	E
contaminate	11	H
continent	12	H
continual	24	F
continually	24	F
continuation	24	F

Word	Lessons	Activity
continue	2	G
continue	24	F
continued	24	F
continuing	24	F
continuous	14	H
continuous	24	F
contradiction	20	E
contrast	2	H
contrast	24	I
contribute	19	F
contributed	19	F
contributes	19	F
contributing	19	F
contribution	19	E
contribution	19	F
contributor	19	F
contributory	19	F
conversational	22	E
convertible	17	E
convict	2	H
cookbook	11	E
corduroy	6	E
corrective	21	I
corrode	6	E
cosmonaut	25	I
costume	5	E
courage	9	G
cowboy	10	E
cradle	9	G
curious	20	I
curtail	3	E

Word	Lessons	Activity
cycle	8	B
cycle	9	B
cyclone	8	B
cyclops	9	B
dash	1	H
daydream	13	E
decay	3	H
decide	9	B
decision	21	I
defective	21	E
deform	4	H
deformity	18	E
defraud	3	H
demanded	6	H
demonstrations	10	H
depart	3	G
departed	6	H
department	15	H
departmentally	23	E
departure	14	H
dependability	21	E
dependence	13	H
depression	21	E
deprogram	4	H
description	16	D
descriptive	15	H
desperate	20	I
destroy	6	H
destroy	22	F
destructible	22	F
destruction	22	F

Word	Lessons	Activity
destructive	22	E
destructive	22	F
destructiveness	22	F
detail	3	H
determination	21	I
develop	18	F
developed	18	F
developer	18	F
developing	18	F
development	18	D
development	18	F
developmental	18	F
developmentally	18	F
dictionary	11	H
difference	13	H
different	12	H
difficulty	21	D
digesting	20	I
digestive	20	I
dim	2	H
disability	11	H
disadvantage	23	D
disagree	1	G
disagreements	24	E
disappear	25	F
disappearance	25	D
disappearance	25	F
disappearances	25	F
disappearing	25	F
disappears	25	F
disappointment	20	D

Word	Lessons	Activity	Word	Lessons	Activity
disarm	7	H	downhill	10	E
disband	1	H	downstream	15	E
discard	4	H	downtown	10	E
disclaim	1	H	dramatically	24	E
discouragement	23	E	drinkable	15	H
discriminate	6	H	economize	20	D
discussion	10	G	educate	23	F
disdain	1	H	education	23	F
disgust	5	H	educational	23	F
disinfectant	12	H	educationally	23	E
disloyal	11	H	educationally	23	F
dismay	1	H	effective	10	H
dismiss	1	H	elbow	9	E
dismissal	11	H	electrical	20	I
disorganization	21	E	electricity	20	I
disorganization	21	F	electrode	8	E
display	1	H	elementary	14	H
disposable	18	D	elementary	22	I
dissatisfaction	23	D	elevator	9	H
dissimilarity	25	E	embrace	9	E
dissolve	20	I	employer	8	H
distant	3	H	encourage	21	I
distinct	2	H	endangered species	24	I
distinction	16	E	endurance	13	H
distract	1	H	energetic	11	H
district	1	H	energy	10	B
disturb	3	H	engineer	11	B
disturbance	13	G	English	22	I
documentary	12	H	enjoyable	15	H
dominates	6	H	enjoyment	12	H
dormant	12	G	enlargement	22	E

Word	Lessons	Activity	Word	Lessons	Activity
enlist	5	G	expecting	21	F
enormity	16	D	expensive	10	G
enormous	14	H	experimental	21	D
entail	5	H	explain	5	H
entertainers	9	H	explanation	23	I
entertainment	12	H	explanation	13	H
enthrone	5	H	explode	8	H
entire	5	H	explorers	24	I
environmentally	25	D	export	5	G
environments	20	I	expression	10	H
escalator	24	D	exterminate	20	E
estimate	16	D	exterminator	22	D
eucalyptus	24	I	extinction	17	D
eventually	22	D	extreme	5	H
exact	5	H	extrinsic	6	H
examination	12	H	famish	7	H
example	19	E	famous	14	G
excellence	16	D	famously	20	D
exceptionality	24	E	fancy	8	B
exceptionally	18	D	fantastic	6	H
excessive	14	H	farmer	8	G
excitement	12	H	fascination	20	E
exclude	5	H	faucet	8	E
executive	19	E	fault	2	E
existence	18	E	feature	24	I
expansive	10	H	female	7	E
expect	21	F	fictional	13	H
expectance	21	F	fifteenth	7	E
expectation	18	D	final	8	G
expectation	21	F	firstborn	12	E
expected	21	F	fishhook	11	E

Word	Lessons	Activity
florist	7	H
flowerpot	9	E
fluke	12	E
footpath	14	E
footprint	11	E
footstool	15	E
forest	7	E
forget	7	E
forlorn	7	E
foundation	21	I
frantic	6	H
fraud	2	E
freedom	7	E
frustrate	5	E
fundamentally	25	E
Galapagos Islands	24	I
garland	4	E
gem	10	B
gemstone	14	E
generosity	25	D
gentle	10	B
gentle	11	B
gently	13	H
gerbil	11	B
germfree	10	E
gigantic	10	H
ginger	11	B
gingerbread	13	E
giraffe	10	B
girlhood	12	E
gist	10	B

Word	Lessons	Activity
gist	11	B
glistening	20	I
good-natured	25	I
government	19	E
governmental	20	D
governmentally	22	E
graduate	6	H
greenhouse	8	E
grocery	11	H
gym	10	B
gymnast	11	B
gypsy	10	B
gypsy	11	B
happiness	6	H
hardness	6	H
hardship	4	E
harvested	9	H
haunt	4	E
haystack	1	E
headdress	15	E
headstrong	13	E
health	14	E
healthy	14	H
helplessness	16	E
heroism	7	H
hibernate	24	I
historical	8	H
hoist	6	E
holiday	4	E
homeland	7	E
honesty	19	E

Word	Lessons	Activity
hopelessness	6	H
host	24	I
huddle	9	H
humanist	7	H
identification	14	H
igloo	11	E
ignorance	17	E
imaginable	24	I
immature	2	G
immediately	23	D
immigrate	22	I
immigration	22	D
impact	2	H
impair	2	H
impart	4	H
imperfectly	24	D
impersonal	18	E
implant	2	H
importance	13	H
importantly	18	E
impose	5	H
impossibility	23	E
impossible	15	H
impracticality	25	E
imprint	2	H
inactive	14	H
inadmissible	21	E
incapable	15	H
incidents	23	I
incomparable	23	F
incompetent	21	E

Word	Lessons	Activity
incomplete	2	G
inconclusive	14	H
inconsistence	24	E
inconsistence	24	F
inconsistent	24	F
inconsistently	15	H
incorrectly	21	E
incredible	15	H
independence	18	D
independently	12	H
indescribable	25	E
indestructibility	22	F
indestructible	22	F
indifferent	18	E
individuality	25	D
inducted	21	I
ineffective	14	H
inexpensive	20	E
infant	2	H
inflexible	15	H
inflict	2	H
influence	13	G
inform	22	F
informant	22	F
information	22	F
informational	22	F
informative	22	F
informer	22	F
ingrain	2	H
inhabit	2	H
injury	11	H

Word	Lessons	Activity
inlaid	2	H
insist	2	H
instruct	19	F
instructed	19	F
instructing	19	F
instruction	19	F
instructional	19	D
instructional	19	F
instructionally	22	D
instructive	19	F
instructor	19	F
instructors	14	H
instrumentalist	25	E
intensive	11	H
intentionally	23	E
interested	7	H
intermission	20	E
international	21	I
intolerable	19	D
intolerant	13	H
intrude	7	H
invalid	3	H
invasion	10	H
invent	18	F
invention	18	D
invention	18	F
inventive	18	F
inventor	8	G
inventor	18	F
invents	18	F
investigation	14	H

Word	Lessons	Activity
investigator	23	D
invitation	20	E
jaunt	2	E
jealousy	23	D
joyride	6	E
kangaroo	12	E
kindness	6	G
knowledge	25	I
koala bear	24	I
lacy	9	B
Laika	25	I
laminate	15	H
landed	6	G
launch	3	E
launder	6	E
leftover	7	E
legalize	15	H
legendary	20	D
letterhead	14	E
lifeboat	10	E
literature	14	H
logical	23	I
loiter	6	E
loophole	11	E
loyalist	8	H
macaroon	11	E
magic	10	B
magnetism	13	H
mailman	1	E
mainsail	1	E
maintain	1	E

Word	Lessons	Activity
maintenance	13	H
manage	9	H
manage	25	F
manageable	25	F
management	25	F
manager	25	F
manufacture	23	I
margin	10	E
marketplace	15	E
marlin	5	E
marshmallow	10	E
marvelous	14	H
maximum	5	E
meadow	13	E
meaningfulness	24	E
meant	13	E
meantime	13	E
measured	24	I
medically	19	E
medicines	25	I
memorial	25	I
memorize	15	G
mermaid	4	E
Mexico	22	I
midday	1	E
midway	1	E
migrant workers	22	I
mileage	9	H
milkman	1	E
miniature	20	I
Minnesota	23	I

Word	Lessons	Activity
mint	1	H
misbehave	5	H
miscast	1	H
misfit	1	H
mishandle	9	H
mishap	1	H
misinform	4	H
misinformation	22	E
misinformation	22	F
mislaid	1	H
mislay	2	H
mismanage	17	D
mismanage	25	F
mismanaged	25	F
mismanagement	25	D
misplay	1	H
misprint	1	H
missionary	11	G
Missouri	23	I
mistake	1	G
misunderstand	13	H
misunderstanding	15	H
monitor	25	I
monorail	15	E
monsoon	11	E
monument	25	I
moonbeam	14	E
multiple	23	I
multitude	24	I
murmur	5	E
nationally	11	H

Word	Lessons	Activity
nitrogen-poor	20	I
noisiest	23	E
nonviolence	22	D
nonviolent	22	I
normalize	15	H
northern	4	E
northwestern	8	E
noticed	22	I
novelist	10	H
numerous	16	E
nutrients	20	I
oatmeal	13	E
oblige	10	E
observant	17	D
obsolete	5	E
obstacles	21	I
occasionally	25	D
occurrence	20	D
oddity	11	G
Olympic Games	21	I
operator	23	E
optimism	7	H
ordain	6	E
organism	22	E
organization	19	D
organization	21	F
organizational	21	F
organize	21	F
organized	21	F
organizer	21	F
orphanage	14	H

Word	Lessons	Activity
outgrow	9	E
outgrowth	10	E
outlook	12	E
overhaul	4	E
oxidize	19	D
oyster	6	E
panelist	10	H
panic	1	E
partner	4	E
passage	12	H
pathway	1	E
pauper	6	E
peacock	14	E
peanut	13	E
pencil	8	B
penmanship	7	E
percent	8	H
percussionist	10	H
perfection	17	D
perfectionist	11	H
perform	4	H
performance	13	H
permanent	12	H
permanently	18	E
permissive	10	H
permit	4	G
persevered	21	I
persist	4	H
persistent	12	G
persistently	20	D
personal	8	H

Word	Lessons	Activity
personality	11	H
perturb	4	H
pessimism	7	H
phenomenon	23	I
physical therapy	21	I
picture	14	G
pigtail	1	E
pilgrimage	21	D
pillow	9	E
playground	8	E
pneumonia	21	I
poison	6	E
polio	21	I
political	19	D
pollution	17	D
popcorn	5	E
population	21	D
portray	20	I
postage	10	H
powerfully	13	H
precaution	11	H
precipitation	23	I
predict	17	F
predictable	15	H
predicted	17	F
predicting	17	F
prediction	16	D
prediction	17	F
predictor	17	F
predicts	17	F
refer	3	H

Word	Lessons	Activity
prefix	4	H
prematurely	21	E
preparation	24	E
prepay	3	H
prescribe	5	H
preserve	4	H
prevent	3	G
prevent	16	F
preventable	15	H
preventable	16	F
prevented	16	F
preventing	16	F
prevention	16	D
prevention	16	F
prevents	16	F
price	9	B
priceless	9	H
princely	12	H
prison	3	H
probably	21	D
proclaim	3	H
produce	17	F
production	17	F
productive	17	D
productive	17	F
productiveness	17	F
productivity	17	F
productivity	24	D
professional	10	H
professionally	22	D
programmer	9	H

Word	Lessons	Activity		Word	Lessons	Activity
prohibit	3	H		reconstruct	5	H
projector	16	E		record	4	H
prolong	4	H		record breaker	24	I
promote	5	H		reduction	17	D
promotion	17	E		redundant	16	D
proofread	14	E		redundantly	24	D
propeller	17	D		reeducate	23	F
proposal	8	H		reeducating	23	F
protect	3	G		reeducation	23	F
protection	10	H		refinance	13	H
publicize	24	E		refreshments	17	E
punish	7	H		refusal	10	H
raccoon	12	E		regardless	6	H
racism	12	H		regenerate	10	H
radiant	24	E		regretful	9	H
railroad	8	E		regulate	6	G
railway	1	E		reinvent	18	F
rainbow	10	E		reinvention	18	F
raisin	2	E		reinvestigate	19	E
random	3	E		rejoin	6	H
ransack	2	E		relatively	11	H
rapid	1	E		relaxing	6	H
reactionary	24	E		remainder	16	D
readjust	5	H		reorganization	23	D
realism	7	G		reorganize	21	F
reason	15	E		repay	4	H
reclaim	3	H		reproduce	17	F
reconnect	16	F		reproduction	15	H
reconnecting	16	F		reproduction	17	F
reconnection	16	F		repulsive	10	H
reconsider	9	H		researchers	25	I

Word	Lessons	Activity
resemble	9	H
resemble	25	I
resist	20	F
resistance	20	E
resistance	20	F
resister	20	F
resistibility	20	F
resistible	20	F
resisting	20	F
resistive	20	F
respectability	25	D
respected	7	H
respectful	8	H
respond	25	I
responsible	15	H
restrain	3	H
restrict	3	H
return	3	G
returnable	22	E
reversible	15	G
riverbank	11	E
roadside	8	E
roadway	9	E
rooftop	12	E
running	6	G
Russian	25	I
sacrifice	22	I
safely	11	G
sagebrush	11	E
sailor	8	H
sausage	9	H

Word	Lessons	Activity
scapegoat	12	E
schoolyard	12	E
Scientific American	23	I
scientists	23	I
scrapbook	12	E
seamstress	14	E
seashell	13	E
seasick	15	E
seaweed	14	E
selfish	7	G
servant	12	H
server	3	E
seventeen	8	E
shadow	10	E
shallow	9	E
shampoo	11	E
shipmate	5	E
shortage	9	H
shortstop	4	E
showboat	11	E
showdown	13	E
significance	13	H
similarity	11	H
sirloin	10	E
smartest	7	H
snowflake	10	E
snowplow	9	E
softness	6	H
southeastern	14	E
southwestern	8	E
Soviet Union	25	I

Word	Lessons	Activity	Word	Lessons	Activity
soybean	14	E	tantalize	24	D
space	8	B	taunt	3	E
species	25	I	teammate	15	E
spectator	8	H	temporary	17	D
spellbound	8	E	Tennessee	21	I
spoilsport	6	E	textile	7	E
stampede	5	E	Thailand	24	I
steamboat	13	E	thirsty	11	G
steamship	14	E	thirteenth	9	E
sterilize	15	H	threadbare	14	E
strain	1	E	thudded	23	I
streambed	13	E	timberline	5	E
streamline	13	E	timid	2	E
streetcar	7	E	tinfoil	15	E
struggle	9	H	toothbrush	12	E
succeed	9	E	toothpick	11	E
successful	8	H	tornado	5	E
successor	9	H	torpedo	15	E
suddenly	18	E	tortoise	24	I
suddenness	17	D	tournament	21	I
suggestive	12	H	township	10	E
sunbeam	15	E	tremendous	14	H
sundown	9	E	tremendously	25	E
sunstroke	5	E	trilogy	11	B
superintendent	25	E	triumph	21	I
supermarkets	22	I	turban	3	E
supplemental	20	I	turmoil	6	E
surrender	18	D	turn	3	E
surround	15	E	turnstile	5	E
sweatshirt	14	E	unafraid	4	H
sweepstake	7	E	unalike	5	H

Word	Lessons	Activity
unattractiveness	24	E
unavoidable	24	D
unchain	4	H
uncomfortable	18	D
unconventional	15	H
unconventionality	25	E
undependable	20	E
understandable	19	D
unemployment	12	H
unexpected	21	F
unexpectedness	21	E
unexpectedness	21	F
unfair	4	G
unfaithful	9	H
unfamiliar	23	I
unfit	4	H
unforgettable	21	D
unfortunate	8	H
unfortunately	22	D
ungrateful	8	H
uniform	7	E
unimportance	20	E
unintentional	10	H
United States	22	I
unlikely	21	E
unlucky	16	D
unmanageable	24	D
unmanageable	25	F
unmentionable	20	E
unmistakable	24	D
unpaid	5	H

Word	Lessons	Activity
unpredictable	17	E
unpredictable	17	F
unpreventable	16	F
unrepairable	25	D
unselfish	7	H
unspeakable	19	E
unsuspecting	19	E
untrusting	7	H
untruthful	8	H
uproot	12	E
urgent	11	B
useless	6	G
utterance	18	E
valid	2	E
vanish	7	H
various	20	I
vault	2	E
vegetables	22	I
verdict	3	E
vermin	4	E
vertical	25	I
vertically	23	E
victim	2	E
vigilant	21	D
vitamin	3	E
void	6	E
voluntary	11	H
vulture	14	H
waist	1	E
waistband	2	E
weightlessness	25	I

Word	Lessons	Activity		Word	Lessons	Activity
weird	23	I				
whirlwind	3	E				
widespread	13	E				
willow	9	E				
Wilma Rudolph	21	I				
windowpane	9	E				
witness	23	I				
woodshed	11	E				
wriggles	20	I				

References

Adams, M. J. (1990). *Beginning to read: Thinking and learning about print.* Cambridge, MA: MIT Press.

Anderson, R. C., Hiebert, E., Scott, J. A., & Wilkinson, I. A. G. (1985). Conceptual and empirical bases of readability formulas. In G. Green & A. Davison (Eds.), *Linguistic complexity and text comprehension* (pp. 23–54). Hillsdale, NJ: Erlbaum.

Archer, A. L. (1981). *Decoding of multisyllabic words by skill deficient fourth and fifth grade students.* Unpublished doctoral dissertation, University of Washington.

Archer, A. L., Gleason, M. M., Vachon, V., & Hollenbeck, K. (2006). *Instructional strategies for teaching struggling fourth and fifth grade students to read long words.* Manuscript submitted for review.

Canney, G., & Schreiner, R. (1977). A study of the effectiveness of selected syllabication rules and phonogram patterns for word attack. *Reading Research Quarterly, 12,* 102–124.

Cunningham, P. (1998). The multisyllabic word dilemma: Helping students build meaning, spell, and read "big" words. *Reading & Writing Quarterly: Overcoming Learning Difficulties, 14,* 189–219.

Just, M. A., & Carpenter, P. A. (1987). *The psychology of reading and language comprehension.* Boston: Allyn & Bacon.

Lenz, B. K., & Hughes, C. A. (1990). A word identification strategy for adolescents with learning disabilities. *Journal of Learning Disabilities, 23,* 149–158, 163.

Nagy, W. E., & Anderson, R. C. (1984). How many words are there in printed school English? *Reading Research Quarterly, 19,* 302–330.

Perfetti, C. A. (1985). *Reading ability.* New York: Oxford University Press.

Perfetti, C. A. (1986). Continuities in reading acquisition, reading skill, and reading disability. *Remedial and Special Education, 7,* 11–21.

Rayner, K., & Pollatsek, A. (1989). *The psychology of reading.* Englewood Cliffs, NJ: Prentice Hall.

Samuels, S. J., LaBerge, D., & Bremer, C. D. (1978). Units of word recognition: Evidence for developmental changes. *Journal of Verbal Learning and Verbal Behavior, 17,* 715–720.

Share, D., & Stanovich, K. (1995). Cognitive processes in early reading development: Accommodating individual differences into a mode of acquisition. *Issues in Education: Contributions from Educational Psychology, 1,* 1–57.

Shefelbine, J. (1990). A syllabic-unit approach to teaching decoding of polysyllabic words to fourth- and sixth-grade disabled readers. In J. Zutell & S. McCormick (Eds.), *Literacy Theory and Research: Analysis from multiple paradigms. Thirty-ninth yearbook of the National Reading Conference* (pp. 223–229). Fort Worth, TX: Texas Christian University Press.

Shefelbine, J., & Calhoun, J. (1991). Variability in approaches to identifying polysyllabic words: A descriptive study of sixth graders with highly, moderately, and poorly developed syllabication strategies. In J. Zutell & S. McCormick (Eds.), *Learner factors/teacher factors: Issues in literacy research and instruction. Fortieth yearbook of the National Reading Conference* (pp. 169–177). Fort Worth, TX: Texas Christian University Press.

Stanovich, K. E. (1986). Matthew effects in reading: Some consequences of individual differences in the acquisition of literacy. *Reading Research Quarterly, 21,* 360–407.

Stanovich, K. E. (1991). Word recognition: Changing perspectives. In R. Barr, M. L. Kamil, P. B. Mosenthal, & P. D. Pearson (Eds.), *Handbook of reading research* (Vol. 2) (pp. 418–452). New York: Longman.

Vachon, V., & Gleason, M. M. (2006). *The effects of mastery teaching and varying practice contexts on middle school students' acquisition of multisyllabic word reading strategies.* Manuscript in preparation.

Woodcock, R. W. (1973). *Woodcock reading mastery tests.* Circle Pines, MN: American Guidance Service.

Woodcock, R. W. (1987). *Woodcock reading mastery tests* (revised). Circle Pines, MN: American Guidance Service.